From acclaimed sommelier Rajat Parr and noted expert Jordan Mackay comes this groundbreaking guide to the iconic wines of Europe. Perfect for anyone who wants to improve their blind tasting skills, gain confidence purchasing and pairing wines, or find a straightforward and visceral way to understand and describe wine, this is a seminal addition to the wine canon. For the first time ever, Parr and Mackay share everything they've learned over decades of tasting wine, including the differences between wines from the seven grand crus and forty premier crus of Chablis, and the terroirs in Barolo and Bordeaux. *The Sommelier's Atlas of Taste* helps you understand wine the modern way—by detailing the features of the tastes, vineyards, and production methods of classic Old World wines, appellation by appellation, soil by soil, and technique by technique. Featuring stunning photography of the faces and places behind the wines, the result is the most in-depth study ever published of the world's greatest wine regions.

THE SOMMELIER'S
ATLAS OF TASTE

A FIELD GUIDE TO THE GREAT WINES OF EUROPE

THE SOMMELIER'S ATLAS OF TASTE

RAJAT PARR AND JORDAN MACKAY

PHOTOGRAPHY BY JOE WOODHOUSE

TEN SPEED PRESS
California | New York

CONTENTS

INTRODUCTION

Blind tasting isn't just a parlor game or a trial meant to torture sommeliers on the path to certification. When practiced by friends around a table with a few good bottles, it can be a wonderful focusing tool that pushes us to think more deeply or, to use a trendy term, be mindful of what's in the glass. It concentrates discussion, tasks the memory, and draws us ever more fully into relationship with the wine in front of us and *wine* in the larger sense.

Rajat, for those of you who don't know about him, is one of the most gifted blind tasters in the world, possibly ever. No one I've encountered tastes annually the colossal, global range of wines every year that Raj does. And when he tastes, he apparently does so with what I've coined an "oenographic" memory, a truly rare kind of mind. Not only does he remember practically all the wines he's ever tasted—the flavors, contours, textures, acid and tannin levels—but he also seems able to recall salient, even trivial details about them—their oak regime, vintage conditions, fermentation vessel, etc. It's a remarkable gift, and a vexing one when you're blind tasting with him (your own copious flailing guesses standing out glaringly against his steady stream of perfect calls).

But Raj also nurtures his talent with a schedule of tasting and traveling few other people have probably ever undertaken. His life is analogous to the kind of regimen you'd expect an elite runner to follow while training for the Olympics. However, instead of marathons at high elevations, substitute weeks-long treks through the vineyards of France. Instead of sprinting on a track, imagine vertical tastings of multiple vintages of one wine. Instead of hours of stretching, substitute daily walks through vineyards with winemakers, picking up rocks, talking about soil structure, wind patterns, and sun exposure. And in lieu of a diet rigorously monitored by nutritionists and coaches, think of tasting all these wines with the cuisines of their regions, whether at a Michelin three-star restaurant or at the kitchen table at a winemaker's home. If wine tasting were an Olympic sport, Raj would be standing alongside the likes of Michael Phelps and Usain Bolt at the closing ceremonies. (As it is, it's probably not a bad idea for him to don some sweats and hit that running track, too.)

Raj's "training," however, comes not from any competitive drive, but from the most heartfelt love of wine and wine culture. When he tastes something that captures his imagination, especially if it's a wine from one of the world's few remaining regions relatively unknown to him, his eyes widen, his attention focuses, and he becomes fixated on knowing its metrics. He'll grab the person who poured it for him by the arm and demand, "Who made this? Where did they work before? What soil is this from? What's the farming like?" Then, you can bet, within the year, he'll arrange a visit to this region, to the very winery that produced the wine. It's a pilgrimage and a compulsion. The investigations and explorations catalyzed by a single taste of wine—the kind that provokes transatlantic and transcontinental travel; requires finding weeks of time in one's schedule; and costs thousands of dollars in travel, lodging, and meals—are the basis for the second reason for creating this book.

This second reason isn't just about blind tasting, but tasting in general. And drinking. And talking. Sommeliers and sommelier culture were the subjects of our first book. At the time, Raj was one of them (I was not, but I hung out with them), and we spent much time in a cadre of wine lovers, eating, tasting, and talking about how wine tastes. But now Raj is no longer a sommelier. He co-owns a few wine brands and spends a lot of time thinking about wine production, which is where his mind was always heading. The natural question after *How does this wine taste?* becomes *Why does it taste like that?*

Why? is the most vexing question in all of wine. Most attempts to explain precisely why a wine tastes the way it does are doomed to fail. But unlike the great philosophical questions—involving life, God, and the universe—with wine you actually can talk to the maker. Like the rest of us, the *vigneron* (a French term indicating the person who grows the grapes and makes the wine, our preference over English's "winemaker," though we will use both throughout this text) may not be able to explain why the wine tastes the way it does, but obviously she can at least offer some detail and perspective.

So this book takes its direction from the way Raj constructs his life—essentially a nonscientific, yet rigorous and impassioned road-tripping inquiry into how wine tastes and why. I've spent much of the last eighteen years of my life doing similar work as a wine and food writer, though certainly not with the same intensity (no one comes close to Raj in that), so it made sense to do this together and record it in book form.

The most important phrase in the previous paragraph may be "nonscientific." Raj and I are both very interested in wine science and look forward to a day when that science might explain some of the phenomena we experience with our senses. But we are not scientists and have only a tenuous understanding of the chemistry, biology, and physical sciences that apply to wine. Nevertheless, in our wine discussions we are often tempted to fall down that rabbit hole, explaining and invoking things with poorly understood or pseudoscientific concepts. That said, we are also aware that wine science still has a long way to go and that the reality of wine's complexity will elude the reach of science's explanatory powers for a long time. Case in point: the controversial word "minerality." Scientists don't like it because it suggests a certain taste or texture is produced by minerals floating around in the wine, minerals that their testing can't find. Non-academics use the term because it powerfully invokes either a taste or smell memory of mineral or rocky substances, or the textural sensation of mineral-rich water. In that unscientific sense we use it as a metaphor and an adjective, not as an actual physical property in a wine. Yet science still hasn't explained what causes that mineral sense.

So our approach is to be essentially old-fashioned. That is, we get our wisdom from the vignerons who produce the wine. If they tell us a certain type of soil in their region usually produces wine of a certain character, we are going to take their word for it and, if finding it useful for learning to taste the region's wines, report what they have to say. If we use the world "minerality," it's as a metaphor, not a physical state of being. If we talk about terroir, it will be with a consideration of cultural practices as well as what we know of soil, climate, etc. We'll discuss this all more thoroughly in Chapter 1, where we look at concepts like terroir, about which our perspectives widened immensely over the course of our travels.

Now, a few words on the title. Traditionally, an atlas is a collection of maps. Thumbing through this volume, you will quickly see it's not a traditional atlas. Once again, we're employing some poetic license and using the word metaphorically, for what we're generally depicting are not roadways or topographies or constellations—the classic subjects of atlases—but the taste of wine—and how do you render a map of taste? You do it in the same confounding way people have always been doing it—with words. Especially when it comes to wine, language is personal and imprecise, but it's all we've got at this point, reminding us of the famous line from music criticism: "Writing about music is like dancing about architecture."

Now, about the other big word in our title—"taste." Taste has many definitions, and in this book, we invoke many, if not all of them. Yes, we are writing about the taste of wine. Yes, we are also chronicling a series of journeys dedicated to the act of tasting wine (and food). Sometimes we had only a taste, though on other occasions we drank the whole bottle. Furthermore—and this is important—the subjects chosen here were curated in accordance with our sense of taste. Some of you might think we have bad taste, and some of the wines we discuss may not be to your taste, but luckily Raj and I have largely similar tastes when it comes to wine, so we readily agreed on almost all of the inclusions in this book.

Taste is a very complicated physical and mental action into which science has invested considerable investigative energy in recent years. Traditional wine writing has been careful to differentiate between a wine's aromas, detected by the nose, and a wine's flavors, detected in the mouth. As we will discuss in more detail in chapter 1, this distinction is in many ways outdated, given that most of a wine's flavors are detected through the back of the throat, by the olfactory system. Furthermore, we really did try to focus in many of our experiences on the wine's texture or mouthfeel, using our tongues to feel for a wine's structure and texture to determine whether certain soils imbued wines with common attributes. So in this case, we were trying to use our tongues more than our noses. But writing about texture is even more "dancing about architecture" than writing about flavor, as our language has very few words for texture.

We are sure to hear many comments about the regions we did and didn't visit, what can be called classic, and the wines and grapes we overlooked. We're sure all such criticism will be valid, and we acknowledge it in advance. So there were entire countries we missed—sorry, Greece, Portugal, and Slovenia. Apologies to Italy's Friuli, Alto Adige, Campania, and Abruzzo; France's Provence, Savoie, and Pays Nantais; Germany's Pfalz; and more. And grape varieties we ignored—e.g., we include Riesling, to the exclusion of Grüner Veltliner, Pinot Gris, and Gewürztraminer; and Nebbiolo, to the exclusion of Barbera and Dolcetto. We chose our "classic" regions using an intuitive equation that took into account our own tastes and our sense of the general worldwide fame, recognition, and appreciation of these regions. It's therefore not a surprise that France dominates this book. When it comes to studying, classifying, and philosophizing about wine, it's the leading culture in the world, and our text reflects that. Other brilliant wine places like Italy and Spain will no doubt reach France's level of saturation at some point.

Finally, I'm writing this introduction to convey my presence as one of the narrators of this story. Raj and I did all the traveling together, spending many, many hours together in cars, cellars, restaurants, and hotels. When we weren't with others or listening to Dan Carlin's *Hardcore History* podcasts on the road, we used the ample spare time (over meals, walks, in the car) to discuss our visits, tastings, and thoughts. That's why I've adopted the plural "we" as the point of view. We've talked it all out together. When Raj says something particularly incisive, I may pull it out as a quote, deviating momentarily from the first-person point of view, to give a sense of the character and dynamics of the situation.

Mostly, what I found remarkable in the creation of this book was how much I learned and, astonishingly, how much Raj learned. Yes, we tasted a lot of wine. But we spent even more time with the vignerons walking the vineyards, where they truly come alive. There were moments of discomfort: huddling against a lacerating wind on a freezing February morning in the Kamptal, perilous car rides on the edge of vertiginous cliffs in Priorat and Mosel, or trying to keep up with vigneron Thierry Allemand as he bounded, mountain goat–like, down his terraces. There were moments of extreme pleasure: eating bread and caillettes (an Ardeche specialty: pork and chard meatballs) made by Pierre Gonon and drinking 1978 and '79 Raymond Trollat St-Joseph in the vineyard by the great character's house; or Easter lunch at the home of legendary importer Becky Wasserman. But, always, always, there were profound, impassioned, mesmerizing conversations with highly philosophical minds, such as when tasting wine in the half-dark of his cellar with Jean-Louis Chave in the Rhône or discussing history over dinner with Peter Sisseck in the Ribeira del Duero.

After every visit, we felt we'd accrued knowledge we didn't have before. And then we forgot half of it (or at least I did) because . . . wine. The overall impression of such a long trip was a palpable sense of the passion driving the small producers of Europe. Certainly, passion can exist in larger-production operations and in big companies. But it's nothing like what you feel from the people who are pruning the vines and tending the wines. In turn, we felt energized and excited about what we witnessed. Despite whatever's going on in the rest of the world, lots of inspiring things are happening in the classic wine regions of Europe. We hope this book gives you a sense of that.

—Jordan Mackay

ONE

TASTE AND TERROIR

In tasting our way across the wine regions of Europe we found ourselves, as one so often does over wine, drawn into fascinating conversations with the people who make it. From the scientific and agricultural to the philosophical and spiritual, these discussions were far-ranging, to say the least. Most of all, we talked about possibility. What can drinking a wine possibly tell us about it and whence it came? And what are we capable of comprehending in that wine?

The answers we sought felt both near and far away. But the length and intensity of our journey—a sort of pilgrimage to the heart of wine—never left us doubting that they could be known, even if those discoveries are difficult to relate in words, facts, or figures. That sense of knowing we craved, and which we hope to pass on, came most powerfully as a feeling of connection to people and place. Thus we found ourselves in Alsace, discussing with Olivier Humbrecht the possibility of water having "memory." Or we stood for hours around an upturned barrel with Jérôme Prévost, wondering out loud if living in close proximity to one's vineyard and visiting it every day can heighten the expression of the wine it makes. And we found ourselves having several memorable meals—such as the one prepared by Jeremy Seysses using pork from a pig he had raised, a perfect match for his Dujac wines—that proved over and over again that what winemakers tend to eat connects to their wines. With great wine it's impossible to tell what aspect begets what feature; the circle is almost always virtuous.

What follows in this chapter is a consideration of those conversations and many more, exploring some of the philosophical territory we found ourselves traversing as we likewise crossed over the Alps and the Pyrenees and Sierra Cantabria. But it all comes down to taste. The attempt to write generally about the taste of wine and the subsequent attempt to connect those tastes to places will inevitably invite criticism. These censures will claim that generalities are of little use, that wine flavors are too subjective to catalog, that the connections between wine and terroir can never be known. Perhaps. But, just as a clear night's sky's grandeur prompts us to ponder the nature of existence, a great wine's irresistible blend of delight and complexity begs us to inquire into its origins (and, implicitly, investigate how to get more). That inquiry must begin with the only and still best tool we already possess. For what is perceivable about wine if not its taste?

Taste is the key to unlocking wine's mysteries. The questions prompted by a taste of compelling wine leads to inquiries of its ontology: the relation of environment to vine; environment and vine to vigneron; vigneron to wine; and wine to drinker. Taken together, those relationships form the equation we use to understand what's more commonly known as terroir, the highly charged word some consider the essence of wine and others see as overused, trite, and pointless. In the investigation, through taste, of terroir, we also examine terms like *minerality* and *typicity*. And we glance into the fascinating and daunting research of human perception, which in the end could be a key to a new understanding of wine.

ON TERROIR

Make no mistake, we are believers in terroir, but we also recognize that it's at once the most meaningless and meaningful term in wine, and still has the power to raise hackles and incite debate. This is somewhat surprising, considering that the term, which was once owned wholly by the French, has now permeated the general vocabulary of wine and food in many other languages. Indeed, terroir has even infiltrated popular culture to an almost absurd degree. For instance, these days, in wide use is the term *merroir* to refer to the impact of specific marine environments on oysters. A 2015 *Rolling Stone* article on basketball was titled "The 'Terroir' of the Atlanta Hawks." In 2017, the webzine *The Awl* ran a piece called "Instagram Has No Terroir." We're still waiting for *hairoir* (the effect of environment on hairstyles) and *fairoir* (a look into expression of locality in music festivals). If you're reading this, you no doubt have some sense of the word, but in case you don't or so we can simply be clear, we'll take a moment to ponder what all the fuss is about, as defining terroir is a messy and unmanageable task.

We're often reminded that *terroir* is a word with no exact translation into English, which faintly suggests that we native English speakers are incapable of ever truly understanding its complex layers of meaning (the French would no doubt agree with this). Perhaps that is so, but we can give it a shot. One thing is clear: Because of its similarity to the familiar Latin root *terr*, meaning earth or land, many people associate terroir first and foremost with soil. "What's the terroir like?" we've heard asked more than once by someone who really just wants to know about a vineyard's soil profile. Of course, if you're already a student of wine, you know the implication of terroir goes far beyond soil. There are many good attempts to define terroir in English, but a classic one can be found in the introduction to the book called *Terroir* (James E. Wilson, 1998), written by renowned British wine writer Hugh Johnson, who elegantly defines the term as ". . . much more than what goes on beneath the surface. Properly understood, it means the whole ecology of a vineyard: every aspect of its surroundings from bedrock to late frosts and autumn mists, not excluding the way a vineyard is tended, nor even the soul of the *vigneron*." With its descriptive flourishes, Johnson's definition captures the all-encompassing sense of terroir. Invoking the vintner's soul is a nice touch to remind us that it will always linger beyond our grasp.

That Johnson prefaces his definition with "properly understood" is disarming. How can we be expected to understand the entire ecology of a vineyard, the impacts of farming methods, *and* the interior life of the farmer? Much less properly? The overwhelming complexities make that equation untenable, which is why some writers have turned to simple, equally inscrutable methods. Wine writer Matt Kramer understood this in coining the term "somewhereness." He wrote (in *Making Sense of Wine*), "Great wines taste like they come from somewhere. Lesser wines are interchangeable; they could come from anywhere." Kramer's definition is helpful because it lassos terroir down into the realm of taste, something we can all relate to. Johnson's definition reaches for the unknowable; Kramer's brings it to our lips.

In his tragically out-of-print *Making Sense of Burgundy* (if you ever see a used copy, buy it), Kramer elaborates on why we should be interested in terroir, calling it "the more beautiful question of wine." Beyond all the myriad aspects of a vineyard, he writes, "terroir holds yet another dimension: It sanctions what cannot be measured, yet still located and savored. *Terroir* prospects for differences. In this it is at odds with science, which demands proof by replication rather than in a shining uniqueness."

That was written in 1990. In the ensuing quarter century, a great deal of wine science has been done, yet terroir still remains at odds with science. By employing definitions that invoke "soul" and "what cannot be measured," terroir believers resist the scientific interpretation of the term. But that hasn't stopped science from trying to prove or disprove terroir. And that's understandable. We're curious animals; we want to explain everything.

The Terroir Controversy

In 2016, Mark Matthews, a UC Davis professor of viticulture, published a book called *Terroir and Other Myths of Winegrowing*. Another respected academic, Victor Ginsburgh of the Université Libre de Bruxelles, has said, "Terroir is not only a myth, it's a joke" (*Decanter*, 2007: "Terroir: The Truth"). Wine writer and historian Paul Lukacs grants in a 2017 article in *Zester Daily* that while "many of the world's best wines convey a sense of place . . . that does not mean that they actually taste of a specific place. After all, tasting a place literally means eating dirt."

The question of terroir's existence is one of those questions pitting empirical evidence against the cold, hard facts ascertainable by science. In this way, the dispute can take on the same shape as those who claim to have seen spirits or ghosts versus the scientists who call it bunk. But while it's only the rare individual who claims certainty about paranormal experiences, those who say they've experienced the terroir of wines are legion; and they have been speaking of it for thousands of years. Yet, the fight rages on.

In a 61-page chapter in his book, Matthews makes an interesting case against terroir. He charts the history of the word's use, noting that hundreds of years ago the phrase *goût de terroir* (taste of terroir) was a pejorative phrase, indicating off or disgusting flavors in wine. He casts doubt on the story of the Benedictine and Cistercian monks' role in spearheading the hyper-specific single-vineyard wines in Burgundy (and many other places) today. He delves into the fascinating economic argument, showing that a pronounced uptick in print of the word *terroir* occurred twice in the last century. Both times correlate to periods in which France's wine dominance was threatened: in the beginning of the twentieth century when France's vineyards were recovering from the blight of phylloxera, and in the 1980s, after the famous Judgment of Paris, in which French classics placed lower than a number of upstarts from California in a blind tasting conducted by experts in Paris. The solution to both threats was for French governing bodies and marketeers to beat the drum of place, pushing the uniqueness of France's wine regions as the most important factor.

Matthews's chapter is very interesting (well, the section on early plant biologists is a bit of a slog) and well worth the read. He writes persuasively that terroir is primarily a cultural construct, yet somehow still fails to convince that it's just myth. That failure is for one good reason: taste.

Talented tasters can often recognize regions, villages, and even vineyards in blind tastings. They can determine producers and vintages. They can identify wines they've never tasted before. Call it terroir, or producer signature, or anything else—but that good tasters can repeatedly perform such feats signals that something exists in some wines that differentiates them. This is not in every wine or available from every producer, but it apparently exists, and *terroir* is a broad and nebulous a term to name it.

Furthermore—and this is one of the big reasons we wrote this book—vignerons who know their land are highly attuned to it. It is the reality of their daily lives, and it's rare to find a good vigneron who won't insist that wines from certain plots regularly taste different from those from other plots, and in consistent ways. Intimately aware of the differences themselves, vignerons will do things like point to a sandy site versus a rocky one, or a steep site versus a flatter one, and tell you the profile of the wines that come from these places year after year. They may not be able to tell you exactly why the differences occur—no one can—but they can describe what they are.

Unsurprising to anyone who knows him, Matt Kramer forcefully rebuts the so-called "scientism" of terroir skeptics like Matthews. In a 2016 *Wine Spectator* column defending the notion of terroir, Kramer writes:

> Is terroir necessarily ambiguous? Sure it is. Everything about fine wine is ambiguous. That's what makes it so difficult to pinpoint precisely why La Tâche tastes different from neighboring Richebourg. No scientific evidence exists, to the best of my knowledge, that definitively identifies and proves the causes of the difference. Therefore, as wine scientists would have it, any differences we find are invalid as they're not verifiable. So we're seen as dupes. Myth lovers. Irrational fools. But we're not. Those of us who credit the existence of terroir, of its legitimacy as a metaphor for understanding the natural world, know that recognizing terroir is no more—and no less—than a way of being alert. We know that the differences we apprehend with our senses are real and far from illusory—or mythical. We know also that soil plays an informing role, in some sites more strongly and clearly than in others.

A key phrase in Kramer's response is terroir as "metaphor for understanding the natural world" and "a way of being alert." In the end, these are also two of the most beguiling aspects of wine itself. After all, so many of us are drawn to it, not purely for literal intoxication, but intoxication in the metaphorical sense. Wine is an exhilarating puzzle for the brain, bringing together so many human and natural disciplines, incorporating diverse landscapes and cultures, stimulating all of our physical senses, and throwing us into conversation with one another. Contemplating wine allows our brains to commune with our bodies, uniting the intellectual and physical. To truly engage great wine requires alertness—mindfulness, if you will. And, indeed, wine is nothing if not a distillation of the natural world. By that token, to engage with wine is to engage with terroir is to engage with life itself.

The Human Factor (Part I)

Most definitions of terroir go the same way. First, they focus on soil type, followed by the other expected details: climate, microclimate, exposition (orientation and exposure), altitude, and so on. The implication is that terroir is something immutable, inviolably created by nature itself. The way it's referred to, terroir is always already there, waiting to be discovered. A common trope from winegrowers is "I'm just doing my best to express the terroir," as if they were photographers capturing the sunset. The underlying impression of terroir is that its fundamental elements are natural, unable to be notably impacted by manipulation. This makes for a lovely vision of wine as a direct expression of nature—unmediated and pure. But, of course, it's a fantasy.

Alcohol exists in nature—it's not uncommon to hear of drunken deer, birds, or bears that have bitten into fallen fruit that's begun to ferment and produce alcohol—but not wine. Winemakers don't even make wine from wild vines, which don't organize themselves into vineyards and often don't even produce much fruit (and when they do, it's known to be quite tart, requiring substantial sugar additions in the wine). It is people who dig the soil and choose the domesticated wine grape variety to propagate. People choose a site to plant and then make such decisions as vine row direction, spacing, and training. People tend the vines throughout the year, making crucial viticultural calls. Upon this consideration, wine lovers inevitably append their stated definitions of terroir: "And don't forget the human factor. The vintner plays a role, too!" The exclamation point is usually implied, something between a wink and a chuckle, a perfunctory acknowledgment that terroir is impossible to conceive without human activity, but nevertheless we'll agree that human intervention is subsidiary to the agency of nature.

And that's just the vineyard. Grapes, of course, still must be harvested and converted into wine. Here, myriad other cascading decisions have to be made, no matter how "non-interventionist" the winemaking: when and how to harvest, to destem or not, type and volume of fermentation vessel, temperature of fermentation, time on skins, cap management, press regime, aging time and vessel, and many more. Obviously, all of these things have a profound impact on the resulting wine.

In considering terroir, our almost inescapable instinct to separate the natural from the man-made results in much confusion. It's best not to even try; they cannot be separated. Matthews, in his terroir takedown, advances this. "Winemaking affects wine," he writes. "This isn't news. . . . When terroir is used to include all factors that can affect grapes and wines, it only means that wines are different. If wines did not differ in a systematic way, wine would not be worthy of reflection, study, or argument."

Certainly, this is true. And, if taken as just a fancy term meaning "wines are different," terroir is not only a useless term, but needlessly confusing. Yet, we all basically think we know what it means. Well, sort of. It turns out there are subtleties to the way French winemakers hear it. As we found while working on this book, the French understanding of *terroir* possesses shades of meaning that are difficult to grasp, given the way most of us Americans have experienced wine. It took lots of time in France, exploring the vineyards with the people who live in them, for some of these realizations to truly sink in. The classical French understanding of terroir incorporates the collective experience of centuries of winemaking history. So, while English-speaking users of the term *terroir* understand it in a rudimentary sense, some of its shades require a greater look at the French sensibility, as we illustrate below.

Terroir vs. terroir

A number of years ago at the Pinot Noir New Zealand conference, the renowned French soil scientist and wine consultant Claude Bourguignon gave a talk, detailing his findings and methods, which deal with the microbiology of the soil. One thing he said to the crowd of hundreds in the audience was that great vineyard expression could not occur if vineyards were irrigated. After the talk, an Aussie winemaker approached and said, "Mr. Bourguignon, in the part of Australia where I work, it would be impossible to grow vines without irrigation." The response was swift and decisive: "Then you have no terroir."

It's an eye-opening response, especially for those of us wine students in the New World, who have only really absorbed the textbook definition of terroir. As discussed above, that definition is clinical and general: the total growing environment and conditions of the grapevine (and don't forget the human factor!). In that understanding, the Aussie winemaker's terroir is simply exceedingly dry and hot, requiring irrigation. To those who take the egalitarian approach to understanding terroir, the wine simply reflects those conditions. In that conception, everybody has terroir.

But clear in Bourguignon's response is a sense that terroir doesn't apply everywhere. It's not an indifferent or anodyne term; it comes with a value judgment. You either have terroir or you don't. Terroir with a capital T vs. lowercase terroir. To the French, some Terroirs are better than others, and there is such a thing as not having any at all, even if you can grow grapes and make wine. Bourguignon's thinking implies that a wine from a place requiring irrigation is not a Terroir wine, but a commodity wine, hardly worth discussing.

This way of thinking is implicit in the way many people whose tastes were cultivated in France think about wine. There is wine, and there is wine of Terroir. A wine Terroir is not any place wine grapes are grown, but a place capable, under the right conditions and management, of producing something unique, something radiant. Is it elitist? Sure, but that elitism is backed by wine history, which the French have in droves (compared to the rest of the world's relatively little).

It explains why many in France, and the Old World in general, are predisposed to be skeptical about much New World wine. Here in the New World, we just don't know yet whether most vineyards or regions are true Terroirs in the French sense. To earn Terroir status takes time and labor on the part of vignerons—among numerous other details: finding the right grape varieties, molding the land, and consistently producing distinctive wine over a long period of time. It doesn't happen overnight and usually takes more than a few decades.

The Human Factor (Part II)

You've probably read that the Médoc of Bordeaux, perhaps the most famous vineyard land in the world, was once but a muddy swamp. Here and there, bits of raised land, used for grazing cattle, protruded from the muck, but the place was essentially a bog. By the Middle Ages, Bordeaux wine meant Graves, St-Émilion, and the high ground known collectively today as the Côtes de Bordeaux. In the late 1600s, Dutch engineers were hired to drain the Médoc, which they did, exposing gravelly soils. They also installed drainage systems, channels, and flumes, which still exist, to usher out excess water. Today, of course, the Médoc's vineyards are heralded as some of the world's greatest terroirs, its wines among the most collectible. Good drainage is a prime reason for this success, and it only occurs there because people literally drained the swamp. They created terroir.

Consider Burgundy, the spiritual birthplace of the concept of terroir. To visit today is an awe-inspiring experience, as you walk down small vineyard paths and roads, which, amazingly, are public and open to anyone. Walking from Musigny to Richebourg is for wine lovers what strolling through St. Andrews is for golf aficionados. Monks in the Middle Ages noticed nuanced differences in wines that came from various parts of the hill and kept these wines separate in celebration of their uniqueness. Thus, through terroir, they honored the voice of the earth on the Côte d'Or. At least that's how the story goes. Yet to hear a more complex tale of this place, it helps to also talk to someone who can read the actual landscape. For that purpose, we meet up with celebrated geologist Françoise Vannier, who today makes a living creating detailed geological studies of vineyards for interested clients like landowners or regional associations.

To walk the slopes of the Côte d'Or with Vannier is a little like visiting the scene of a crime with a CSI. She studies the layers of sediment in a pit, the angle of a hill, or the rocks protruding from a vineyard and ruminates on cause and effect like a forensic scientist. Every so often, she points out gaps in the vine-covered slopes. "This was surely a quarry below here," she says, gesturing to one sharp dropoff. "There was geologic faulting here until about twenty-three million years ago, and since then erosional processes have continued and smoothed the relief. But very often when you have reliefs here along the Côte, it's because of human activity and not tectonic activity." At one place, we stop, peering down over a sheer wall. "This huge cliff below, about 50 feet down," she says, "is a former quarry that has been used by the monks of Citeaux to build the Clos de Vougeot. And it is called Perrières."

The vineyards in Burgundy called Perrières, which people think means "stony place," were indeed stony places, but not so named for the stony ground that supported grapevines. They were quarries, and their output can be found throughout the region as buildings, roads, and walls. Over the centuries, as vineyards became more prevalent and profitable than quarries, the quarries were filled. But filled in with what? Soil, Françoise says, but not necessarily soil from the same hillsides. Tests have revealed that replaced soil may have come from other places, suggesting neighboring vignerons wouldn't part with their Côte d'Or dirt willingly. Even some very famous vineyards might be composed to some degree of soil from outside that spot.

In our minds, the fact that human activity intrinsically contributed to shaping the landscape for the purpose of viticulture should not diminish the greatness of the wines of Burgundy or Bordeaux. Terroirs are not "discovered." From the beginning, they are constructed. They are lasting and evolving collaborations between human, earth, and vine. Terroir is neither the unmediated expression of "what nature wants to give us" (as some winemakers are fond of saying), nor the specifically designed product of an individual's intentions.

Terroir takes time. Topography is shaped, water redirected. Rocks are removed. Soils and rocks may shape the vines, but vine roots twisting deep down for centuries also shapes the earth. Children are born. Viticulture changes. Vines are replanted as wine styles change. And they are replanted again in another generation. All of this is requisite to achieve what the French consider Terroir. And thus the resulting wine is a collective achievement—the sum of the realities of the site and the will of the people working it: neighbor influencing neighbor, over generations and centuries. This process happened in Bordeaux and Burgundy, but also throughout all these places, from Etna to the Wachau. It is in large part how a wine comes to taste of a place and why we've yet to see it much, except maybe superficially, in the New World.

If terroir is more than just rocks or soil or vine selections or farming techniques, how do we make sense of it? At what moment does a vineyard or a village become a terroir? How do we incorporate time and human action into the equation of the soil and geology and climate? The philosophical and scientific theory of emergence offers a useful way to at least try to grasp terroir. The overarching idea is easy to comprehend. Emergence is a process of creation in which something new emerges when smaller, discrete components interact and self-organize. It can be applied to lots of systems. Recently, theoretical physicist Geoffrey West invoked it in his pioneering work on cities. In a 2017 interview, he explained it as such:

A city is not the sum of all the people in it, and it's not the sum of all the roads and all the buildings. It's not the sum of all the events that take place in it. There's something much more than that; it's some integration of all those. And it's useful as a concept to think of it as some collective phenomenon and talk about its own individuality. And we do, obviously, talk about New York and San Francisco, and so on. It does have a sense of individuality. . . . And so you come to this concept, which is inherently the idea of complexity and complex systems. Yes, it is made of constituents. But if we start to delineate them, it's almost an infinite number and associated with them is an infinite number of equations. And of course that means you can't come to terms with that. It becomes conceptually not a . . . way of deriving the idea of what a city is.

Substitute "terroir" for "city" in that formulation, and you get a helpful template for understanding it. Like a city, all the constituents of a vineyard—soil, vines, climate, vineyard management—become La Tâche or Cannubi or, one step further, the resulting wine. Predicting an outcome by simply looking solely at individual constituent parts—be it the soil type, the underlying geology, or the clone—is impossible, though there may be recognizable features.

In wine, the leap from constituent parts to emergent whole seems to be the crux of the rift between academics and writers over terroir. Writers are willing to accept the hopeless complexity and focus merely on the emergent phenomenon of what they taste in the glass. Academics examine individual components in order to explain terroir. And when they can't measure the impact of any component, they deny terroir's existence.

The "Terroir" Alternative in Describing Wines

Because of the complexity and indeterminism of the word *terroir*, we may use the word *typicity* to describe the character of a wine or set of wines. Terroir works for describing a place or set of conditions, but not a wine's taste. It may be a pedantic point, but saying "I can taste the terroir in this wine" sounds clumsy and creates confusion (especially in literalists)—you can't actually taste the dirt in a wine. Typicity is helpful here, as it describes the common qualities wines (from a site or a vintage, for example) might express. So: this wine shows "great typicity," rather than "great terroir." It's a fine point, we admit, but worth noting. We use the typicities we find in certain groups of wines to draw conclusions about wine's more ephemeral aspects like soil type, fermentation, etc.

Typicity is derived from the French *typicité*. *The Oxford Companion to Wine* defines typicity as "a wine's quality of being typical of its type, geographical provenance, and even its vintage year. . . . [I]t is perhaps because typicality is a subjective notion, rather than a physical attribute that can be measured by analysis, that it is so much discussed." It's a broad definition for a broad word, but basically refers to the way a wine expresses some greater, overarching character (like terroir), without having to say, "I taste the terroir in this."

Another helpful definition, stated by writer Jennifer Fiedler in the online magazine *PUNCH*, notes that typicité "sorts through all of winemaking's variables—the oak barrels, the grape composition, the fermentation styles—and comes up with an acceptable range for what wine from a certain region is supposed to taste like. In France, for example, we associate a specific flavor profile and style of winemaking with, say, chardonnay from Chablis. Wines made in this general, accepted profile for the region are said to have typicité."

We like typicity because it takes its cues from other wines, which is truly where we derive all our knowledge. Typicity describes a (shared) experience and understanding of a group of wines, while invoking terroir presumes a knowledge of the truly unknowable and unquantifiable. Typicity observes, rather than judges. A wine's lack of typicity is not necessarily a criticism or a strike against it, but merely an observation of its deviation (whether intentional or accidental) from the generally understood profile of a certain locale. Yes, it's inexact (what in wine isn't?). But it takes into account received wisdom, consensus, time, and the collective wills of places and peoples to arrive at a sense of typicity.

The Bedeviling Minerality Question

The terroir expert and winegrower Pedro Parra (he holds a PhD in terroir and a master's in precision agriculture from the Institut National Agronomique Paris-Grignon) explained to us that these days he tries to avoid using the term "minerality." Why? "Every time you mention it," he says, "the soil scientists and geologists go searching through the wines for examples of minerals that we can taste. Of course, they never find any and then make a big stink."

To Parra's point, the geologist and well-known wine researcher Alex Maltman wrote in a 2013 takedown of minerality as a wine descriptor that though tasting "minerality" in wine is suddenly fashionable, "whatever minerality is, it cannot literally be the taste of minerals in the vineyard rocks and soils."

Literalism in popular wine rhetoric vexes Maltman, because the language tasters use makes it seem as though there's a direct connection between geology and flavor. He notes that suggestion of the flavors of hay or leather in wine doesn't lead people to think those things are actually dissolved in it. Fair enough. But does this make it foolish to use them? If you're talking to an old friend on the phone and you say, "It's good to hear your voice," you're not actually hearing that person's voice; you're

THE ROLE OF CLIMATE

While soil is talked about ad nauseum by many students of wine (including us), most people who study it seriously believe climate to be a greater determining factor of the nature of wine. We agree. Climate controls which grapes you can grow in a region more definitively than soil does. If we don't write about climate as extensively as this notion might suggest, it's just that in each section we're focused more on the dynamics within a region rather than between regions. Therefore, when significant climactic differences exist in one region—such as between Spain's subregion of Rioja Baja and Alavesa, or in Austria's Spitzergraben, or on the various faces of Mount Etna—we will mention it. But, in general, when the climate of a region is consistent throughout, we focus on other questions.

hearing a reproduction of it thanks to signals sent over thousands of miles and reconstructed by a miniature speaker. Yet you don't feel obligated to say, "it's good to hear a reproduction of your voice." Or, as another example, upholsterers don't get flummoxed when we describe wines as "velvety." Perhaps we can all agree that what we call minerality in wine is not the direct taste of minerals, many of which have no flavor. But can minerals in the soil, feeding the vines and ultimately the grapes, create a signal that is ultimately picked up by our sense of taste? Who knows? It seems plausible, at least, even if we're not responding directly to the "taste" of the minerals, but tasting some effect they have on the wine.

However, people can't even agree on what minerality is. We've heard it variously described as a flavor, a texture, and an energy. In his book *Postmodern Winemaking*, winemaker and consultant Clark Smith defines it as resembling "the aftertaste of a half-shell oyster or of a tiny electrical current in the throat." For others, it can be the slightly grainy texture exhibited by mineral-rich water or licking a wet stone. Some people associate it with a smoky characteristic like sparked gunpowder.

Instead of the problematic word "minerality," Parra says, "I use the word 'electricity.'" He refers to it as a physical sensation and says it can manifest in wine in numerous ways. He equates it to an electric sensation that produces tension in the wine. It arises, most of the time, from vines planted in intensely rocky sites, he says.

We agree with Parra and Maltman that minerality is a tricky and controversial word for various reasons. More vexingly, however, is its slippery usage. Much like terroir, it means different things to different people, and is thus hard to define and perhaps of questionable value. Yet, for those who sense it—whatever *it* is—minerality is a terribly compelling and powerful component of wine to deserve all this fuss. Minerality, electricity, or whatever you want to call it ("salinity" and "saltiness" are now fashionable)—it has some connection to a wine's vitality.

Thus, minerality's value is not as a scientific term, but as a metaphor. We don't speak of literal minerals in wine; we speak of a poetic characteristic that *reminds* us in some way of stones, rocks, metals, and minerals. Maltman helpfully lists the most common mineral cues: flinty taste/smell, or flintiness; gun-flint aroma/struck flint and matches; earthy smell; smell of warm/wet stones; seashells and fossilized shells; and metallic smell. It turns out, many of these notes might arise from organic compounds in wines (or wineries) and from bacteria and molds found in nature.

HOW WE "TASTE"

One area that doesn't get much attention yet in the greater wine conversation is *how* we actually taste, and what we are capable of sensing. While we subscribe to Matt Kramer's belief in terroir and its resistance to science, we are still fascinated by what science can tell us about what and how we taste. After all, if a glass of wine sits in a forest and no one's around to taste it, who cares if it has minerality?

Understanding more about how our tongues and noses and brains interpret the cues in wine (and food) may ultimately give us more of a sense of what we perceive in wine and why. For example, what if our mouths are discovered to possess a previously unrecognized ability to detect microscopic traces of minerals that our brains encode into a sensation of minerality? The minerality debate would become moot, as it could be proven we have a taste for "mineral," just as we have for bitter and sweet. Fortunately, serious work is now being done on human taste perception, and both journalists and food-loving scientists are writing about it in ways we laypeople can understand.

The recent books *Neurogastronomy* (2012) and *Neuroenology* (2017) by Gordon M. Shepherd, a professor of neurobiology at Yale, detail advancements in the study of taste. Shepherd's ideas about how we taste are put forth in *Neurogastronomy*:

> Up to now the focus of food science has been on relations between the composition of the food to the perceptions of the flavors. Some of the explanations have begun to reach into the mechanisms of the brain. What is now needed is to begin with the brain, and show not only how it receives the sensory stimuli, but how in doing so the brain actively creates the sensation of flavor. It is important to realize that flavor does not reside in a flavorful food any more than a color resides in colorful objects.

We won't go too heavily into the science here, but it's important to understand why this new area looking into how taste is created (as noted in Shepherd's *Neuroenology*, "by the brain and the biomechanics of the mouth and respiratory system") could be a powerful tool toward a better understanding of wine. It bridges the chasm between the literalists and the philosophers, by moving beyond what is literally, consciously tastable in the wine and into the way our brains interpret these elements. To start, we must recognize the magnificent tasting and smelling machines we all are. It's a shift in thinking, as so much of science's attempts to demystify wine rely on telling us what we *can't* taste.

It's a commonly held belief that humans' senses of smell and taste are inferior to other animals'. While indeed, physiologically, we have fewer taste and smell receptors and fewer types of them than other animals, the story doesn't end there. Our brains, which process the information our sensors provide, are much more expansive and fast. As Shepherd writes, "Despite the declining number of receptor genes, the brain processing mechanisms of the smell pathway . . . bestow a richer world of smell and flavor on humans than on other animals." The cameras on modern smartphones provide a good comparison, using processing power to create photos that far exceed their minuscule image sensors' capabilities.

Furthermore, it's commonly held that modern technologies can better analyze the specific components of foods. However, in some ways, our sense of taste is even more formidable. As Mark Schatzker notes in his excellent 2015 book about flavor and nutrition, *The Dorito Effect*, "The best aroma-sensing equipment money can buy—a 7890 Agilent chromatograph paired with a LECO Pegasus HRT mass spectrometer—will run you $350,000. It can take that equipment hours to 'taste' a single substance, and it can't even say if it tastes good or not. It can tell you only what's in there. And even then it will still miss stuff. The human nose is instant. The human nose is technology money can't buy."

Shepherd details the two major ways in which we smell. Orthonasal smell is the direct kind that comes in through our nostrils—sniffing the air while inhaling. Retronasal, which "contrasts in so many ways with orthonasal smell that it can truly be considered a separate type of smell," takes place inside the mouth, throat, and head. For example, retronasal smell occurs when you breathe out and engage in all the other activities of wine tasting—sloshing, chewing, feeling—"and thus is intimately tied to, if not inseparable from, the sensations of taste and touch." Furthermore, our saliva also acts on the wine to release certain scent molecules not obtainable solely by the nose.

Swallowing, Shepherd explains, is also integral to the experience of tasting. After swallowing which "the coating of the wine on the throat has a direct input to exhaled air. . . . Repeated swallowing thus contributes to the sustained activation of the olfactory receptor cells through retronasal smell, providing the most powerful input for sensory discrimination of the wine." This is good news for those of us who relish drinking wine—not just "tasting"—as the best way to try to understand it!

Even after swallowing, we are not done "tasting" the wine. Researchers have found that taste receptors similar to ones on our tongues exist elsewhere in the body, too. A 2014 article in *Nature* noted that receptors are "distributed throughout the

EARTHY OF A SECOND LOOK

Some human noses can instantly recognize TCA (trichloroanisole), the compound that makes wine taste corked, in *parts per trillion*. And that's just one particularly noxious aroma we've been trained to recognize. Who knows what other things we sense that fly beneath our conscious radar but may affect the way we feel?

The obscure, lovely word *petrichor* is variously defined as an "earthy scent produced when rain falls on dry soil" or "a pleasant smell that frequently accompanies the first rain after a long period of warm, dry weather." We all know that smell. It's ethereal, transporting, and . . . not exactly the smell of rock dust or earth. Rather, it's a scent conjured by biology. Actinomycetes are a group of bacteria that live in soil. When they die, they secrete geosmin, a chemical with that familiar earthy scent. Geosmin settles onto the ground, and when rain pelts the surface, it is stirred up into the air, along with dust, exuding the petrichor. Hence our sentimental and entirely reasonable association of geosmin with wet rock. (Incidentally, geosmin can often appear in tap water as the same unpleasantly "dirty" flavor that also shows up in freshwater fish like tilapia and catfish.)

Petrichor aside, other mineral misnomers include "flintiness." Flint has no aroma unto itself, but its hardness can be used to create a spark against iron, igniting particles of the metal and creating a smoky smell. The scent is not of flint, but flint is a contributor to the reaction. The point is that the suite of flavors, aromas, textures, and electrical sensations now falling under the umbrella of minerality have their root in natural phenomena. Minerality may not be literally or directly the flavor of minerals derived from vineyard rocks and soils. So be it! When someone says flinty, we know what they're saying.

Let us take a moment to marvel at the wonder of human sensation. So sensitive is human smell that it can reportedly pick up geosmin at levels lower than ten parts per trillion! However, if this is the case, such a statistic must give us pause in blindly accepting conventional wisdom about what we cannot perceive in wine. When so much about olfaction and wine and the brain is unknown, how can you write anything off?

stomach, intestine and pancreas, where they aid the digestive process by influencing appetite and regulating insulin production." Since then, receptors have been found in other parts of the body, too. Receptors in the stomach can detect sugar and amino acids and secrete a hunger hormone at the detection of carbohydrates and protein, encouraging us to eat when nutrients are sensed. This kind of sensation may not be the same as consciously savoring a note of Meyer lemon in a glass of Chablis, but if automatic physiological reactions play a part in the way a certain wine makes us feel, even subconsciously, then we may have to expand our concept of what taste is. Perhaps our bodies are "tasting" things our tongues don't and sending signals to the brain that spur it to create images, feelings, and sensations that figure into that greater emergent sense we know as taste.

THIERRY ALLEMAND
Domaine Thierry Allemand, Cornas

TASTE AND TOUCH ⸺⸺⸺⸺⸺⸺◇

One aspect of taste we're particularly interested in is the category of mouthfeel, in which we include wine tasting concepts like shape and structure. Given that we've just described how so many aspects of sensation work in concert to create flavor, to separate this perception of wine from other aspects may in the end be futile, but it's worth discussion. Mouthfeel is massively important in wine. Case studies have observed mouthfeel to subconsciously be more important to wine drinkers than flavor. Indeed, how many times have you found yourself draining a bottle of a mild but nice-feeling wine, while the more flavorful or aromatic bottle remains full on the table?

In their recent book *Mouthfeel: How Texture Makes Taste* (2017), Ole G. Mouritsen and Klavs Styrbæk (Danish physicist and chef, respectively) note, "Of all the different contributors to the total flavor experience, mouthfeel is probably the most neglected. We rarely pay attention to the actual mechanical aspects of eating." Why might this be the case? Perhaps it is because the body is immediately preoccupied with smell and taste. When it comes to mouthfeel, they surmise, attention is usually only triggered when it runs counter to expectations—a mealy apple, for instance, or a stale piece of bread.

We like to think that wine tasters are more attuned to mouthfeel than most people. Perception of texture is taught from the beginning of wine training, but discernment must be keen. The textural difference between a tender tomato and a chewy piece of beef jerky is obvious. But given that all wine is liquid, we need more granular measures. Still, remarking on the texture of a wine is incredibly difficult, perhaps because we don't have enough words. Japan has 406 discrete terms to describe texture, English a paltry 78. Given that only a handful of those probably apply to liquids, our vocabulary is severely limited. Thus, we recruit touch sensations from solid materials we sense with our bodies—silky, leathery, gravelly—to describe liquid in our mouths. Like minerality, these are metaphors. What's incredible is that to our minds, the metaphors make perfect sense. In some beautiful way, our brain registers the interaction between our mouths and liquid similarly to the way our skin touches physical surfaces.

We sense the texture of wine in our mouths via mucous membranes on our cheeks, tongues, and even through nerve endings in the teeth. But what in wine produces our sensation of texture? Tannins and phenols play an important role, as they give a sense of astringency. Acids create a feeling of tartness, bite, and even energy. Sugar, ethanol, and glycerol offer a feeling of body. Alcohol and glycerol convey body and weight. Carbon dioxide bubbles can make a wine feel prickly, coarse, or smooth. In concert, the sensation of all these elements gives rise to what is called a wine's structure, though, again, using structure to describe a liquid is about as confounding as calling it "dry."

The astringency in tannins go a long way to determining our sense of texture and mouthfeel, even if it's a bit of a trick. Tannins work by binding with proteins in the saliva and on the mucous membranes. As they bind they create bigger particles, which are stripped off the cheeks and tongue and out of the saliva. We feel this as a rough and abrading surface, since important lubricants have been removed. This coarseness creates a grain or texture that makes it feel like the wine has substance that can be rubbed by the tongue or even chewed. Lack of astringency means the wine is not binding with proteins and thus glides smoothly across the mouth. Astringency can create many different semblances of texture, from powdery and chalky to grainy, sticky, or grippy.

Some acids and tannins and phenols connect with sensors in different parts of the mouth, creating localized feelings in places like the back of the tongue, sides of the cheek, and so on. We talk about the front, mid, and back of the palate, and sometimes the experience of receptors firing across these locales gives the wine a sense of movement, sweeping across in a wave. Foremost, the combination of acid and tannin, along with alcohol, can often seem like an organizing element in the wine, giving it shape, dimension, and volume. All of this falls into the camp of structure; all of it is hard to describe in words!

Of course, this isn't the full story. Taste and smell are crucial to detecting texture. To get a sense of this, try the old trick of holding your nose while tasting a wine. Of course, you'll notice that you don't perceive much flavor. But you should also note that your sense of the wine's texture is also dulled. Specific flavors also influence the perception of texture and vice versa. For example, the authors of *Mouthfeel* point out that the scent of vanilla creates a sense of creaminess in food. It seems reasonable that vanilla may have the same impact in wine, perhaps explaining one of the reasons rich, oaky Chardonnay is often described as creamy. Sweetness enhances the sense of viscosity, while sourness decreases it, and bitterness appears to have no effect on texture. Tannins can add a bitter flavor or lessen a fruity sensation in a wine. Acidity diminishes the perception of sugar and therefore also the sense of the wine's body. This is intriguing, as our perception of texture and structure in wine appears to exist outside of what we'd call the primary flavors—texture being the feeling of the wine on the surface of the mouth, structure being a combination of factors that appears to create the experience of the wine's "shape."

Some experts believe the nature of a wine's mouthfeel is determined by the place where the vines grow, a sort of direct connection to site. This connection has nothing to do with the flavors (fruit and otherwise), but is all about texture and structure. In an interview with *Wine and Spirits* magazine, soil scientists Claude and Lydia Bourguignon spoke to this. "In fact it's not an olfactory analysis of a wine but the mouthfeel that's a function of the place the vine was planted," Lydia says. "We hold terroir tastings called 'geo-sensorial' tastings. They were first practiced in 1312 by Philippe le Bel. It's a sort of taste-training, in which you actually touch, even taste, different rocks to then be able to find the same sensations on the palate with the wine. For example, touching granite gives a cold impression, while limestone seems warm."

HOW TO TASTE

People have written entire books on how to taste, so we won't go into such detail here. But it's helpful to remember a few things to have the best experience. Wines should be served at proper temperatures—not too warm for reds (best at about 60°F to 65°F) and not too cold for whites (best at around 50°F to 60°F). While it's not necessary to have a glass specifically designed for what you're tasting, it's nice to have a large enough glass that the wine's aroma can expand. Clean glasses are a must: before pouring, smell the glasses for off aromas. If they've been sitting for a long time in a box or in a wooden cupboard, they can take on those smells. Likewise, if they've been washed with dirty water or a dirty sponge, those off aromas can get into the wine, too.

When the wine is in the glass, pay attention to the color, which can correlate to such things as grape variety, age, and winemaking style. Is a white wine golden, or straw-colored, or greenish? Is the color dark or bright? Is a red wine bright ruby or more purple-black? Next, smell the wine and pay attention to the aromas. Are they fruity? If so, what kind of fruit, and how ripe? Or are they earthy and, if so, what kind of earth—wet, rocky, woodsy? If floral aromas are present, do they remind of violets, roses, or lavender? Is the wine simple or complex? (That is, does it only have one or two standout notes or can you spend minutes with the glass to your nose trying to single out all the aromas?) These are the kinds of questions you should be asking yourself.

Take a sip and hold the wine for a moment in the mouth. Let it gently slosh on your tongue and across your palate. Is it heavy or light? Get a feel for the texture—is it smooth, grainy, lush, slick, or something else? Get a sense of the shape of the wine (structure): Does it feel big and round? Or is it long and linear? Or does it seem angular and pointy? Look for dryness or sweetness, astringency or juiciness. Do the acids seem to jolt your nerves and make you salivate? Or do astringent tannins seem to grip the back of your tongue? Do you feel it mostly at the front of the mouth or does it finish long into the back of the palate?

Wine tasting is an incredibly stimulating and complex activity, giving the mind a lot to think about, so don't be intimidated if it takes a while to start paying attention to all these things. Finally: spit or swallow? Well, that depends on what sort of tasting you're doing. If there are a lot of wines and you want to make it clear-headed to the end, don't hesitate to spit. But, if you want to get the fullest and truest impression of the wine, we think it's important to swallow at least one sip, to feel what it's like going down. Then note how long the flavor lingers on your tongue, as extended length can indicate quality and intensity. Do you feel like a dragon, exhaling a burst of fusel heat after you swallow? The wine may be unbalanced in its alcohol. And finally, it's simply important to experience how your body (beyond the mouth) experiences the wine, something referred to as digestibility: Is your body happy to receive this wine? If so, there are few better qualities in a wine.

Can the type of soil or rock in which vines grow imprint wines with some sort of common and consistent source code? Given what the scientists say, it seems doubtful. However, intriguing examples of this exists. For instance, Chablis and Sancerre from Kimmeridgian marls, despite being 70 miles apart and from different grape varieties, are more similar in the mouth than different. It's something we explored while researching this book, and sometimes we came to conclusions worth talking about, while other times we came up empty, such as trying to understand the impact of the famed *galestro* soil of Tuscany (more on this in the Italy chapter). But we're far from the only people interested in this matter. It's also a major focus of winemaker and terroir specialist Pedro Parra, whom we mentioned above. Parra spent years training his palate, studying vineyards and rocks, and tasting over and over again for similarities and differences in the wines from similar geological substrates. Simply by being alert, he has noticed commonalities.

Parra is employed all over the world as a vineyard and wine consultant. His job is, at the most basic, to help people better understand their vineyards. Over the years, he's become a firm believer in the importance of stones in the soil and of pure rocky subsoils. Standard, crumbly topsoil doesn't really interest him. It's the rock underneath and the vine's ability to interact with it that ultimately determines whether a wine can express terroir or minerality (though, remember, he prefers the term "electricity"). And, indeed, Parra can often sense consistent differences between various rocky subsoils in wines. (Not all wines express their rocks—either due to inexpressive soil types, indifferent farming, or other factors.)

If this sounds far-fetched, a blind tasting with Parra, as he sometimes gives to audiences during lectures, can be convincing. Before the wines are poured, he'll describe in detail the ways different kinds of rock can impact a wine. Granite, he says, offers a very acidic sensation, with a huge amount of energy/minerality in the front of the mouth. He doesn't feel much impact on the sides of the tongue. Wines growing in schist also have acidity, he says, but it is felt more in the cheeks. The wines feel bigger—not round, but with more energy than granite felt in the cheeks and sides of the tongue. "Schist is always about power," he says, "a mineral bomb." Limestone is easier to identify because of its distinctive short tannins and energy. Limestone wines aren't round, but more long down the tongue. They're elegant with a fine granularity and subtly tense electricity. Finally, he says, volcanic substrates tend to be a little flat and rustic, lacking electricity.

In describing these tastes, Parra only talks about texture and structure. Flavor, which can be dictated overwhelmingly by variety, not soil, doesn't enter his descriptions at all. After giving that brief introduction into how he perceives different rock expressions, the wines are poured. As the audience sips, chews, and considers the mystery wines, he reminds that each one seems to focus itself on different parts of the mouth—forward, back, sides, and on the cheek and tongue. For one the impression may be of power; for others it might remind of zippy energy or gossamer finesse.

Then he goes through each wine, one by one, asking for conclusions as to the rocky origins of each wine. Sure enough, even an inexpert audience will get some right, based on his descriptions. A Barolo from La Morra expresses the vibrance and energy of limestone. A Cahors from the south of France shows the density and power of Kimmeridgian marl. A Pinot Noir from Oregon grown in basalt expresses its impact on the front of the mouth with big, dry tannins. Another wine, a Nerello Mascalese grown in basalt on Etna in Sicily, has a surprisingly similar feel. Of course, this is simply an exercise—and, of course, Parra has chosen the wines—but there's enough correlation to be intriguing. And Parra, with his own well-practiced palate, does very well in blind tastings we've administered to him.

FRONTIERS OF TASTE

We've dipped into the terroir disputes—some say it's obvious, and others say it's a convenient cultural/economic construct that can't be supported by science. Squabbles over minerality likewise pit scientific literalists ("we cannot taste actual minerals in the wine!") against those who use the word as a metaphor for a quality in wine that reminds of stones or minerals. For the record, we're believers in terroir and see its expression in wine as an emergence of factors and interactions too complex to be measured and explained by contemporary science. Will people ever find common ground between these positions? We think so, as research on taste, wine, and viticulture continues to provide tantalizing new paths of inquiry.

Primary among new taste insights are the discoveries of taste receptors on the tongue, mouth, and inside the body. For generations, we all accepted the four major tastes—sweet, salt, bitter, and sour. Now that's been amended, and most accept that we have five major tastes, including umami, our sensation of deliciousness via savory glutamate molecules.

All of this is based on solid physiological study. Scientists suggest the existence of a new "taste" when they discover on the tongue a receptor dedicated to receiving a particular stimulus. Many scientists believe the number of tastes we have will well surpass five. In recent years, they've found receptors for starch, fat, and water. Taste receptors for metals and blood are actively being sought. Further research may likely produce awareness of senses we didn't even know we had. For instance, have you heard of kokumi?

Another Japanese discovery, in 2010, kokumi is more a sense than a flavor. The *Mouthfeel* authors describe this Japanese word (with no direct translation) as combining three distinct elements: "thickness—a rich, complex interaction of all the taste impressions; continuity—the way in which long-lasting sensory effects grow over time and only taper off slowly; and youthfulness—the reinforcement of a harmonious sensation throughout the whole mouth."

At a lab in Japan, food scientist and author Harold McGee tasted kokumi stimulants added to food in the microscopic amounts of two to twenty parts per million, and this is what he had to say: "The flavors seemed amplified and balanced, as if the volume control had been turned up and an equalizer turned on. They also seemed somehow to cling to my mouth—a tactile feeling—and to last longer before fading away. And the effects extended to aroma as well as taste, though I imagine indirectly through the taste effects."

The Japanese researchers discovered that kokumi sense is activated by a series of compounds that engage calcium-sensing receptors on the tongue. Among those compounds are calcium, as well as the sulfur-containing compounds alliin (found in garlic) and glutathione (found in grapes and in wine). It just so happens that wine contains the *mineral* calcium. Glutathione is not a byproduct of fermentation, but rather transferred from the plant, and it's known in winemaking to be a powerful antioxidant.

Debate on kokumi as an official taste is ongoing, but it sounds surely like an element of what we'd call mouthfeel, and further muddies the distinctions between taste and texture. Nevertheless, kokumi's implications are intriguing. It has no taste or smell on its own. We're hardwired to detect it, which means we get it almost instantly, first at a subconscious level. It produces a desirable effect. And its catalysts occur in grapes and wines. More work needs to be done, but it's hard to escape the feeling that we're just at the tip of an iceberg. How many other receptors will be discovered? How many more "tastes" do we have? How will they impact our discussions of wine?

Receptors are not the only area where fascinating work is being done. Our other senses have an enormous impact on the way we perceive taste, and these have profound implications on wine. For instance, a 2015 *New Yorker* article detailed the research of Charles Spence, a professor of experimental psychology at Oxford University. Head of the Crossmodal Research Laboratory, which studies how our brains merge data from our five senses to produce our experience of reality, Spence argues that "in most cases at least half of our experience of food and drink is determined by the forgotten flavor senses of vision, sound, and touch." To wit, he's discovered such oddities as "coffee tastes nearly twice as intense but only two-thirds as sweet when it is drunk from a white mug rather than a clear glass one . . . that bittersweet toffee tastes ten per cent more bitter if it is eaten while you're listening to low-pitched music . . . and a cookie seems harder and crunchier when served from a surface that has been sandpapered to a rough finish." Most wine drinkers know that seeing the color of a wine influences our expectations of it, and that the shape of the wine glass can influence the way we perceive it. How deep does this go?

In *The Dorito Effect*, Mark Schatzker notes the phenomenon of volatile-enhanced sweetness. He writes about it in the context of tomatoes. A researcher had noticed the surprising ability of some tomatoes to taste up to twice as sweet as others, even though they contained less sugar, and wondered what was going on. Then she remembered that scientists discovered something they called "volatile-enhanced sweetness" in the 1970s, when they demonstrated that adding fruity aromas to sugar water made it taste even sweeter. Tomato researchers had failed to notice this. Certain volatiles and combinations of aromas can intensify flavors, such as that of tomatoes and strawberries, conferring a sense of sweetness not caused by the presence of sugar. What might this mean to our understanding of the flavor of wine? Perhaps it may explain the propensity of New World wines like those from California or Australia to taste sweet compared to Old World wines that seem dry—even if neither contains residual sugar and are therefore technically dry. New World winemakers do tend to make fruitier-tasting wines, often pushing ripeness past the norms of many Old World regions. Is volatile-enhanced sweetness the reason even dry wines may taste cloyingly sweet to some tasters?

Finally, things taste different depending on our physical states. If you're hot and thirsty, a drink will taste different than when you're not. Airplane food has to be loaded with salt and other flavorings because our senses are dulled, not by cabin pressure, but by the roaring sound of the engines and the vibrations in the plane. Our sense of taste is completely subject to so many things beyond our consciousness and ability to control.

All in all, taste is a sense that humanity is just starting to examine with real rigor. We chose *The Sommelier's Atlas of Taste* as the title for this book because we were going all-in on the idea of taste—an incredibly powerful, personal, and subjective sensation. We each sense taste through our mouths, bodies, and minds. This chapter has been a brief discussion of taste and how it relates physically and philosophically to wine, before we get to the meat of the book, which is all about exploring individual regions. For those of us believers, taste provides the unassailable guarantee that terroir exists and the proof that minerals and rocks in the vineyard are somehow shaping the taste of wine, even if we don't know how. From here on, as we journey through the classic wine regions of Europe, we look at all aspects of wine, but our overwhelming focus is taste.

This pursuit gives the form to the chapters, each dedicated to a different country, and then to select regions within that country. In the introduction to each region we offer a synopsis of the current state of the region with regard to the way we and sommelier culture in general looks at the wines. In the section entitled "Particulars of Place," we detail salient features defining each region's terroir or typicity. And then in "Questions of Taste," we ask and attempt to answer one or two of the principal questions tasters of these wines are likely to have. The section called "Rajat's Top Producers"? Well, that's self-evident, though he adds that these are but a few of them: in many regions he could have listed more.

TWO
FRANCE

We're trying to follow Cornas vigneron Thierry Allemand through an ancient vineyard whose terraces he's reconstructing. Allemand is hard to describe—sort of a cross between aging superhero, mountain goat, and crackpot genius. Anyway, he simply exudes energy, which he's using to bound up and down tall stone terraces he somehow built himself despite the fact that they're made of boulders stacked into shoulder-high walls. Some of the jumps and landings on this tour are treacherous, and Raj almost goes over the edge, planting his foot wrong and wrenching his ankle, an injury that will plague him for many weeks.

Our goal is to learn as much about the relationship between various important places and the wines that they produce. But risking death and cracking ankles isn't supposed to be part of the deal. For his part, Allemand seems to be amused, seems to wickedly enjoy leading these softies over the brutal terrain he traverses every day. People think studying wine is easy, but when you get down into it, dangers abound.

The boulders Allemand had been stacking with his superhuman strength were enormous, craggy pieces of white limestone (a complement to the dominant granite of Cornas). We are reminded of something Allemand's importer, Kermit Lynch, told us as we tasted a few wines in his sitting room. "France has so many different soil types," he said, "but the one that recurs most frequently is limestone."

Of course there is the granite of Beaujolais, the schist of Anjou, the clay of the Jura, and the gravels of Bordeaux. But even in these places, limestone manages to make cameos, and as we travel more and more we come to relish the glint of this form of calcium carbonate both on the ground and in the wines, that signature spark that animates everything from Champagne to Burgundy to Saumur and St-Emilion. We learn that one of the primary dynamics in French wine—from vineyard to glass—is the interconnection between limestone and its contrasting element, clay. Limestone soils make wines with focused, linear, tight acidity and a lifted structure and body.

Wine words often associated with limestone-heavy wines are *straight*—indicating the path very high acidity charts down the middle of the tongue and deep into the back of the throat—and *bony*, which describes a fairly light wine with an angular structure and brittle, crunchy texture. Clay soils provide descriptors we associate with the non-skeletal parts of the body—*flesh, girth, muscle*. The more clay in the soil, the more the resulting wine gains heaviness and body. Too much clay and the wine becomes ponderous and flat; not enough and it cracks and shatters in the mouth. Many of the greatest French wine zones, from Burgundy to St-Emilion and everything in between, are the ones with the most compelling balance between these two poles.

And within that lesson was another. The relationship between soils and the taste of wine is complicated. And while the French have gone farther than any other place in exploring and constructing their wine regions around it, it's never as simple as one soil and one taste. But in searching out the classical taste of wine you have to start somewhere, and the vineyards of France are still the best option.

LOIRE VALLEY

Loire Valley wines have forever been mainstays in blind tasting flights for young sommeliers. After all, the Loire is a classic, a true standard of French wine as stated by the textbooks we all studied as we fell under the seductive spell of wine. But, going back just ten years ago, even if Loire reds and whites made frequent appearances in blind tastings, they rarely received much attention beyond that (excepting Sancerre). That is, we tasted them and studied them, but didn't really drink them. Of course, all that has changed now, and dramatically so. Today, we drink them lustily.

Why weren't Loire wines more popular? It's a good question, and there are several reasons. Burgundy was more accessible and available in previous decades than it is today. Loire wines were—and still are—cheaper and more available, perhaps making them less glamorous to people just cutting their vinous teeth. Burgundy had the big names, the global superstars—DRC, Jayer, Dujac, Lafon, Leflaive—while the celebrities of the Loire were less heralded and far fewer. Also, Loire wines may have unique, exotic, savory, and even just somewhat green or herbal flavors that don't always satisfy a young palate's desire for sweeter, fruitier tastes. But it's also true that Loire wines have gotten much better over the last fifteen to twenty years. Greater global interest in the wines of France, generational change, the rise of natural wine, and the emergence of a few new stars have illuminated the vast, hidden potential of the region, invigorating a spirit of even higher quality and achievement.

The turnaround is miraculous. In recent years, no region of France has captured the fancy of sommeliers and young wine lovers like the Loire Valley. Tastes are changing. Wine drinkers are more open to those once unfamiliar Loire flavors—grassy, herbal, occasionally bitter. They are developing an appetite for the Loire's thrilling acidity, crispness, and lighter body. And, let's face it, yesterday's hippest French wines, Burgundy and the Rhône, have been "discovered" by the wider wine-drinking population, and the best of those bottles have only become more expensive and harder to find.

Another reason the Loire has gained cachet among a new generation of wine drinkers: it's been the epicenter of the natural wine movement. Whatever you think of the movement or the wines, natural wine and its passionate adherents have galvanized a segment of the industry and ushered new people into wine, while bringing attention to previously peripheral regions (like the Jura and Beaujolais). In the Loire, where but a few years ago no one was interested in its more obscure wines like Coeur-Cheverny or Jasnières, the occurrence of a new natural winemaker can suddenly vault these names onto the lists of the hippest wine bars of Brooklyn or Paris.

So, for those who seek some of the classic qualities of northern French wine—earthiness, vibrance, complexity—but want to enjoy them without having to do deep reconnaissance in wine shops and spend extravagantly, the Loire makes perfect sense. It also serves the interest of those who want to be on the cutting edge. Perhaps it still doesn't produce a majority of France's most epic or iconic wines, but it more than makes up for the lack of top end by supplying scads of great drinking wine. And, as the wine-consuming population outside of Europe grows and grows, great drinking wine becomes ever more crucial. "Don't let the perfect be the enemy of the good" could well be the motto for the Loire, and we're in favor of this spirit. That said, there's no shortage of absolutely incredible winemakers operating in the Loire—many of them young—who in the coming years will be challenging the supposition that the Loire's ceiling for greatness is lower than other regions'.

In this coming era, the Loire's other great asset is its versatility. Diverse styles abound, from sparkling to sweet and everything in between. Light, mineral-driven whites are a specialty from both ends of the appellation (Muscadet and Sancerre), while medium to heavy-bodied whites can be found in appellations like Vouvray, Montlouis-sur-Loire, and Savenièrres. The reds—whether Pinot Noir or Cabernet Franc, the Loire's two great red specialties—are earthy and dry, medium-bodied at the heaviest, and perfect for today's burgeoning preference for lighter, more versatile red wines.

Sancerre

Sommeliers have a love-hate relationship with Sancerre. They love it because it sells, sells, sells. As one wine director told us, "If we put it by the glass, it's all anyone orders!" For sommeliers, it's never bad to have a reliable cash flow. But if you sense a hint of exasperation in the above quote, it's for the same reason. Sancerre is the knee-jerk selection of people who don't bother to engage with wine. It's the same as saying, "I'll have a Bud" or "Give me a gin and tonic" without bothering to look at a menu.

In a similar duality, Sancerre can be sublime—one of the great white wines of the world—but more often it's simply humdrum at best. It fell victim to its own success. The commercial strength of the village's brand led to overplanting, overcropping, and formulaic, industrial winemaking. For decades, these ordinary Sancerres have deluged grocery store shelves and generic wine lists.

When, straight from Charles de Gaulle Airport, we set out for Sancerre, we were looking for great, category-defining wine, not dreck. Sancerre's a convenient first stop after a transatlantic flight: land in the morning, grab a coffee, rent a car. If all goes well, in less than three hours you'll be sitting down to lunch, a cold bottle of that famously dry, pert white wine on ice.

PARTICULARS OF PLACE

Sancerre is a classic hilltop village with vineyards spreading out into and throughout the valley below. So successful are the wines from here that it's become a monoculture—vines, vines, vines, as far as the eye can see. From the top of the village, vineyards unfurl, billowing like a blanket over gently rolling hills. Immediately to the town's east is the stately Loire River, languidly flowing north here before it heads west to the Atlantic. Across the river, you can see the vineyards of Pouilly-sur-Loire, flatter and more exposed.

To visit Sancerre in the early spring, when the vines are but denuded scraggly skeletons, is to get the measure of two important things. Without expanses of green leaves to distract your eyes, the bleak landscape first tells you which vineyards are being farmed organically and which are not. The organic ones show life between the vines in the form of bursting cover crops of grasses, flowers, and legumes. Herbicide-treated vineyards are obvious—cold, hard, desolate ground beneath and between the vines—and by far the majority, as the overwhelming extent of industrial farming here is an inescapable fact.

The person showing us around does not farm the latter way. Rather, he's strictly biodynamic. Jean-Laurent Vacheron, of Domaine Vacheron, is an old friend. A fervent fellow with an impish sense of humor, he has an eternally youthful energy, even as he enters middle age. Under the stewardship of Jean-Laurent and his cousin

SAUVIGNON BLANC OUTSIDE SANCERRE:

POUILLY-FUMÉ, MENETOU-SALON, REUILLY, AND QUINCY

Sauvignon Blanc is by no means exclusive to Sancerre in this part of the Loire Valley. It's grown in several other nearby villages, each with something different to offer. We mentioned the area directly across the Loire to the east that produces Pouilly-Fumé, the second most famous wine of the area. The Fumé ("smoke" in French) has often led people to associate the name with a smoky characteristic in the wines, but the word evidently refers to the morning fog that comes thickly on the river, resembling smoke. This area has much the same soils as Sancerre, but in reverse—silex is concentrated near the river to the west, and limestone and Kimmeridgian marl begin to predominate moving east.

To the west of Sancerre are three notable villages for Sauvignon Blanc: Menetou-Salon, Quincy, and Reuilly. None of them stand up to the juggernaut to the east, but they can be solid wines and good values. While Kimmeridgian marl of the same ilk as Sancerre's can be found in the villages, more of the Sauvignon Blanc is planted upon gravelly and sandy alluvial terraces, making for less interesting wine. Grapes here generally ripen a bit earlier and produce slightly more imprecise wines with less cut and definition. Nevertheless, especially for the lower cost, they can be brisk, refreshing, and delightful. Look for producers such as Domaine de Reuilly in Reuilly, Sylvain Bailly and Domaine Villalin in Quincy, and Domaine Pellé in Menetou-Salon.

Jean-Dominique, the domaine has become one of the elites of France, producing both whites and reds of amazing purity and nuance.

At this time of year—early March—the leafless vines allow an unobstructed view of the soils. In case of a clear day, bring sunglasses, as this landscape (more like moonscape) is blindingly bright, thanks to the reflection of the pure white *caillottes* (the chalky stones that cover much of the area immediately around Sancerre). Caillottes are an important formulation of the taste profile of Sancerre, as they make up more than 50 percent of the region. Indeed, for everyday Sancerre—the kind enjoyed at bistros and airports around the world—it is the caillottes that provide the template. Millions of these small, jagged chunks of Oxfordian limestone litter the ground's surface, reflecting light onto the vines all summer. Caillottes produce the light, bright Sancerres you're familiar with. Not especially deep or profound, but vibrant and perky, these wines are meant to be drunk young. The best of them have an undeniably mineral texture and energy that make them absurdly refreshing.

"This wine always gives me a smile," Vacheron says of the wine from his caillottes-heavy Le Paradis vineyard, "because the acidity is so sharp and crazy." Le Paradis, with but a few inches of topsoil over the limestone bedrock, is a laser-focused,

citrus-infused wine with acidity that pleasantly sears the tongue, leading to a long, pure, buzzing finish. "The chalk gives chalkiness and saltiness," explains Vacheron. "The less clay you have, the more mineral the wines."

The contrast of clay can be felt in Chambrates, another vineyard, which has a thick layer of clay and organic matter above the chalk. Chambrates has similar flavors to Le Paradis—classic citrus, green apple, grassiness—but the shape is different—broader, more muscular. There is still minerality, but it's wrapped in a powerfully sinewy body. The difference between these two wines can be compared to that of a marathoner's body versus a sprinter's. Paradis is the long-distance runner, lean, long, and angular; Chambrates is the sprinter, ripped, thicker, and rounder.

Vacheron next shows us Les Romains, which demonstrates another, very different sort of rocky soil, the second of the appellation's three major rock types: silex. Composed of flint or chert, silex occupies the far eastern part of the appellation and then continues on across the Loire, where it's a signature soil component for the neighboring Pouilly-Fumé wines. Even though it's the minority rock type in Sancerre (just 20 percent of the surface), silex is important, as it makes an epic style of wine—brooding, dense, powerful, deep.

"Our fathers bought this land," says Vacheron, "and it was thought to be potentially less interesting than the limestone. But in reality, it's not uninteresting. It's just more complex to make great wine here. You need to really listen closely to the terroir. The wines are very mineral, but in a different way. The . . . *elevage* of the wine [maturation before bottling] is more complex to achieve. With limestone wines it's much easier."

Vacheron continues, "*Le calcaire* [limestone] is easy to enjoy, obvious. With silex you need to work. It doesn't try very hard to make you like it." The silex wine is much rounder. It's short and compact with formidable density. Many people invoke the scent of gunpowder or flint stone as a classic indication of Sancerre from silex. And Vacheron demonstrates this by cracking two pieces of silex together, creating a little hint of smoke. Any smoky note in the wine doesn't come directly from flint, but the metaphor is apt—sometimes there's a hint of matchstick smoke in the wines.

Lastly, we drive to the village of Chavignol for a look at Sancerre's third important rock type: Kimmeridgian marl, a tight fusion of limestone and clay. (You'll also hear about Kimmeridgian marl in our sections on Chablis and Champagne, as this type of rock does star turns in these locales as well.) Chavignol is famous for Sancerre's most epic whites. It's also famous for its renowned goat cheese, *Crottin de Chavignol*, which happens to be smashingly good with Sancerre. For our tour of Chavignol, we had an appointment with the great François Cotat, whose eponymous wine is one of the icons of the region.

JEAN-LAURENT VACHERON
Domaine Vacheron, Sancerre

At the end of a tight valley west of the Sancerre hill, Chavignol is surrounded on both sides by steep hillsides, one of which is preposterously abrupt; standing atop it and looking down is not for the acrophobic. Coming to mind immediately is how painful it would be to climb this massive, brutally vertiginous hill. Unsurprisingly, the ancients named this place *Les Monts Damnés*—"the damned mountains!"

Those cruel jokesters knew what they were doing, however. Les Monts Damnés, and neighboring super-steep vineyards Le Cul de Beaujeu and La Grande Côte, produce a singular style of Sancerre, one that is hard to confuse with the wines from pure caillottes or silex. Kimmeridgian is key, as no matter where it pops up, it produces a unique stamp on a wine. The melding of limestone and clay together in a marl somehow produces a wine different than if the clay and limestone had just been layered on top of each other. The wines reflect the dense, seamless integration of clay and limestone particles, somehow offering the robustness of clay and the mineral energy of limestone at the same time. The wines can be brooding and thick with earthy aromas, a far cry from the bright citrus and grass of mainstream Sancerre. Indeed, in years past, these Chavignol wines have been denied the Sancerre appellation in tastings by the region's wine board because they are so atypical.

Cotat, who farms only 4.25 hectares (10 acres), is a soft-spoken man, as you'd expect for someone faced with the ruminative daily task of working these vines. At the base of the damned hill, we stagger over the loose rocky terrain of Cotat's vineyard on the Côte d'Amigny, unable to gain a steady foothold. Back at his winery, we taste Cotat's current releases and some older vintages. One of the unique characteristics of this style of Sancerre is its ability to age. Most Sauvignon Blanc in the world, let alone most Sancerre, is not the kind of wine you'd want to drink more than two or three years past its vintage date. But these powerful Chavignol wines have a closed, inward-looking quality when young and often need many years to blossom into full expression. A 1990 La Grande Côte proved that to us. It was Sancerre, but also not . . . it was something more. From a great, albeit warm vintage, almost thirty years old at the time of tasting, its fruit had evolved to wild, exotic notes like passion fruit and cantaloupe, while the aromas veered from honey to a deep earthy scent of mushrooms. A mushroomy note is not uncommon in wines from Kimmeridgian marl, which puts its stamp on any vines that touch it. The crazy fruit notes—well, those are just an expression of the great diversity that is Sancerre.

What are the differences between the tastes of Sancerre from limestone, silex, and Kimmeridgian marl?

Limestone, the Oxfordian kind known as caillottes in Sancerre, is the most common soil type and yields a bright, energetic, high-pitched wine. High limestone content in the soils emphasizes acidity in the wine and excludes fleshiness, creating a texture considered bony, straight, sometimes piercing.

Try: Domaine Vincent Pinard, "Florès."

Silex, aka chert or flint, provides a wine with more flesh and roundness than wines grown mostly on limestone. Some attribute a smoky characteristic to these wines, but it doesn't always appear and is likely more due to winemaking than terroir. Mostly, the shape of the wine in the mouth is round, and the structure is more short and compact than limestone, and not as linear. Think density, with a mineral streak running like a spine through the body. Flavors go to stone fruits and florals.

Try: Domaine Vacheron, "Les Romains."

Kimmeridgian marl, a tight mashup of clay and limestone, puts a similar signature onto Sancerre as it does to Chablis: a singular interweaving of taut minerality with fleshy roundness. Whereas silex provides both sensations too, they feel more separate there—like a cable whose rubber tubing (the wine's flesh) surrounds the metal wire (the wine's mineral sensation). In Kimmeridgian wines the two sensations seem miraculously interwoven like a fabric. It's truly a wine of texture, especially in youth, when flavors and aromas may be suppressed.

Try: Domaine François Cotat, "Les Monts Damnés." For fun, try alongside a Chablis from a similar soil type like Domaine William Fèvre, "Montée de Tonnerre."

FRANÇOIS COTAT
Domaine François Cotat, Chavignol

◇ **DOMAINE VACHERON** In Sancerre, there's Vacheron and then there's everyone else. Since Jean-Laurent and Jean-Dominique took over, Vacheron's been one of the most consistent wines in the Loire, if not in all of France. The cousins work biodynamically in the vineyard and precisely in the winery to make wonderfully drinkable but terroir-expressive wines. And a big nod to the Vacheron rosé, perhaps the greatest rosé in existence.

◇ **FRANÇOIS COTAT** The master of the Kimmeridgian, Cotat's wines are wonderfully traditional. In hot vintages, they can come off as a little flabby, high alcohol, perhaps slightly off-dry. But when they're on point, they capture the density, minerality, and power that come from the incredibly stony, steep Kimmeridgian slopes of Chavignol.

◇ **PASCAL COTAT** The cousin of François also makes very good wines. When their families' holdings were passed down, the two cousins split the holdings, and it's a shame that they don't really speak. (We made the mistake of asking François if his cousin made his wines the same way, and he curtly answered, "I have no idea.")

◇ **GÉRARD BOULAY** Another great of Chavignol, the Boulay family's first record of farming grapes there date to 1380, when the Clos de Beaujeu was already recognized as a great white wine. It still is today. Wines from these Kimmeridgian-soil vineyards often have the density and earthiness of Chablis.

◇ **DOMAINE VINCENT PINARD** Not well enough known in the States, this is a very good domaine, making razor-sharp Sancerre that doesn't shy from intensity of acidity. Their practices are good—low intervention, organic viticulture—on vines averaging fifty years, mostly planted on caillottes.

◇ **DIDIER DAGUENEAU** The most well-known producer in Pouilly-Fumé, Dagueneau is loved by all, and rightly so. The wines are powerful expressions of silex, rich and mineral at the same time. The domaine carries forth the indomitable personality of Didier, who tragically died in a plane crash in 2008. Now the wines are made by his son and daughter, and they're carrying on his legacy ably. The wines are pure, but not as idiosyncratic as Didier's, which had a little more funk.

Previous Page:
The town of Sancerre viewed from Les Monts Damnés

Touraine

From Sancerre, we head west into the heart of the Loire, where new soils, topography, and grape varieties await. To enter the section of the Loire Valley known as the Touraine—anchored by the city of Tours—is to be welcomed into the kingdom of Chenin Blanc and Cabernet Franc, the white and red pillars of the area's wines. The Touraine is a whopping 120 miles west of Sancerre (with yet another 160 miles or so to the Atlantic), giving a sense of how extended the Loire winegrowing area is. As you move west toward the ocean, the climate becomes more maritime and less continental, meaning more temperate and humid, but without quite the highs and lows of Sancerre.

We are focusing on the two signature grapes of the region. Among sommeliers and other wine hipsters, there are hardly two more popular wines these days. This turnaround is well deserved; Cabernet Franc and Chenin Blanc have long gone underappreciated. Sommeliers learned them, but rarely drank them. That's all changed now, likely because their quality is better than ever, and Burgundy has gotten too expensive. If in the past, you knew Loire Chenin Blanc for teeth-stabbing acidity and wacky flavors, and Loire Cabernet Franc for thin, weedy wines low on pleasure, you'll appreciate the changes.

Our first stops are the towns of Vouvray and Montlouis-sur-Loire: ground zero for Touraine Chenin Blanc. Chenin has a unique talent; it's able to make every style from super sweet to bone-dry, from fat and round to piano-wire tight. We love most the dry wines, which carry a medium to heavy weight with lots of concentration. At its best, Chenin provides exotic, unfamiliar flavors—litchi, anyone? Lanolin?—and its acidity is on another plane of existence compared to most wines.

Vouvray and Montlouis

In a Tale of Two Towns, Vouvray may be the bigger name, but Montlouis-sur-Loire (known colloquially as "Montlouis") has been the more compelling wine in recent years. Sitting just across the river from one another, the two appellations are close, perhaps too close. They vinify the same grape, Chenin Blanc. Their soils are similar. Heck, wines from Montlouis were bottled as "Vouvray" until Montlouis received its own appellation in 1937. However, Vouvray was always seen as the great wine, the one written about in books.

But in the most recent generation things shifted, and Montlouis is suddenly the more interesting wine. In its fame, Vouvray became complacent, failing to keep ties with the current scene. Vouvray is large, with more than 2,200 planted hectares (5,400 acres) and only a small fraction of it organically farmed. Montlouis, by contrast, is small, with only 400 planted hectares (980 acres), yet almost half is organic. Vouvray turns over 50 percent of its grapes into cheap sparkling wine, failing to make the most of Chenin Blanc's complexities. Montlouis, rather, has made a name for itself in recent years with innovative dry still wine. To put it bluntly, Vouvray is old school, while Montlouis is the cutting edge. Not that there's anything wrong with old school— the wines of Vouvray pillars Domaine Huet and Philippe Foreau's Domaine du Clos Naudin (we'll just refer to it as Foreau, which is printed more boldly on the labels than the domaine name) are some of the greatest Chenins on the planet. The problem in Vouvray is that there's not a lot of energy or creativity beyond those two and a few other producers.

The closely entangled and somewhat seething relationship between Vouvray and Montlouis boiled over in 2013, when a ridiculous law was passed ruling that any wine labeled Vouvray must be vinified within the appellation boundaries, effectively disqualifying anyone whose winery is just across the river, in Montlouis—even though the grapes were grown in Vouvray. The incident was a low moment for the more famous and entitled commune of Vouvray, exposing its slack aristocracy as threatened by those hungry, energetic, middle-class strivers across the river. The law effectively targets two prominent, ambitious producers whose winemaking facilities are in Montlouis but who make famous wine from grapes grown in Vouvray: François Chidaine and Jacky Blot. Unless they chose to build or rent a winery in Vouvray, they are now prevented from labeling these wines Vouvray; instead, they must use the humble catchall term *Vin de France.*

The class difference between the two communes is apparent in two visits we make, one on each side of the river. In Vouvray, we stop into Philippe Foreau's stately domaine. Foreau is an immensely charming man with an incredible grasp of his wines and terroirs. Domaine du Clos Naudin has a lovely gate, beautiful grounds, and some ornate buildings, as you would expect of a high-brow producer in a high-end region. We taste with him in his dark, very cold subterranean caves and are treated to a range of styles—from very dry to very sweet—and vintages. "Often the wines with the important terroir—when they are young they are quite austere and offer few aromas. But they are always dynamic on the mouth," he notes, supporting our thesis for this book, "and the length shows through. If you don't have length when it's young, you'll never have the length when it's old!" He also treats us to a grand disquisition on wine and food pairing, a jovial yet also deadly serious part of his approach. "It's true, I do love to eat," he admits, while telling us that his 2010 sweet wine would be perfect matched against lobster with citrus, lemongrass, and coriander.

In contrast, when we head across the river to François Chidaine's cellar in Montlouis, there are no flourishes. The winery is bare-bones, as is the cellar, both chiseled out of the limestone hillside. Speaking of chiseled, one could say the same for Chidaine's wines, which are uniformly terrific, fusing the laser-sharp acid of Montlouis with the rich, full capabilities of Chenin Blanc. While Foreau does not make *parcellaire* wine—wine from a single plot or vineyard—Chidaine makes a plethora of them, as he is interested in the finest gradations of site in his wines. The origins of the gulf between Montlouis and Vouvray, he tells us, have always been there, going back

FRANÇOIS CHIDAINE
Domaine François Chidaine, Montlouis

to the politically motivated division of the appellations in 1937. The elites of the region have always lived in Vouvray and looked down on Montlouis. Despite that, Montlouis is a more compelling appellation these days. However, its prices still reflect the historical norms. So enjoy great Chenin while it's still cheap!

PARTICULARS OF PLACE

Given that Vouvray and Montlouis used to be considered one region, you won't be surprised to learn that their general soil and exposition profiles are quite similar. Vouvray lies on the Loire's north bank and Montlouis on its south. However, the better part of Montlouis faces the smaller Cher river, a tributary, right before it joins the Loire.

Historically, when people have written about this region, they have mentioned *tuffeau*, the local name for the particular kind of limestone that defines the area. Tuffeau is a porous, soft lime with low density, strong but also malleable and well draining. Tuffeau underlies everything here, as the Loire has cut through it over the millennia, leaving sheer cliffs and steep slopes beside the river. Spectacularly, quarries and other hollows at the base of the cliffs have been made into wineries, wine caves, and even residences. If the well-draining tuffeau is the connection between the vineyards of Vouvray and Montlouis, then the soils atop it play a big role in defining the difference. While a range of topsoil exists, it comes in two main families. The first, called *perruches*, is clay mixed with silex (flint), which creates wines of tension and flinty minerality, with flavors (subtle in young wines) of white flowers and citrus with hints of licorice (look for Chidaine's Montlouis Clos du Breuil). The second is *aubuis*, a yellowish clay mixed with limestone and flint, producing wines of more presence, density, and power than perruches does (try Clos Habert). Aubuis is much more common in Vouvray, as is chalky clay (perruches is almost nonexistent). In Montlouis, you find more Perruches as well as much more sand.

The question is not just which soil type defines a vineyard, but how deep that soil is before the tips of the vines make their way into the tuffeau underneath. In general, heavier clay returns heavier, rounder wines with more fruit. A preponderance of clay and aubuis atop the tuffeau is what gives Vouvray its famous weight. It's the presence of limestone in the vicinity of the vines' roots, François Chidaine tells us, that slows Vouvray's maturation of the grapes and allows vignerons to take them further in terms of richness. Montlouis, lying in the convergence of two rivers (Loire and Cher), features soils more eroded and washed out, therefore containing more sand and pebbles, less clay, and deeper, warmer soils that ripen the grapes earlier and faster and to higher sugar levels.

Limestone cliffs at Domaine François Chidaine

What does Chenin Blanc from Vouvray and Montlouis generally taste like?

In its most classic form, Vouvray beautifully marries voluptuousness with mineral strength. It often feels round and fleshy in the mouth—especially for wine with its feet in limestone—but, at its best, is neither plump nor sluggish. Rather, it takes its energy from a mineral footing while piling on waxy richness and stature. Flavors vary, but giveaways are fruit notes that run from peaches to quince. Chenin Blanc also often has a telltale lanolin aroma: think wet wool, like a sweater that's been caught in the rain.

How do you tell the difference between them?

When blind tasting or trying to determine the differences between Vouvray and Montlouis, consider both style/culture and what you can pick up from the texture. Both have the ability to produce rounded, medium-to heavyweight white wines, both with strong mineral cores. However, Montlouis may be slightly lighter in stature, thanks to pebbles and sand, and its most prominent producers tend to favor the style of bright, forward acidity and intense dryness. Vouvray, on the other hand, given its old-school leanings, may often show as plumper, rounder, and heavier. For the great Vouvray producers, acidity is never a question, but it is usually presented on a wine with rounder, broader shoulders than Montlouis. To experience the contrast, try a rich, powerful, classic Vouvray from Domaine du Clos Naudin (Philippe Foreau) or Domaine Huet against a Montlouis from Chidaine or Jacky Blot. You will taste Chenin Blanc's breadth and power in both, but the Montlouis will likely be racier and more cutting.

- ◇ **FRANÇOIS CHIDAINE (MONTLOUIS & VOUVRAY)** The pope of Montlouis and Vouvray—just a sublimely great producer. He knows his vineyards better than anyone, and he styles his cuvées to the contours of each vineyard. He lets the vintage dictate the wine, meaning he has no formula, but determines each year the length of fermentations and duration of aging. It's a classic and very honest way of making wine old-school style. He uses big barrels and older barrels to add no oak flavor to the wines, and allows them to mature at a slow, even pace in his extremely cold cellars. The wines are pure and clean, yet profoundly expressive. And they're still phenomenal values, many available for under $30.

- ◇ **JACKY BLOT (TAILLE AU LOUPS—MONTLOUIS & VOUVRAY)** Amazingly, Blot has been quietly making exceptional wines for many years, but is still an under-the-radar producer. His wines are terroir-driven and sharp, always interesting, always saying something new. His use of barrels new and old can sometimes make the wines lush and soft, but they always have great aging potential.

◇ **LA GRANGE TIPHAINE (MONTLOUIS)** Coralie and Damien Delecheneau run this fourth-generation family domaine set on a beautiful plateau in the Montlouis subdistrict of Amboise, overlooking the Loire. Damien is an excellent winemaker, crafting terrific cuvées from not only Chenin Blanc, but also the red grapes Gamay, Cabernet Franc, Côt, and Grolleau. Some of the vines are very old, but the sense of experimentation and play is alive here. To a one, the wines are fresh, energetic, and exciting.

◇ **DOMAINE HUET (VOUVRAY)** The 2003 sale of the majority of this eminent domaine to the American family of Anthony Hwang created much controversy and intrigue, and speculation that another precious French heirloom wine estate was finished. However, that hasn't been the case. From the outside, at least, the wines are as polished and precise as they've ever been and have remained true to the style of Huet, which is rich and round, with ripe notes of quince and honey, but lots of energy coming from the acid and stony core.

◇ **DOMAINE DU CLOS NAUDIN (AKA PHILIPPE FOREAU, VOUVRAY)** The great gourmand of Vouvray maintains his elegant time capsule well. These wines are throwbacks in their adherence to simpler times, when wine wasn't about single vineyards and micro expressions, but about the general style of the domaine overall. The sec is always bone-dry, the sparkling always magical. Wine comes in the Foreau style, rich and precise though never heavy, and it's always consistent—not cutting edge, but always reliable. Every vintage and every wine is true to place.

Chinon and Bourgueil

When it comes to red wine in the Touraine, it gets no better than the two towns of Chinon and Bourgueil. (A third, St-Nicolas-de-Bourgueil, an adjoining appellation of Bourgueil, is good too, but smaller and less significant than its neighbor.) Indeed, when these wines are good, few reds in France are better value. Cabernet Franc shines here, taking its greatest star turn as a solo, unblended variety. Nowhere else in the world does pure Cabernet Franc reach the heights it does here (well, except for next door in Saumur). These wines' brilliance lies in their ability to deliver the earthy red fruit perfume, acid, and elegance promised by Cabernet Franc, but with more of the body that its critics ding the variety for lacking. While these wines won't be confused structurally for Bordeaux, they have body, tannin, and a remarkable ability to age. More than merely great lunch wines, as some might accuse them of being, they're brilliant table wines—gulp-worthy on their own and versatile with food.

Chinon and Bourgueil share many of the same dynamics as Vouvray and Montlouis. Both are specialists in the same grape, this time the red Cabernet Franc. Both share similar soils. And the two villages are on different rivers. Bourgueil looks over the Loire, while Chinon faces another Loire tributary, the Vienne. One element these two villages lack is the animosity Vouvray feels for Montlouis. Talk to producers in either town, and they only seem to have friendly things to say about one another, almost to a fault. Matthieu Baudry, the ardent young vintner of Domaine Bernard Baudry in Chinon, says, generously, "I really believe Bourgueil has great terroir. Chinon has a great terroir. And I won't tell you that Chinon has the best, because I don't believe it."

Of course, while mutual admiration is high, a subtle hierarchical ranking has Chinon at the top of the heap as the most celebrated appellation of Touraine reds. How did such a hierarchy arise? There's no clear reason, but it might be a simple case of star power. Importer Kermit Lynch (thanks to a tip from Jacques Seysses of Burgundy's Domaine Dujac) found Charles Joguet in 1977 and was blown away by his freshly made wine. Shortly thereafter, he started importing Joguet and turned the domaine into a star (he still imports it today). Also in Chinon's favor, we can't even begin to describe how to pronounce Bourgueil (it's a mouthful, even in French).

Just as Chinon is fortunate to have Joguet, Bourgueil is fortunate to have Domaine de la Chevalerie. This domaine, founded in 1640, is tragically unknown in the United States. Early one morning, we visited the lively, hilarious young proprietor Stephanie Caslot, who had only a year earlier assumed responsibility for the historic domaine (with her brother, Emmanuel) after the death of their father, Pierre. The wines here are as traditionally made as they come ("traditionally made" or "classically made" will be recurring phrases in this book). Traditional winemaking styles can vary from region to region and country to country. In most places, though, including many regions in France, this simply means natural-yeast fermentations and aging in large, old, neutral casks that don't impart any flavor of wood) and the young duo brings extraordinary pep to what could otherwise be a relic.

After a tour, we step out into the brisk morning air. Stephanie surveys the long driveway leading down to an enormous subterranean limestone cellar (so vast and roomy it could serve as a New York subway station). "We will taste from here to the cellar," she says, dragging a barrel over to one side of the drive to serve as a makeshift table. We have no idea what she means, but take wineglasses in hand, as, arms full, she carries half a dozen bottles out. It's freezing, but the wines taste good, dark, and strong. After we taste the wines from the current vintages of 2014 and 2013, she walks the length of the drive and disappears down into the cellar for a few minutes, returning with a few bottles of older vintages. We taste the 2010, 2009, and 2008. The bottles begin to crowd the top of the barrel. Then she disappears again, returning with another armful of bottles: 2006, 2005, 2002. Soon the barrel's top is too crowded, so she begins to line bottles on the cement drive. She vanishes again and returns with yet another bushel of bottles. Now another time. And another. As the trail of bottles grows, wines from the nineties beget wines from the eighties, seventies, and sixties. How far can this possibly go? The answer is exactly as promised: The wines stop when the trail of bottles reaches the end of the drive,

50 feet away: our last tasting is a vintage 1946. "I told you we'd taste to the cellar door!" she says.

Not a single wine has fallen apart; at most, the wine is barely faded. It's a tour-de-force tasting and proves the remarkable longevity of the amazing Cabernet Franc from these soils. As we get into the older wines, their flavors change in fairly expected ways—primary (fresh) fruit flavors fade, replaced with more nuanced, dried fruit notes and earthy aromas; tannins soften and the wines in general become tamer and more gentle. The only astonishing part is how youthful the oldest wines are—a phenomenon that you sometimes see when tasting wines from cold regions stored in cold underground cellars. Low temperatures and lack of movement slows down the reactions in the bottle that cause it to age.

"I tell my customers, the wine tastes like the soil looks," Matthieu Baudry says, as we climb into his car to survey Chinon's soils. "It's as light or heavy as the texture of the soil." When it comes to these soils and their arrangement, Chinon and Bourgueil are quite similar, almost mirror images on long hillsides in neighboring valleys. Most important to know is that there are three main soils—sand, gravel, and clay limestone—each occupying different bands of the hillside like layers of a cake.

At the base of these hills, as one would expect of a river valley, are mostly gravels and sands. From here come the lightest wines, meant for quaffing. Domaine de la Chevalerie's is called Les Galichets; Baudry's is Les Granges. "When you taste Les Granges, you look at the soil . . . it's light, sandy, well drained," says Matthieu. And the wine? "It's light and fruity too. Easy to drink. You can't expect to have lots of minerals, limestone, saltiness in a wine, when it's just planted on these simple sands and gravels." Both domaine's wines are lighter, though Les Granges from Chinon is perhaps a bit more generous at this young age, offering more flesh and youthful fruit, while Chevalerie's Galichets is still quite tense and hard.

We climb back into the car and drive a short way up the hill, gaining only slight altitude. "So we are only 1,650 feet between each vineyard," Matthieu continues, "but they are very different." He points at the vines. "That is Les Grezeaux, our oldest vines at sixty years. Here are more gravels, but with much more pebbles and stones. There is clay in the subsoil, so it makes a deeper wine with more tannin and a lot of concentration."

The soil changes considerably where we next stop: higher up the valley's side, up on the slope. "This is Le Clos Guillot," Matthieu says. "There is clay and limestone here. Lots of shells in the limestone and some sand mixed in. It makes a very finely textured, long wine, as you would expect from limestone." The limestone, he explained, is yellow limestone—a younger type than in his other nearby vineyard, La Croix Boissée, which is white limestone. At La Croix Boissée, Matthieu makes both a white (from Chenin Blanc) and a red (Cabernet Franc, of course). The effect of the difference in a limestone's color is unclear. The Chenin Blanc comes from a white, pure limestone section, where there's hardly any topsoil, resulting in a wine that is very elegant and mineral. The red, which comes from an area with more clay, is perhaps the domaine's top wine. It is fuller than the gravel wines, as would be expected, but still boasts the fineness of structure of limestone. Powerful dark berry and cherry notes fill the mouth upon tasting, but it also has a lot of crunch from plentiful, if polished tannins. This is a wine that can age decades.

We summit the hill, coming to a plateau. The soils here go back to a lighter profile—a hard bedrock of limestone covered with sand. The wine made from the top of the hill is simply called Le Domaine, and is a basic (but delicious), easy-drinking red.

DOMAINE BERNARD BAUDRY
Soils from various vineyards at Domaine Bernard Baudry, Chinon

We've been through the similarities of Chinon and Bourgueil, but how are they different? The most easily observed difference is one of climate. Even though they are close together (just 10 miles), the difference in river valleys makes an impact. Bourgueil sits on the side of the grand Loire at a place where the valley opens up. This subjects the vineyards of Bourgueil to the maritime weather effects coming up the river from the Atlantic (cool, rainy springs to warm, sticky summers and unpredictable wet and windy autumns). In contrast, on the smaller Vienne river, Chinon's valley is narrower and tighter, offering it a little protection from the weather and some added warmth. "Here in Bourgueil we have a sort of oceanic influence," Stephanie tells us. "Chinon can be a little more dry and continental. Sometimes when we have a big rain, you can see the difference. It can be pouring here and it's dry there."

Consequently, the wines in Chinon can be more supple and fruit-forward, drinkable at a younger age. Bourgueil wines tend to have more structure, with heavier tannins, and may take a bit longer to open up, but can age a very long time, as we found out.

QUESTIONS OF TASTE

What do Chinon and Bourgueil taste like?

While the profiles of the wines vary in terms of producer and soil, these Cabernet Francs often tend toward red fruits with notes of cherry and raspberry that may ultimately lead to darker blackberry flavors. Savory secondary flavors recall licorice, violets, or other meadow flowers. Often an earthy note pervades, reminiscent of chalk dust or wet stones. The grape, after all, is Cabernet Franc, so look for some classic Cabernet notes, too—not necessarily the cassis (blackcurrant) so closely associated with Bordeaux, but redcurrant. Furthermore, a whiff of that leafy, slightly herbaceous side of the Cabernet grape is often a dead giveaway in a blind tasting.

While rarely reaching heavy-bodied status, these Loire reds can vary considerably in weight, from lithe, light-bodied affairs that explode with bouncy fruit to more substantial, crunchy reds that have darker tones and denser tannins.

How to tell Chinon from Bourgueil?

Telling the two wines apart is not easy! Yet, if you're trying to make the call in a blind tasting, a greater suppleness and ripe, warm fruit might indicate a wine from (slightly) warmer Chinon, while heavier structure, thicker, grainier tannins, and slower evolution could indicate Bourgueil.

The cellar at Domaine Bernard Beaudry

STÉPHANIE AND EMMANUEL CASLOT
Domaine de la Chevalerie, Bourgueil

◇ **DOMAINE DE LA CHEVALERIE (BOURGUEIL)** This little-known domaine makes some of the best Cabernet Franc wines in the world. We see firsthand the aging potential of this estate, which practices winemaking that is as old school (traditional) as possible: wild yeast ferments, maturation in big, old oak casks. Vinification and aging in extremely cold, underground limestone cellars makes for wines with incredible fortitude and longevity. Priced in the $20–$50 range, these wines are incredible deals, given how long they can age.

◇ **CATHERINE & PIERRE BRETON (BOURGUEIL)** One of the most beloved producers in France and with a great presence in the United States thanks to Kermit Lynch, this great domaine is just down the hill from Chevalerie. Thanks to early participation in promoting natural winegrowing practices, the domaine is considered a star of the natural wine movement. The husband-and-wife team produces incredibly delicious and honest wines with lots of character. Their sparkling and Vouvray are also exceptional.

◇ **DOMAINE DU BEL AIR (BOURGUEIL)** This incredible domaine, with hand-farmed, handmade organic wine from the Gauthier family, is a gem. The Clos Nouveau is one of the oldest pieces of land in the area, and makes a luscious, stony red—ethereal Cabernet Franc. Jour de Soif is their breezy, easy-drinking entry wine.

◇ **BERNARD BAUDRY (CHINON)** This estate represents so much of what can be great in French wine today—a fantastic family, vineyards and winemaking worked by the owners, and an obsessively terroir-specific drive to capture all of Chinon's facets. The reds are structured and firm, but also sport a mineral, chalky deliciousness. Do not miss the rosé and the rare, beautiful Chenin Blanc.

◇ **DOMAINE LES ROCHES (JÉROME LENOIR, CHINON)** This is a wine to cherish and love. So old school, this is as raw and naked as Cabernet Franc gets (in a good way). It's profound, rustic and transparent, made from old vines (most own-rooted, meaning they are growing on their original roots and haven't been grafted onto American rootstock to protect the vine from phylloxera) on bony limestone soils, the wines mature for years in a deep, cold, mold-covered limestone cellar. Just one cuvée, Les Roches, is made, and it's spectacular, soulful, and heartwarming. Sometimes older vintages are released dating to the 1980s or 1990s.

◇ **CHARLES JOGUET (CHINON)** He put Chinon on the map, thanks to Lynch's discovery of him in the 1970s, and has always set the standard with ripe, soft, rich Chinon, a wine that can be drunk young or aged. It remains today as solid and scrumptious as it's ever been.

◇ **DOMAINE ALLIET (CHINON)** Another wonderful Chinon, made in a richer, more modern style that impresses a bit more flesh and plumpness into the wines. Some time in new oak barrels smooths them out, resulting in appealing wines that are a bit more juicy and fruity than others from the area.

Saumur and Saumur-Champigny

The name Saumur has many associations in wine. Foremost, Saumur is a gorgeous, vibrant town on the Loire with a stunning castle, limestone cliffs, waterfront strolling, great shops, and wine bars. As a wine region, it's sprawling, but easy to unpack.

While officially a part of the Anjou region of the Loire, Saumur (and its adjunct appellation Saumur-Champigny) could easily be connected to the western part of Touraine, to which it is very close. While the topography is different, the soils are fairly similar—lots of limestone, clay, and tuffeau. We are on the very edge of what was geologically the Paris Basin, that vast, ancient inland sea that gave the gift of so much limestone. But that ends in the Anjou and what follows comes from the neighboring geological feature known as the Massif armoricain, which trades in dark igneous and metamorphic rock. Indeed this western side of the region is known as "Black Anjou" for the color of the rock, while the Saumur area is referred to as "White Anjou" thanks to the bright, reflective glare of chalk.

If the soil here has much in common with Chinon/Bourgueil and Vouvray/Montlouis, the topography is different. While those vineyards are situated on terraces climbing out of the river valley, Saumur is fully on the plateau. Here, the larger effect is of flatness, even if the landscape is really composed of gently undulating hills. But flatness equates to easier farming, and fairly rich clay-limestone soils with ample groundwater can equate to higher yields. And those two qualities often go hand in hand with lower-quality wine and inexpensive sparkling from Chenin Blanc, which is exactly what Saumur is known for in France. Saumur's area is huge, covering almost forty villages and three different *départements* (governmental regions), and it produces wines ranging from white and red to sweet and sparkling.

Saumur-Champigny is an appellation within Saumur featuring red wine only, predominantly from Cabernet Franc. It was created in 1957 in an attempt to elevate a brand of red wine from the more vague offerings (white, red, sweet, and sparkling) of Saumur. The strategy worked, and Saumur-Champigny wine became popular in the seventies and eighties in Parisian bistros, where it was known as a bright, fruity, easy drinking *vin de soif* (drinking wine—casual, uncomplex, inexpensive). Many French people still see it that way. However, these days, many good producers are making quality red wine in both Saumur and Saumur-Champigny, so it's not ironclad that the latter is always superior.

While it's true that oceans of industrially farmed, indifferently made wines can still be found in Saumur, there are also a number of resplendent wine areas, and some of the Loire's greatest bottles are made off them. Now a new generation of young vignerons are taking inspiration from famed domaine Clos Rougeard to produce some of the Loire's most electrifying wines.

CHÂTEAU DE MONTSOREAU

Samur

BRÉZÉ

VINEYARD FOCUS

"The Greatest Forgotten Hill" is the name our friend, California wine importer Ted Vance (The Source Imports), memorably gave to Brézé in one of his essays. The good news is that Brézé is on the rise, today producing some of the most arrestingly mineral, intense Chenin Blanc on the planet. The tale of how Brézé became forgotten highlights France's struggles in the twentieth century.

On the generally flat plane of Saumur, the hill of Brézé stands out. Not monumental in height or stature, it can still be seen from a distance as a large, sprawling mound topped by a UNESCO World Heritage Site castle, a perennial tourist destination. Beneath and around the castle, spanning 360 degrees, is a sea of vines, many of them enclosed behind walls as separate clos. For at least five hundred years, these vines produced some of the most profound wines of France. They were regularly exchanged, barrel for barrel, with Château d'Yquem, the nectarlike sweet wine from Bordeaux that today still sells for thousands a bottle. They were a favorite at Versailles under the Sun King, Louis XIV (because owner Thomas de Dreux-Brézé was the Grand Master of Ceremony at the court).

But things, as they do, declined. Two world wars didn't help, as Nazis occupied the château during the second. The Marquis de Brézé of that time had three daughters, and, through marriage in 1959, Brézé fell into the hands of the Comte de Colbert, who didn't value it as much as the original family. By then, the focus of the great vineyard had become quantity, not quality, and the soils were farmed chemically.

"From 1945 to 1965 there was a crisis of Chenin Blanc," Romain Guiberteau, the great Saumur winemaker, tells us. "There was so much produced, so badly produced. It became an ocean of sparkling wine—more like sparkling water with alcohol. During the crisis, they planted more and more Cabernet Franc, as a fashion had developed especially for rosé and also some red wine." In an effort to capitalize on the new taste for Cabernet Franc and to emphasize a wine that could fetch the higher prices that could pull Saumur out of the gutter, the appellation of Saumur-Champigny was created in 1957.

Perhaps Brézé would have regained renown if it had become part of the new, elite appellation, as it was indeed invited to join the other eight prestigious hillside areas forming Saumur-Champigny. But there was a problem. The new appellation was only for red wine, and Brézé's great reputation was for Chenin Blanc, to which, before World War II, 90 percent of its soils were dedicated. Out of respect for its illustrious past, the château's owner declined the invitation, and Brézé remained lowly Saumur, fetching half the price of Saumur-Champigny. But in doing so, the marquis may have secured Brézé's future. And that future is Chenin Blanc.

"More and more people are still planting Cabernet Franc in Brézé today," says Arnaud Lambert. "If it had joined Saumur-Champigny, there would probably be no Chenin left." And Lambert is very glad it didn't. He and his late father jumped at the opportunity to sign a long-term lease on the Comté de Colbert's vineyards in 2009 (many had tried over the years, but the Lamberts were the first to succeed). The lease included land in eight of the clos of Brézé, very old vineyards, each with different soil configurations and expositions. When Arnaud finally got in the vineyards, he found soil that was barely alive thanks to decades of chemical farming. He rolled up his sleeves. "It's a lot of work to improve the quality of the soils," he said in 2016, "but now after seven years of organic farming, the soils are showing progress and we will begin biodynamic farming next year."

Today, out of 400 total hectares (980 acres), only four producers are bottling the wine as Brézé, accounting for about 10 percent of the vineyard area. The rest gets issued by the co-op as just sparkling or Saumur Blanc or Saumur Rouge. Arnaud Lambert has 21 hectares (51.5 acres), and makes stunning single-vineyard whites from Clos du Midi, Clos David, and Clos de la Rue. These are precise, crystal-sharp wines in their youth, with enough snap to shock the tongue, but still possess the weight and resonance to expand and slightly soften with age. The reds come from Clos de L'Etoile and Clos Mazurique. He also makes a sparkling brut and rosé. While differences in each vineyard lead to wines of distinctive character, Lambert's style arcs toward grace. His wines are stripped down and elemental, ripped with acidity and verve. They plug into the electricity of Brézé's limestone soils.

At the other end of the style spectrum, the wines from Clos Rougeard and Guiberteau are much richer. They use lees contact and new oak to produce a rounder, more opulent style, one with undeniable power. Certainly, Brézé's signature acidity and minerality are forcefully present, but the bodies of these wines are rounder and richer. The last estate bottling of Brézé, Domaine du Collier's whites and reds, charts a style in between Rougeard and Guiberteau. All of Antoine Foucault's wines are worth seeking out, from the Saumur Blanc ($35) to the reds and whites from century-old vines labeled as La Charpentrie.

The inclination of such new, relatively young producers as Romain Guiberteau, Arnaud Lambert, and Antoine Sanzay is to follow the parcellaire model of single-vineyard wines, rather than the larger estate model practiced by Bordeaux. "We are just the first generation in at least fifty years interested in organic farming, terroir, single vineyards, and we are not many," says Arnaud Lambert. "Most people here still just make red wine."

Indeed, the roster of people making compelling wines in Saumur is quite short. For instance, even today, out of the 200 hectares (500 acres) and dozens of owners in the commune of Brézé (one of the most historical places in Saumur; for more on Brézé, see page 65), only four producers are bottling wines themselves; all the rest disappears into the vast tanks of the local cooperative. But things are very slowly changing. It helps to have a domaine of the stature of Clos Rougeard as a guiding light. Founded in the late 1600s and only ever farmed organically or biodynamically, this small, humble domaine is known as one of France's best. Today, its wines sell for north of $200 a bottle. Following the death of one of the two brothers who ran the domaine, Rougeard was sold in 2017 to Martin Bouygues, one of France's richest men. We shall see how that affects the domaine. But in the meantime, its success drives others forward.

PARTICULARS OF PLACE

South of the town of Saumur, the intertwining appellations of Saumur and Saumur-Champigny occupy a series of villages and hillsides. Saumur-Champigny lies within Saumur and is made up of vineyards around the towns of Saumur and Champigny, and six other nearby villages. Given that Saumur-Champigny is an appellation only for red wine, any white produced there will just be labeled Saumur Blanc. There are not obvious differences in soil or terrain between the two appellations. The areas of Saumur-Champigny were simply plucked from areas that were known to produce more distinguished red wine—typically they have slightly higher elevations and more pronounced slopes.

Very much like Chinon and Bourgueil, the bedrock of Saumur is limestone—tuffeau. In many areas, these will be covered with stony clays mixed with sand or stones. But these are certainly wines of limestone. The major difference between the appellations is that Saumur-Champigny doesn't have much of the alluvial gravels present in some of the lower terraces of the two Touraine regions. The access to limestone here means two things. One, limestone affords the ability to make supple, fruity reds, which is what Saumur-Champigny made its name on thirty years ago, when it was the fruity, chilled red of Parisian bistros. That's now changed, and wines of substance are produced, though they usually remain of moderate alcohol and medium body, even if they're powerful and occasionally tannic. Two, the limestone soils of Saumur-Champigny are exceptionally good for Chenin Blanc (here called Saumur Blanc).

The advantages of Saumur-Champigny's slopes and elevations? Better drainage (already a strong suit of tuffeau) and thinner topsoil. Winemaker Romain Guiberteau tells us his grandfather's rule was "plant Chenin Blanc when there's 3 feet or less of topsoil; plant Cabernet Franc when there's more than 3 feet." Consequently, the thin topsoil in Saumur-Champigny could be great for Chenin, but the white grape is not favored there, as it doesn't get the appellation and consequently sells for half the price of red of similar quality.

QUESTION OF TASTE

Tasted blind, how do you distinguish Saumur Rouge and Saumur-Champigny from Chinon and Bourgueil?

Even though their soils are similar, Saumur-Champigny has historically made a lighter, fruitier wine than the other two nearby regions. It gained that reputation in the 1960s through the 1980s, despite the epic, unique reds of Clos Rougeard. Perhaps Saumur-Champigny grows on soils with higher limestone content, making them less powerful than Chinon and Bourgueil. However, in the last ten to fifteen years, more and more exacting, high-caliber reds have emerged from Saumur-Champigny. If Chinon and Bourgueil speak to berries and spice, the heavier wines of Saumur tend toward chocolate and wild strawberry.

RAJAT'S TOP PRODUCERS

◇ **ANTOINE SANZAY** A great young up-and-coming producer. He follows the lead of Clos Rougeard, but has found his own way of making wines of wonderful purity and expression. His Les Poyeux is superb, not far off from Clos Rougeard's. His whites are likewise delicious—textural, flavorful, and alive—look for the Saumur Blanc Les Salles Martin.

◇ **CLOS ROUGEARD** One of the great domaines of France; for decades it remained in relative obscurity, as so many wine lovers ignored the Loire. But now the secret's out. Nevertheless, we're lucky to have lived in the long age of this incredible property. Wines from the 1900s, 1920s, and 1930s have held up amazingly in recent tastings. Le Bourg is the most tannic, Les Poyeux a little smoother, and the Clos Rougeard is a blend that's almost accessible on release. The white is a rare, beautiful bird.

◇ **ARNAUD LAMBERT** One of the bright stars of Saumur, Arnaud has made wines under two labels, Château de Brézé and Domaine de St-Just, though his plan is to consolidate those under his own name. A very serious winemaker and farmer, he loves wines of elegance and restraint. He is ever trying to peel away the evidence of his own winemaking, leaving as little of his own imprint as possible, to purely express his vineyards. Lambert is a Brézé specialist; it's where most of his vineyards lie and the origin of his strongest wines: look for whites from Clos David and Clos de la Rue vineyards and reds like Clos Mazurique. While his wines are wonderful today, there's no doubt that his best is yet to come.

◇ **DOMAINE GUIBERTEAU** Romain Guiberteau's white wines made him famous. When they hit the mainstream, they blew everyone's minds with their power, energy, and sharpness. The style embraces acidity, much like Arnaud Lambert, but there has been a tendency to use more new oak (something we've noticed less in recent vintages, however). These wines are so potent and high energy as to require some time in the bottle, so don't open too early. The standout white is Le Clos de Carmes. The reds are great, too. Some contend Romain Guiberteau is in fact a better red-wine maker, despite his white-wine fame.

◇ **DOMAINE DU COLLIER (ANTOINE FOUCAULT)** Antoine's father and uncle owned Clos Rougeard, but Antoine started his own label in 1999, working 7 hectares (17 acres) in Brézé. The wines are well priced for their incredible quality. If you can't get Clos Rougeard, they are a good substitute, and at a fraction of the price. They're restrained, soulful, and pure. In particular, the bottlings of red and white called La Charpentrie are stellar.

◇ **CHÂTEAU YVONNE** This newer estate, founded in 2007, has been biodynamic since 2012. Yvonne's wines are absolutely delicious—very taut, wonderfully made, with finely wrought texture. All are great, but the basic Saumur Blanc is an exceptional deal.

◇ **THIERRY GERMAIN (DOMAINE DES ROCHES NEUVES)** Domaine des Roches Neuves is famous as a producer of wonderful biodynamic Saumur; Germain has for years been making some of the region's more compelling wines. A disciple of Charly Foucault of Clos Rougeard, he looks for similar purity and clarity, aiming for the cleanest expression of fruit without delivering rustic tannins or underripe flavors.

Savennières and the Anjou

What is the profile of the great Chenin Blancs of Savennières? Depends on whom you ask and which wine they've had lately. At one time, decades ago, the wine was often sweet. Then it became famous as a dry wine, powerfully austere and caustically acidic. Then it changed again in the nineties, fattening up with more ripeness, honey flavors, and flab. Today, it's a dry wine but still can be found in different styles, from the lean and mean to the plump and droopy.

The one thing that binds all these wines is schist. The schist of Anjou Noir is particularly evident in this pristine village on the north bank of the Loire, just 10 miles west of Angers. You see it on the three great hillsides basking in front of the river, you see it on the roofs of local buildings, and you feel it in the wines, where it provides a stern, stony spine. Most who write about Savennières write about Coulée de Serrant, the Loire's most famous vineyard (historically, along with Montrachet, Yquem, and Château Grillet, its whites have been France's most treasured). They write about its owner, Nicolas Joly, who became the face of biodynamic farming for wine worldwide, and its most ardent proselytizer. But we were interested in tasting with Thibaud Boudignon, a younger upstart vigneron and an outsider, whose bold vision for Savennières (and nearby schistous soils in Anjou) stakes out a different claim.

Thibaud makes exceptional wines—in his own style. A rather large and imposing guy and former judo champion, he makes wines that are also powerful, focusing the acidity and minerality into a powerful beam. "For me," he said, "the taste of the schist and the sensation in the mouth is very different than in Saumur. Saumur has the limestone and the clay, and the wines are round. Here, the wines are straight and sharp, but broad and deep, as well." Thibaud's wines are incredibly focused and piercing on the tongue. If anything, they seem to have more physical force, a bigger size in the mouth, than most Saumur wines, to which limestone bestows a lightness of touch. As Pedro Parra told us in chapter 1, "Schist is always about power." Thibaud's wines support that.

Not far away, just across the Loire river, the gilded expanse of Anjou has used its own schistous soils to foster another evolution, the natural wine movement. Thanks to protection from Atlantic rains, but a humid atmosphere and moisture from the Loire, sweet, botrytized wine (affected with the "noble rot" that makes some of the world's most famous sweet wines) from the Anjou was historically one of France's most celebrated. But, as sweet wine went out of favor and postwar France temporarily lost its wine culture, the Anjou faded from memory, farming with chemicals and producing oceans of rotgut rosé. A place with great history, lots of cheap land, and a broken wine tradition proved to be the perfect environment for hungry, curious winemakers like Jo Pithon, Mark Angeli, and Patrick Baudouin (and later, Richard Leroy) to experiment with organic farming and winemaking with fewer and fewer additions.

With the freedom of just starting out—no expectations, no obligations—they could take wines to the limits of non-intervention. Which they did, and along the way they ignited a zeitgeist of people looking for something more analog, anti-establishment, and liberating in their wines. The handmade labels, irreverent brand names, lack of pedigree, and even the sometimes brilliant, sometimes flawed wines themselves were reminiscent of the garage rock movement in which musicians threw out the rules and made something based on raw emotion and contradiction. With Joly shaking up staid Savennières and evangelically touting biodynamism, the Anjou became the center of natural wine, a movement that today has spread all over France and the world. The irony for the Anjou is that some local producers (like Stéphane Bernaudeau and Kenji Hodgson) have found it easier to steer clear of winemaking regulations by not even labeling their wines as Anjou. Instead, they opt for the catchall Vin de France.

But, politics aside, here in the pastoral Anjou, it's still possible to find the gentle spirit at the heart of it all. Though the natural wine movement has become an

The limestone aging cellar at Domaine Arnaud Lambert

THIBAUD BOUDIGNON
Savennières

international cause célèbre, Anjou comfortingly remains a bit of a backwater. Such is the feeling when we mosey our way out into the country village of Martigné-Briand, where Stéphane Bernaudeau, in his little rustic shed, allows us to taste from his few barrels. A former assistant to the famous Angeli, he takes us to his prize vineyard Les Nourrissons and its gnarled, beautiful hundred-year-old Chenin Blanc vines. The wine he makes from them is stunning—round, full-blown, but complex and vibrant. And it's completely clean, thanks to meticulous farming and precise winemaking, even without modern equipment. In this one beautiful, delicious wine is the promise of natural wine, the essence of Anjou's dark, igneous soils, and a wonderful experience of the Loire's magic and variety.

PARTICULARS OF PLACE

Savennières is one of the rare Loire wines from the northern bank, with Anjou extending down in the rolling hills south of the river. The story here is largely about that transition between Saumur and Anjou, from limestone to schist and alkaline to acid soils, and the profound change it makes in the wines. Whereas the limestone provides zip and a lithe, crisp structure for wines, the schist makes wines of a thicker, more smothering texture whose power feels more like an ambient electric hum buzzing in the skull.

In Savennières, the single vineyards of Coulée de Serrant and the hill of La Roche aux Moines dominate the scenery with their dramatic hillside facings against the Loire, but beyond that Savennières expands on shallower hills and rolling expanses. The soil structure can go from dark schist to a curious blue, one with volcanic debris and granite.

Across the river, Anjou is much less dramatic. A lush, bucolic countryside, it has gentle slopes that rise from small, flowing streams, interrupted by periodic stands of trees and small villages. It looks like rich, easy country, a quality that can be reflected in the wines, which are generous, full, and dangerously easy to drink.

QUESTION OF TASTE

How to recognize Savennières and other Chenin Blanc derived from schist?

While Savennières can come in many forms—from a round, floppy, alcoholic style to steely and minerally—it's not hard to make a guess on it. First, look to the texture. There is a full, powerful form derived from the schist. And even if the wine is big and round, there should be a core of edgy acidity keeping it aloft. Next, look to the flavors, which tend to capture the full exoticism of Chenin Blanc, bringing in pear, spice, herbs, wet wool, and other sheeplike aromas, as well as scents of rock and earth. Look for a solid structure based on power and weight supported by a mineral acidity and then often laden with wild Chenin flavors.

◇ **THIBAUD BOUDIGNON** Boudignon's wines are the revelation of modern Anjou. He does not appreciate the rampant volatile acidity, acetic acid, and other flaws that can characterize much of the natural wine movement, and his wines express this clearly. They are razor sharp, with finely wrought precision, lightning acidity, and lots of well-toned muscle. Yes, they're marvels to behold, but they're also incredibly satisfying to drink, especially A François(e), a steely cuvée named for both his grandfather and his mother. Thibaud's rosé shows his sweet, soft underbelly.

◇ **RICHARD LEROY** This natural producer makes some of the most fiery, energetic white wines on the planet. Always imbued with a powerful blast of TLR (see page 155), they hum with vibrancy and flavor. Hard to find nowadays, so always purchase on sight!

◇ **STÉPHANE BERNAUDEAU** A small, rustic producer and a new discovery, his wines are hard to find, but beautiful in composition. Like meticulous carvings from rock, they've been sculpted so skillfully that they appear soft and gentle, though they're firm and centered within.

◇ **MARK ANGELI** He was a groundbreaking figure in the organic and natural movement and a true visionary of Anjou. Sometimes his wines can be slightly dry, but they are always complex, full of life, and delicious.

◇ **BENOIT CORAULT** This young, committed producer doesn't just farm his own vineyards—he lives in them. He farms only with a horse and his hands, but is meticulous in the cellar, producing pristine, clean wines.

◇ **DOMAINE AUX MOINES** A mother-and-daughter team run this tiny domaine in Savennières, putting out a small amount of finely wrought wine that runs the stylistic path between the cutting, sharp style and the more relaxed, rounded version. They also release back vintages, and it's still possible to find bottles from the 1990s at great prices.

BURGUNDY

Burgundy—the spiritual home of terroir, the mecca of minutia—is where wine asks you if you're ready to take the next step in your relationship. Do you really love me? Are you just a drinker, looking no further than your next glass? Or are you serious, ready to ask questions and listen, ready to study topographical maps and memorize vineyard names? What's your commitment?

Don't feel threatened that Burgundy just wants to be real and mature. Yes, we can still go out and party—occasionally. But maybe it's time to start thinking about settling down, having a relationship. Think about what you'd be getting.

Obviously, the wines speak for themselves. Pinot Noir and Chardonnay—what more needs to be said? These wines come from a series of villages lined up neatly on a north–south running escarpment called the Côte d'Or, "the Golden Slope." The plethora of styles and tiers in Burgundy meet all demands: red, white, and rosé; plump and lean; dark and light; power and finesse; ludicrously expensive and just expensive. Burgundy can be both hedonistic and intellectual at the same time. Just like life, these wines can be enjoyed youthfully, but also gain pleasure through the wisdom of age.

The place itself is welcoming and accessible (you can reach Burgundy's heart in less than three hours by train from Paris's Charles de Gaulle airport). Hospitality is part of the Burgundian mentality. Good meals are easily found—this is not true of all great regions (ahem, Rhône Valley)—and service generally welcoming and friendly. Beaune, Burgundy's beating heart, is a pristine and beautiful village, well preserved, clean, and approachable. It's small enough to be walkable, but sophisticated enough to support excellent restaurants, hotels, shops, and attractions. The vineyards—even the most elite—are just a few minutes away, available to be strolled, ogled, and photographed to your heart's content.

Of course, Burgundy is experiencing perhaps its greatest prosperity. Thanks to global demand and limited supply, prices are at an all-time high, as interest in Burgundy is peaking worldwide. This shows in the crowds of BMWs filling Beaune's tiny parking zones and the occasional challenges of getting lunch reservations in the better spots. Yet, at the same time, the wines have likely never been better. The ease of selling Burgundy doesn't appear to be lulling most producers into complacency or laziness. Indeed, the opposite. After decades of murdering their soils with chemical farming, winemakers have turned more and more toward organics and beyond. Vineyard work has never been better; winemaking, more conscientious. In Burgundy's endless generational churn, the young people assuming control of their family domaines are obsessed with improving everything. Rather than resting on unearned laurels and settling into an unexamined life, they've been open to the world, working harvests everywhere from Tasmania to Sonoma, making connections.

Perhaps most encouraging in a region that has been exhaustively studied and chronicled (earning more ink than anyone but Bordeaux), discoveries are there to be made. These may take many forms, from a new producer who has somehow managed to find grapes (Pascal Clement, for instance) to exciting wines suddenly emerging from places that had been written off (St-Romain is one). As the prices of the great Grand Crus drive these aristocratic bottlings beyond the reach of all but the wealthiest, Burgundian vignerons seem just as committed to producing great village or Bourgogne wines.

All in all, Burgundy's doing everything right. So what could be left to say about it? Well, for one thing, we came to some interesting realizations with regard to the region's ever-so-famous terroir. The clay-limestone blend that covers the Golden Slope is celebrated (and envied) worldwide. Regarded by many as a perfect subsoil, it mixes, in various proportions, the fleshy, water-holding capacity of clay with limestone's bones, grace, and electricity. Open any serious Burgundy book and you'll see endless references to soils with smile-inducing names like oolite, Bajocian, and Bathonian. Less often—or never—you'll read what impact the soils have on the wines . . . because no one exactly knows. So what's the point of endlessly mapping the soils and subsoils of these vineyards?

We put that question to one expert who does geology work for many domaines. "Should I be honest with you?" he asks. "In my opinion, my job is to help vignerons communicate with their clients. I think between the two world wars, people were quite lost, and they needed to keep in touch with their traditions. Because there had been some advances in the natural sciences, they became convinced that natural features were the explanation." With all the attention on Burgundy today, he says, more and more people inquire about the differences among the wines and the vineyards, the great differences in price, and so on. "The vignerons need something to tell the people, and I'm here to help the conversation dwell on something more scientific-minded, beyond the age-old knowledge."

As mentioned in chapter 1, we also spent time with well-known geologist Françoise Vannier, which helped us realize how much more complex the story at ground level and below can be. The impact of human activity on the slopes of Burgundy (and most every other place) cannot be understated. For thousands of years, sometimes side by side with vineyards, quarries of varying sizes have existed up and down the Côte, from which huge amounts of stone were extracted. Centuries ago, as the land became more valuable for wines than for stones, the quarries would be filled up to reconstruct the hillside. But filled up with what? Soil from somewhere, nearby probably, but presumably not dug from the very same hillside. This happened up and down the slope; some people even suggest that massive amounts of imported soils may have something to do with the unusual and idiosyncratic behaviors of some vineyards given the setting around them.

GEOLOGIST FRANÇOISE VANNIER
looking at crinoidal limestone at Bonnes Mares in Chambolle-Musigny

However, for as much as we heard about the small differences among vineyard soils in Burgundy, we also heard several times from Burgundian vignerons both past and present how consistent the Burgundian soils are. They gave the impression that, while the soil is undeniably wonderful for Pinot Noir and Chardonnay, it's not minor shifts in soil type that create the vast differences between the flavors of the wine. If it's not soil, what might it be?

"I feel like my colleagues are so obsessed with soil to explain how their wines taste that they really seem to overlook that terroir is not just soil. There's many other factors in there, too." This is how Jeremy Seysses of Domaine Dujac in Morey-St- Denis opens our conversation as we prepare to spend a rainy spring afternoon with him driving among the vineyards of the Côte de Nuits. While we're obsessed with vineyard soils ourselves, here we're going to adopt Jeremy's sentiment. The soils of Burgundy have been documented over and over in countless books and articles. Instead, we're going to peer into a couple of other intriguing, less-discussed factors influencing the classic tastes of Burgundy.

"The obsession with soil makes sense," Jeremy continues, "because that's the part where you're having the biggest impact with things like cover crops in winter, ploughing, etc. It's where your practices truly make a difference. But I think not enough attention is paid to climate." To that end, he notes how the nearby Jura region is a somewhat mirror image of the Burgundian slope across the Saône valley (it was split from the same plateau and then pulled away to the east). "We have soils so remarkably similar to the Jura across the way, yet we make wines that are so different, and that's a climate thing, keeping in mind the degree to which geography dictates climate."

Tall and pale, Jeremy is half American and half French, an Oxford-educated, quick-talking, wide-ranging conversationalist, who leaps easily from keen observations about Gevrey-Chambertin to some recent bit of gossip about pop culture. Consequently, he's a fascinating guide to the villages of the Côte de Nuits, in most of which his family owns at least a few vines.

One aspect of the Burgundian topography whose influence Jeremy suggests is underemphasized is the *combe*—the French word for a small valley in the edge of the plateau. It's where water running down from the plateau has created a streambed that empties into a larger valley. The Côte d'Or is the east-looking face of a big plateau, Jeremy explained. "During the glacial ages, when the permafrost thawed and made these giant rivers, you had these big canyons that became small canyons (or big chasms)." The combes are the lasting remains of these waterways, even if water is not constantly flowing today. The Côte de Nuits, he says, boasts four big combes, at the villages of Gevrey-Chambertin, Marsannay, Nuits-St-Georges, and Chambolle-Musigny.

GRAND CRU, PREMIER CRU, AND OTHER CLASSIFICATIONS

Many European wine regions have endeavored to classify their vineyards into some sort of hierarchy. Always messy and disagreement-prone, such systems nevertheless help organize what are basically large, sprawling, overwhelming masses of information—the villages, vineyards, and producers in a region. Frankly, no perfect way exists to do this, but the classifications do help us remember names, sort quality levels, price wines, and shop accordingly.

Burgundy's classification system divides vineyards into categories of quality, from highest to lowest: Grand Cru, Premier Cru, Village, and regional. In order for a ranking to appear on a label, all the grapes in a bottle of wine must be from vineyards owning at least that ranking. For example, wines labeled Grand Cru must be from vineyards ranked as such. A blend of wines labeled Premier Cru must be from at least Premier Cru–rated villages, but could include some Grand Cru wines. And so on. Village wines just state the name of the village—Meursault, Gevrey-Chambertin, for instance—while a regional wine will just be called Bourgogne (Rouge or Blanc). Chablis follows much the same practice, but below Village (Chablis), Petit Chablis is a fifth category.

These rankings are not guarantors of quality, but rather suggestions of potential. The skill of the producer still makes a huge difference, as a Premier Cru or even a Village wine from an elite producer may outstrip a Grand Cru from a mediocre one. For instance, many think Les Perrières vineyard in Meursault, a Premier Cru, is deserving of Grand Cru status. As we said, it's messy.

Other regions have their own classification systems. Champagne ranks entire villages as Grand Cru or Premier Cru, not merely certain vineyards within them. Naturally, this can lead to a lot of hand-wringing over the placement of village boundaries and such. Beaujolais classifies its land simply as regional (Beaujolais—good—covering around 100 towns or vineyard areas), Village (Beaujolais-Villages—better—and available to 39 different villages/areas), and Cru (the best, and only referring to 10 villages/areas).

Bordeaux's classification scheme is a little different. Famously done in 1855, it classifies the producers of the Médoc region in tiers of Crus or Growths, from First Growth to Fifth. Originally, there were only four First Growth producers, but Château Mouton-Rothschild was elevated from Second to First in 1973. To lovers of Burgundy, whose classification is based on terroir, the Bordeaux system seems somewhat silly, as it does not pertain to land, but to brand. But, despite the criticism it's held up, and still after 160 years the First Growths are generally the most desirable and expensive, and on down the line.

Many other regions have discussed classifications—Barolo and Barbaresco, particularly—but haven't gotten much past delineating their vineyards and deciding what can be called a single-vineyard, village, or regional wine. While in some ways the classifications are meaningless—what matters is in the bottle—they do give a sense of how, collectively, a particular region views its land, producers, and wines. And, in that, these rankings can be very revealing and provoke much spirited discussion.

Combes differ in size and shape. The combes in the Côte de Nuits tend to be narrower and deeper than those in the Côte de Beaune. Beneath the plateau, the combes significantly impact the vineyards on the slope (the Côte d'Or). For instance, they remain conduits—mostly for cold air to pour down the hillsides from the forests atop the plateaus, but also for water and other debris. Given that Burgundy is divided into village communes, it's significant that villages are built inside or beneath combes. As clefts in what could otherwise be imposing cliffs, combes provided villages with quarrying opportunities, water, and pathways to the Haute Côte atop the plateau.

"They affect weather patterns in a major way," Jeremy says of the combes. He notes that the hailstorms pushing up from south of Burgundy that have ravaged the Côte de Beaune in recent years haven't hit the Côte de Nuits, because "they get sucked up the big combe at Savigny-lès-Beaune, go all the way around, and reemerge in Marsannay." That is, the big combe separating the Côte de Beaune from the Côte de Nuits whisks away the storm and transports it behind the vineyards of the Côte de Nuits before spitting it back out through another combe at the end of the slope. Almost the entire Côte de Nuits avoids catastrophic damage.

Just as crucially, the combes affect vineyard microclimates. The shape of a combe reflects the hardness of the stone being eroded over millions of years and also determines how that air and water get distributed down below. A tighter, narrower combe may result in fast-rushing winds that cool a narrow band of the hillside, but reach far below. A wider, shallower combe might affect a broader swath of vineyard, but mostly higher up on the hillside. Likewise, vineyards directly beneath the combes receive more water, a boon during dry years, but a death knell in wet years.

Combes influence sun exposure, too. The Côte d'Or's combes run west-to-east, creating exposures with south and north faces. "Vineyards with north exposures, which are fairly unusual, are exceptionally cold locations," Jeremy says, since the air coming through the combe is cold, and a northernface means limited exposure to sunlight. "The cold really sits there as well because the forest is cool and at night the cold air just pours out."

On the other hand, he sees an interesting consistency among south-facing vineyards. "Coming out of a combe, a slightly southeast exposure is, for me, always one of the most elegant crus in the village," he says. "You see it over and over again. In Gevrey that vineyard is Clos St-Jacques. In Morey, it's Clos St-Denis. In Chambolle it's Les Fuées or Les Cras. If you move further south the next combe is Combe d'Orvaux, so the vineyard that is premier cru is Les Petits Musigny. Moving down to Vosne, it's Les Suchots." The common theme among them all is elegance, precision, and fine tannins, perhaps because the vineyard has the benefit of great sun exposure, but also extreme cooling via the vent in the

THE HUMAN ELEMENT IN BURGUNDY'S TERROIR

The "human element" of terroir creation, which we referred to in Chapter 1, is a frequent topic in Burgundy these days. Call it a Caterpillar invasion—not insects, but backhoes, dozers, and excavators. In many villages, forest has been smashed over to make way for vineyards. More often than not, this draws the ire of existing producers, and for good reason. Jean-Marc Roulot notes that someone was given permission to extend an existing vineyard. "See how stupid this is," he says, pointing at a bare, white scar of hillside on the crown of Meursault. "They had to take out the forest and make terraces, and the soil is nothing here. The only things that grow naturally here are forest weeds."

Roulot points north to the top of the hill of Corton, where we can see bulldozers in the act of clearing forest. In Chassagne, Alex Moreau tells us some landowners are creating new plantings by removing the topsoil, deploying excavators to pound the hard limestone bedrock into rubble, and then replacing the topsoil—all to hasten the vine roots' descent into the bedrock. Jeremy Seysses tells of a similar maneuver at the top of Gevrey-Chambertin. A landowner returned the removed topsoil to a vineyard at the top of the hill. But the act of removing it had literally ungrounded the earth; at the first heavy rain, it all washed away, leaving him nothing but bare bedrock and the vignerons beneath with a lot of mud in their vineyards.

In a place where nuanced, low-impact vineyard work is the name of the game, the insertion of heavy machinery and disruptive work is jarring. Also, planting vines where great wine cannot be made only has the effect of devaluing the appellations of the region. The toll of greed is levied on everyone. At the same time, this is how terroir has been constructed for centuries, even in Burgundy (minus the bulldozers), and just goes to show that even if the origins aren't pretty, future generations may have no sense of the disruption and questionable taste behind the new vineyards.

hillside. "I'm not sure if it's slightly bigger temperature swings," Jeremy says, "or if it's a matter of more rocky surfaces, since most of the topsoil or small rocks have fallen down the slope."

Another piece of the puzzle that gets far less play than soil or geology when talking about Burgundy is the vines themselves. Pinot Noir is the dominant variety of the Côte de Nuits, but is it the same everywhere? Hardly. Just as the soils here are not monolithically expressive of one type, neither is the gene pool of the vines. They may all fall under the category of Pinot Noir, but within this total are thousand—millions, even—of different individual expressions of the plant.

A grape variety—Pinot Noir or Chardonnay in the case of Burgundy—is just a collection of almost identical plants descended from a single vine. Most of the plants in this family will be the same, but the genotype (the genetic code contained within the cells) is always changing, even within a single vine. Sometimes a mutated genotype results in a divergent phenotype (the physical expression of a trait, such as, say, smaller berries). In some cases this mutation might be manifested on a certain branch of the plant, but it can also end up altering the genotype of the whole plant. Genetic instability is a given—that's nature (especially for Pinot Noir). Now imagine slight genetic changes (which usually result in no physical change in the plant) in concert with the environmental impacts of a plant living in one place for a long time. Those impacts take many forms: climate, chemical composition of the soil, and farming methods are the obvious ones. Less obvious are the impacts beneath the surface, where roots encounter all sorts of entities like viruses, bugs, bacteria, and fungi. In response to all these relationships, vines can change over time. It's so complex as to be unreproducible in a lab and almost impossible to fathom. But just as we are products of the microbiome in our bodies, so vines are products of their own local ecologies. Through careful observation, the vigneron may note when a vine has reacted to something in its environment and changed itself. If it's a change in a desirable direction, she may take a cutting to preserve the genetic traits. This is called massal selection, and we find it a touchstone in Burgundy and throughout Europe.

Massal selection is simply an elegant term for recognizing vines with desirable characteristics in a vineyard, taking cuttings, and then propagating them for later replantation or to start new vineyards. The goal is the same as horse or cattle breeders'—to improve the genetic stock and diversity of the collective. In vineyards, this may mean selecting for qualities like smaller berries, loose clusters, low vigor, disease resistance, early or late ripening, thick skins, and so on. As we traveled for this book, we found the second-most passionately discussed subject by top vignerons (after organic farming) was the importance of preserving and expanding their own vine selections through *selection massale*.

Globally, new plantings over the last thirty years have been fueled primarily by clones (vines reproduced through cuttings in which the new plant is identical to the original) that have been sanitized and de-virused in a lab. These are safe choices, but also (by definition) lack individuality, providing a monolithic block of genetic character versus the multifaceted complexity of a vineyard planted via massal selection. Understandably, many vignerons zealously protect and refine their own vineyard genetics. This, after all, is a component of their wines' uniqueness. And, though we're talking about plant material here, the so-called "human factor" looms large, as it's human selection that shepherds the traits of the vines (although you could also make the argument that humans are just as likely being manipulated by the vines . . . but that's another story).

How does this specifically relate to Burgundy? One of the recurring questions when it comes to the taste of Burgundy has to do with the signature of the villages. Routinely, great blind tasters (and even some not-as-great tasters) can make a reasonable conjecture about the village where the wine in question was

Auxey-Duresses, Côte de Beaune

grown, suggesting that each village has a unique identity or taste signature. If each unique vigneron is working only with his or her own set of vines, how does the imprint of an entire village arise? Is it because of unique soils? That's a tempting argument. Were it so simple as one village being on gravel, another being on limestone, another resting on granite, it would be easier to ascribe the differences to each village's makeup. However, geologists tell us that, despite subtle shifts, throughout Burgundy, soils are a fairly consistent medley of the same components.

A more compelling answer to the question of village identity lies in the human factor of vine selection. The famous, small villages of Burgundy—Gevrey, Nuits, Chambolle, Vosne, etc.—make some of the most renowned wine in the world. Just a handful of miles from one another, travel between them takes only a few minutes by car on the existing fast, paved roads. But back in time, it's easy to imagine that travel or communication among them wasn't so easy. The 3 miles between Morey-St-Denis and Vosne-Romanée would take at least an hour to walk, perhaps longer if one was hauling a heavy load by wagon. It seems fair to imagine that until the twentieth century, travel between these villages was not as rapid or common as it is today. If each village was more isolated, it's also not hard to assume that the local vignerons drank more of their own (and each other's) wines, shared information, and shared vine material. Given a more insular culture in each village, could it be possible that a combination of factors—springing from specific local ecologies, local vineyard practices, a somewhat shared taste in local wines, and a somewhat unique and communal bank of vine genetic material—could give rise (as an emergent phenomenon) to what we now think of as a recognizable village signature?

We put the idea to Jeremy Seysses. "There seems to be a certain phenomenon of memory in the soil or the plant," he says. "It can be good or bad at times. If you plant a clone in a soil that's been long cultivated and given rise to vines of certain characteristics, you can often see a 'clean' or new vine gradually adopt those traits, even if it didn't have them when it was planted. That could be the return of a virus. But it could also be if you plant a clone that produces big berries in a vineyard that gave you small berries, ten to fifteen years later you might see small berries coming back."

In that vein, Jeremy tells us of research from the University of Dijon that suggested vines retain a pattern imprinted on them. Take a cutting from a vine in a vineyard and grow it in a highly confined space, and it will become a dwarf vine. If you then replant it in its original vineyard, it will remain small for a few generations. Why doesn't it immediately adapt? Because it retains in its genotype, its operating system, the imprint of growing in confinement. "In a place like Morey-St-Denis," he says, "where most people would have been replicating their vineyards from, say, Clos de la Roche and replanting there, you would have a gradual building of the memory of that place. So if you moved these cuttings into a vineyard nearby, you're bringing some Clos de la Roche

JEREMY SEYSSES
Domaine Dujac, Morey-St-Denis

character to another place. Over long periods of time and multiple generations, a vine memory develops perhaps alongside a sense of soil memory, for it is also a living thing." In a situation in which neighbors shared cuttings (or stole cuttings from one another—it happens), "this notion of a shared vineyard memory could conceivably arise in a place, creating this macro village kind of character." Conversely, he notes, "introducing clonal selections would constitute a big loss of patrimony."

This sense of patrimony is on many vignerons' minds these days. Simultaneous with his triumph in gaining UNESCO World Heritage status for the vineyards of Burgundy, Aubert de Villaine, the stately, octogenarian director of the Domaine de la Romanée-Conti, has organized (along with Denis Fetzmann, former vineyard manager of Louis Latour) what he calls a Pinot foundation project. This, he tells us when we visit him one cool morning at the domaine in Vosne-Romanée, has involved bringing forty like-minded domaines to comb through their old vineyards in search of *Pinot Fin* ("fine pinot"). What is Pinot Fin? A unique variety? Not exactly. Rather, it refers to a collection of Pinot Noir specimens found in old vineyards (uncontaminated by lab-created clones) that strongly display quality-oriented characteristics. "Fine Pinot," de Villaine says, "is that which gives relatively small clusters, not too tight so there's some aeration (to prevent mold), small berries, giving naturally low production of maximum thirty hectoliters per hectare."

Aubert de Villaine sees another goal beyond low yields in his Pinot project. "It's important to be fine," he says, "but we also want diversity. When we arrive in five to six years to what I hope will be the success of this project, the vignerons of Vosne-Romanée, Morey, Gevrey, Volnay—everywhere—will have a selection, something like three or four hundred lines from old vines from which they can choose. But the key besides the fineness is the diversity. In those two qualities, along with the land, you can find the essence of Burgundy."

Côte de Nuits

The northern half of Burgundy's famous Côte d'Or runs from Dijon south to the village of Nuits-Saint-Georges, from which it gets its name. Along the way, it offers the famous wine communes of Gevrey-Chambertin, Morey-St-Denis, Chambolle-Musigny, Vougeot, Vosne-Romanée, and Flagey-Échézeaux. Pinot Noir is the star here, as these vineyards produce the greatest red wines of Burgundy.

Marsannay and Fixin

These two northernmost villages of the Côte d'Or are on what used to be referred to as the Côte Dijonnaise, though not in reference to a sandwich spread. Rather, the old name refers to the proximity to Burgundy's capital city. And if, as you're driving through its shopping centers and subdivisions, Marsannay feels a bit like a Dijon suburb, it's because it is. Sprawl from Dijon has overtaken Marsannay and its neighbors. Over the decades vineyard land has been lost to development, never to return. Don't fret, though, as there's still plenty of land to produce wines that in recent times few sommeliers have actively sought.

When asked what she thinks of Marsannay and Fixin, one retired sommelier tells us, "I've never really thought of them before, because, frankly, we never had to drink them. Up until ten years ago, I rarely even bothered to try Bourgogne Rouge or Bourgogne Blanc. Burgundy just wasn't that special or hard to get." That may be changing now, she admits.

For several reasons, it's time to pay attention to these wines. The first is improved quality. Several talented young producers exist in these villages, and new ones emerge occasionally in the churn of generational change. The second reason is price. As costs for the rest of Burgundy continue to rise annually, some of these wines can scratch that red Burgundy itch at a lower cost (but still run in the $30–$50 range). On the flip side, by dint of the fact that they're Burgundy, Marsannay and Fixin prices have also risen, and the wines worth drinking here are not exactly cheap.

Marsannay didn't even receive appellation status until 1987 and possesses no Premier Crus, let alone Grand Crus. While its subsoils are classic Burgundian clay-limestone, its topsoils—sometimes quite deep—are a mess of washout from the river Ouche, which flows into Dijon. This washout includes silts, gravels, and clays. Remember above when we mentioned that one of the large combes empties onto Marsannay? It's massive, and not only has it brought a slurry of topsoils, but it also blasts the cold air that historically kept Marsannay from developing optimal ripeness. Those are the knocks. But the upside is that in warmer vintages, Marsannay can perform quite well. And winegrowing today is better than ever, as is vinification, and good producers are able to suss out sometimes rustic, but juicier, richer, and spicier wine than ever before.

Marsannay can be counted upon for floral red wines that remind the drinker of strawberries and cherries, occasionally inching toward black fruits. They're not often substantial, but can be quite pithy and satisfying. Marsannay's twentieth-century reputation, however, was made on Pinot Noir rosé, which is often excellent. The challenge is that it's Burgundy, so the cost is always much greater than rosé from a sunny warm place that produces it in abundance with ease.

If Marsannay is a good alternative to higher-priced Burgundy, Fixin (pronounced *fee-sahn*) can also provide a modest fix. And driving through it, too, is a swim through Dijonnaise. However, the vineyards, far off the road, have more in common with Gevrey-Chambertin to the south than with Marsannay to the north. Fixin wines have a reputation for being hard and somewhat wild, savory without a guarantee of redeeming fruit. The wines are not as deep in body as top crus—more lean and wiry, yet still have firm tannins. In short, they tend to lack the instant pleasure that much of the rest of Burgundy delivers, perhaps because of a preponderance of weathered stone without enough clay or marl to provide as much roundness and flesh. However, Fixin does have Premier Cru–rated vineyards that can produce wines of distinction and complexity. Furthermore, these vineyards produce wines with enough stuffing to age. With time, they can soften into gentle and beguiling bargains.

QUESTION OF TASTE

How to taste the difference between Marsannay and Fixin?

Marsannay reds tend to be medium-bodied, expressive of red berry fruits like strawberry, cherry, and redcurrant, with accompanying floral and stony notes. They can be delightful, though rarely impressively deep or complex; juicy and satisfying, but rarely profound. Fixin wines are typically crunchier. More lean and bony, they have less flesh, leaving the tannin and acid to dominate the wine. Marsannay has a little more weight, flesh, and density.

RAJAT'S TOP PRODUCERS

◇ **SYLVAN PATAILLE (MARSANNAY)** Pataille is considered quite a superstar winemaker; he also consults for many other properties. He's a great taster (geologist Françoise Vannier told us how he recognized the presence of clay in a wine's subsoils that she didn't think existed, until eight years later a soil pit she dug confirmed his observation). A former lab oenologist, he started his domaine from nothing in 1999 and has built it up into a source of lovely, vibrant wines. His Bourgogne Rouge is one of the best in Burgundy.

◇ **BRUNO CLAIR (MARSANNAY)** The true king of Marsannay, this historic domaine's Marsannay wines are rarely talked about because of the magnificence of the rest of its Côte d'Or holdings. But here, as in every wine from the domaine, the winegrowing is meticulous and the winemaking solid, resulting in well-crafted, tasteful Marsannay.

◇ **DOMAINE BERTHAUT (FIXIN)** Young Amélie Berthaut has taken the reins at her family's domaine. It was already in good hands with her father, but it will be interesting to see what her touch brings to the generally bony, austere wines of Fixin. Early results show vibrant, fresh wines that channel Fixin's sometimes-unruly nature into wines of great energy and perfume.

Pruning at Domaine Dujac

Gevrey-Chambertin

One of the most iconic villages in Burgundy, Gevrey-Chambertin is in some ways an outlier. Its placement at the far north of the appellation makes it somewhat remote from the cluster of villages to the south. And its wines are usually Burgundy's most powerful, muscular, deep-bodied, and longest-lived. Its vineyards are populated by the Côte d'Or's greatest concentration of old vines, which buttress the concentration and depth already brought forward by the high preponderance of clay in these soils.

No doubt, it's the character of these wines—potent, physical, serious—that led to the designation of nine Grand Cru vineyards here, the largest number of any Burgundian village. However, these days, some are questioning if all the vineyards are worthy of this mighty status. There is strength in numbers, as these Grand Crus line up next to each other mid-slope like a phalanx of soldiers. No one doubts the mighty vineyard of Chambertin, center of them all, nor Clos de Bèze, its right-hand man. But the rest of the family—Charmes-Chambertin, Mazoyères-Chambertin, Chapelle-Chambertin, Griotte-Chambertin, Latricières-Chambertin, Mazis-Chambertin, and Ruchottes-Chambertin—don't always convince they've earned their lofty designation (and price).

PARTICULARS OF PLACE

The irony of having so many "underperforming" Grand Crus is that Gevrey also boasts a great number of the most "overperforming" Premier Crus. These all huddle together on the other side of the village, far from the cluster of Grand Crus, as if rival factions at a concert, not sure how to engage with one another. The Grand Crus occupy the main floor, dominating the area front and center. The Premier Crus, lesser in status, are forced off to the back and over on one side.

They may not know it, but theirs is actually a great position, for they climb deep into the mouth of the famous Combe Lavaux, which provides cool air and southerly exposures. The Premier Crus seated here are top notch: Combe de Laval, Lavaux St-Jacques, and the unimpeachable Clos St-Jacques. Down below, you have areas that can be prone to mildew and rot, but high above where these Premier Crus live, you have wonderfully elegant crus. In cool vintages they may lack the heat to achieve optimal ripeness, but in warm years like 2009 and 2015 the wines are beautiful and meaty, with fine tannins and abundant fruit.

On the other, southern end of the village a Premier Cru has attached itself to the Grand Cru cluster: Aux Combottes. Squeezed in just next to the Morey-St-Denis border, it clings right on the backs of Grand Crus Latricières and Mazoyères, as if trying to hear what they're saying. Combottes lies right in line with Chambertin itself, so why is it not Grand Cru? Again, it's the combe effect. "Combottes" is the diminutive of combe, and indeed, it sits right on a hollow at the end of the small

Combe Grisard. This microclimate makes it cooler than the Grand Crus, which aren't exposed to the wind. Heavier soils have also deposited there, and the poorer drainage seems to affect ripening, so the wines are never quite as full-blown. In warm, dry vintages, though, Aux Combottes can be every bit as great as the others with a grace and suppleness to accompany potent cherry fruit. Lignier and Dujac are great exponents of this vineyard.

And then there's the odd question of Griotte-Chambertin—the outlier, the darling. This little Grand Cru vineyard, just beneath Clos de Bèze, beguiles all tasters with its ethereal delicacy, redolent more of a Chambolle than a mighty Gevrey. Griotte means "sour cherry" and some think the name was chosen for the flavor of the wine. Others contend the word was also used for a certain kind of small stones found in the vineyard. Still, the reason behind this vineyard's anomalous wine escapes us. Geologist Françoise Vannier has a theory—the place where Griotte sits was a quarry. After all, it is inset and slightly below the road, leaving it not hard to conceive that stone was dug out of this hillside here. If that was the case, and the quarry was later filled with earth taken from somewhere else, perhaps that might answer the question. Griotte is different because its soil is alien!

QUESTION OF TASTE

What is the taste of Gevrey-Chambertin?

Gevrey-Chambertin is often recognizable in a blind tasting. Classical traits are a darker, more purple color and, consequently, flavors along the darker fruit spectrum compared to villages like, say, Vosne-Romanée, which are more typically on the red fruit side. Gevrey's darker fruits are often accompanied by deep savory flavors suggesting dried herbs, spices, and even a little gaminess. Structure is another big clue. At its most classic, Gevrey-Chambertin is a densely packed, tightly woven wine. Tannins may not be rough or jagged, but there will be a lot of them, making for a concentrated, chewy experience. Despite this, there's usually good acidity, holding the wine's powerful body up in a good posture.

◇   **DOMAINE ARMAND ROUSSEAU** The top producer of Gevrey-Chambertin, Rousseau is incomparable—one of France's greatest producers, period. Rousseau's wines fall in the middle of the red-black fruit spectrum that characterizes some villages. They're red in color and sometimes in fruit. But at other times, they have the dark, savory earthiness that's a hallmark of Gevrey. Nevertheless, these are wines of pleasure that equally satisfy the mind. These wines are renowned for their purity, and their honesty and sincerity always shines through.

◇   **DOMAINE FOURRIER** Jean-Marie Fourrier is a very smart winemaker, a top producer, and also now a négociant (someone who buys grapes or wines, vinifies and/or blends them, and puts them out under his or her own label). His wines tend to express the dark, savory side of Gevrey, but in a style that is texturally light for the village, avoiding the trap of heavy, dense wines other producers fall into.

◇   **PHILIPPE PACALET** A Beaujolais native, and nephew of the late, great Marcel Lapierre, Pacalet is a natural wine producer, a négociant who farms and purchases grapes and makes them in a low-intervention style with no sulfur, bringing out their fruitiness and vitality (but perhaps compromising their fortitude for long-term aging). He could be listed in many villages, but he's strong in Gevrey, making beautiful vibrant versions of Gevrey-Chambertin village, Premier Crus Bel Air and Lavaux St-Jacques, and Grand Cru Ruchottes-Chambertin.

Morey-St-Denis

Moving south from Gevrey-Chambertin we come to the humble village of Morey-St-Denis, so named when the quaint town of Morey decided to attach its name to the greatest attraction in its vicinity, the Grand Cru vineyard of Clos St-Denis. We take a moment to weigh the savvy of this idea, since today Clos St-Denis is considered by exactly no one to be the greatest cru in the village (it was a century ago). But merging Morey with Clos de la Roche or Bonnes Mares just sounds weird, so perhaps it was the best decision.

Morey's other two Grand Crus (for an impressive total of five) are Clos des Lambrays and Clos de Tart, a near *monopole* (single owner monopoly) and a true *monopole*, respectively. The irony of Morey-St-Denis is that despite the splendorous holdings of really top-notch Grand Crus, it's not really well known as a village, crammed between two more famous villages in Gevrey and Chambolle-Musigny. Also, there didn't use to be a preponderance of great producers in the village outside of megastars Domaine Dujac and Domaine Ponsot, but that seems to be changing now, as a few other names have crept back into the picture. All in all, Morey-St-Denis is one to keep an eye on, as we will likely start seeing more and better village wines emerge over the years. There's room to grow.

Vineyard-wise, Morey is a neat and orderly place. All the Grand Crus lie mid-slope above the town, in one line. Just beneath them dwell most of the Premier Crus, with the exception of a few perched high on the slope. Up there in the rafters is Domaine Ponsot and its famous Clos des Monts Luisants vineyard where it grows Aligoté, a novelty in the red-dominated Côte de Nuits. (Dujac also produces a racy Monts Luisants from Chardonnay.) The soil is incredibly thin and rocky, producing a white wine of opulence and minerality.

Situated between Chambolle and Gevrey, Morey makes wines that are similarly located between the styles of the neighbors—elegant, if not as ethereal as Chambolle, yet not as structured and brawny as Gevrey. Of the Grand Crus, Clos de la Roche is the most famous and the most suave, with an ever-pleasing lushness that never goes over the top, but also never becomes too hard and dense. Its personality doesn't fade over time (as we later learned at dinner over an astonishing magnum of 1978 from Dujac, a wine at its absolute peak). Clos St-Denis, the title town, makes a lovely wine itself, often with a cloud of earthy perfume and a supple texture, though rarely as robust or memorable as Clos de la Roche.

How do the two great vineyards of Morey-St-Denis, Clos de la Roche and Clos St-Denis, compare?

Both wines channel the spice and warm fruit of Morey-St-Denis, but there are crucial differences. The soils and position on the slope are fairly similar. Morey-St-Denis has a very small combe, but it empties out right in the middle of the appellation, and Clos St-Denis is just in its path on the favored northern side. Clos de la Roche typically displays more structure, firmer tannins, muscle, and a strong, mineral core. On the other hand, Clos St-Denis, perhaps because of the gentle cooling air, shows silkier tannins and a lighter, more elegant touch. In a way, Clos de la Roche is a spicier, "warmer" wine compared to Clos St-Denis's cool, floral elegance.

◇ **DOMAINE DUJAC** Founded only fifty years ago, thanks to brilliant insight, commitment, and great taste in choosing vineyards, Dujac has ascended to the top tier of domaines in France as fast as could ever be imagined. Based in Morey, their holdings extend from Vosne to Gevrey, with exceptional results everywhere. The style here trends toward finesse and purity with a mind toward an ability to age well.

◇ **DOMAINE PONSOT** This famous domaine has long stood for quality at extreme levels. It is reliably one of the last to pick in all of Burgundy, and uses no new oak in creating dense, powerful, and expensive wines. However, in 2017, its leader and winemaker Laurent Ponsot abruptly stepped down, so we shall see what becomes of this profound estate.

◇ **DOMAINE DES LAMBRAYS** The domaine and the vineyard share the same name. Long acclaimed as one of the great sites of Burgundy, Clos des Lambrays sadly underperformed for some decades under less-than-stellar management. Now under new ownership, this historic domaine is back to producing wonderful wine in its poised, somewhat austere, and mineral-driven style that blossoms with bottle age.

◇ **CÉCILE TREMBLAY** The two generations before her had ignored the family vineyards, so it was a big step in 2003 when Cécile, grandniece of the legendary vigneron Henri Jayer, decided to step into winemaking and take back the vineyards from the renters. Converting the vineyards to biodynamic and organic cultivation after years of chemical farming has taken time, but what's emerged is a delightful new domaine, making gentle, lightly extracted wines that prize finesse over concentration.

◇ **HUBERT LIGNIER** A wonderful producer, the family has gone through some hard times following the untimely death of young Romain Lignier, who had taken over the estate. But Hubert came out of retirement to right the ship and the wines are now made by Romain's older brother Laurent, whom, it turns out, has a deft hand himself. The wines are as pure and precise as they ever were.

Clos des Ruchottes at Ruchottes-Chambertin, Gevrey-Chambertin

Chambolle-Musigny

So small as to barely qualify as a village, Chambolle nevertheless enjoys an outsize reputation for the quality of its vineyards and its producers. Only two Grand Crus are here, but they are heavy hitters, Bonnes Mares and Musigny. There's also a so-called Super Second in Les Amoureuses, a Premier Cru, which many think is Grand Cru level much of the time. Other strong Premier Crus are Les Fuées, Les Gruenchers, Les Charmes, and La Combe d'Orveau.

The most celebrated aspect of Chambolle-Musigny, however, is the style of wine, which is considered to be ethereal, graceful, and the very embodiment of finesse that ushers drinkers to Burgundy. It can show power too, but always in the sheen of elegance, decorated with airy red fruit and the aromas of flowers and stone. Musigny and Bonnes Mares can be tannic and even burly wines in their youth. But after a decade or fifteen years, eventually they too can find their way to that heavenly Chambolle music.

The standout producers in this tiny village live up to the loftiness of the territory, be it the stalwart, skillful, soulful Christophe Roumier, the serious and graceful Frédy Mugnier, or the aristocratic Comte de Vogüé.

PARTICULARS OF PLACE

How does Chambolle come by its elegant, finely knit wines? Is it the local winemaking style, epitomized by Frédy Mugnier? Or is it a matter of terroir? On the terroir front, there can be no doubt about a few facts: The village sits higher on the slope than any of the other villages, so it's reasonable to surmise that its vineyards are slightly cooler and, being higher up, there is more exposed limestone, leading to lighter wines. It also sits in the maw of the large combe de Chambolle-Musigny, which keeps things cooler still.

The darker soils exist mid-slope on the northern end, in and around Bonnes Mares, which also borders Morey-St-Denis. These soils are known as *terres rouges* (red earth), reddish-brown in color, carrying more clay to produce a more muscular, denser wine. In contrast, the southern part of Bonnes Mares is formed of *terres blanches* (white earth), a limestone-rich marl, and makes a much gentler, high-toned wine of greater finesse. Christophe Roumier has holdings in both soils and vinifies them alone, before making a blend of the two together.

Also of interest here are the Premier Crus Les Cras and Les Fuées, both on the northern (south-facing) side of Chambolle's large combe. It's these vineyards that are often the most elegant crus, showing lighter tannins and body carrying a pool of delicate red fruits. The grapes are warmed by the sun in a good, south-facing exposure, yet cooled by the funnel of cold air through the combe. Indeed, the air from this combe spills out mostly to the southern end of the village, which is also hemmed in by forest, keeping it, and its elegant crus of Musigny and Les Amoureuses, well chilled.

What is the classic taste of Chambolle?

Chambolle is considered to be the epitome of the light, ethereal expression of Pinot Noir in Burgundy. That's expressed at its most extreme in the wines of Frédy Mugnier, who has cool vineyards and extracts his grapes very lightly (not churning them around too much as they ferment in the tank) to produce wines that almost look like dark rosés and may carry the delicate perfume of strawberries and raspberries. However, in less extreme examples, even the more extracted, darker wines of the cru usually have some grace. Take the Musigny (if you are ever lucky enough to even find one, much less afford it) of Christophe Roumier. It's a powerful, often tannic wine, but no one can doubt its suppleness.

- ◇ **DOMAINE GEORGES ROUMIER** Few people are more respected in Burgundy than Christophe Roumier, who embodies the Burgundian spirit more than most. His domaine is tiny, and he produces very little wine. But what he does make is of the utmost quality and from the greatest crus, like both Bonnes Mares and Musigny. The wines are sturdy, strong, and made to age.

- ◇ **DOMAINE JACQUES-FRÉDÉRIC MUGNIER** Frédéric (Frédy) Mugnier, a former oil engineer and then airline pilot, is meticulous to the extreme. In making very light-colored wines of low extraction, as described above, he comes across as a certain type of artist, dedicated wholly to his craft and vision for his wines. Lucky for all of us, that vision is brilliant and his singular wines are always a blessing. These wines have less power and density than Roumier's, but that's the point, as they never feel thin or fail to beguile.

Clos de Vougeot

Clos de Vougeot is a wonderful icon of Burgundy, expressing in equal measures its profound history, its contradictions, and its brilliance. Let's take those in order. Founded in 1100 by Cistercian monks, this is a very old vineyard indeed, and hallowed ground for anyone who cares about wine. To walk around this place is to be humbled by the thought of a millennium of people tending vines here. Rated a Grand Cru, the Clos de Vougeot also presents some headaches. At around 50 hectares (123 acres) in size, it's the largest Grand Cru vineyard in the Côte de Nuits, with some eighty different owners. On a hillside that reaches high up the slope and descends down to the foot of the highway, the conditions change dramatically throughout the vineyard. That it all gets to be called Grand Cru, no matter whether the vines sit in a privileged exposure on the hill or sit in mud down near the road, is maddening to some, but recognizes the physical, cultural, and economic realities of Burgundy. Yet when it's good, a great wine from Vougeot can compete with any wine of the region.

While both village-level and Premier Cru vineyards exist in the commune of Vougeot, the site is dominated by the Grand Cru clos, which occupies more than 80 percent of the total land. Covered with small pebbles, the topsoils have very little clay and a lot of limestone. Working down the slope, one will encounter more clay and a shift in the type of limestone. Toward the bottom of the hill, the soil becomes alluvial and much heavier, not draining nearly as well.

In researching this book, we ventured into the Clos de Vougeot with David Duband. It was a rainy day, and all we can say is that there is quite a lot of clay, as our shoes sank heavily into the mud. Anyway, that's just to say that Vougeot has indeed some heavy soils. However, good wines are made in the heavy soils. And some contend that classical wine made from throughout the vineyard would include wine from the better-draining soils at the top of the slope as well as wines from the heavier, lower regions.

QUESTION OF TASTE

What are the essential qualities of Clos de Vougeot?

It's hard to say, given there are so many producers and it's such a large vineyard. However, in a blind tasting, a Clos de Vougeot call might come from a wine with soft dark fruits and an earthy cast. Structure-wise, it can have a fairly large body and significant tannins, but they're not as fine as in nearby Vosne and not as sharp as in Gevrey. It's the sort of wine that you identify when you can't pin it decisively to any other village.

RAJAT'S TOP PRODUCERS

⬦ **DOMAINE LEROY** So vast is the hand of cards owned by Domaine Leroy, it would be possible to list it as a top producer of almost every village in the Côte d'Or. But the Clos de Vougeot really is special. An amazingly complete wine, it always shows finesse and elegance, while still having a satisfyingly dense, full core.

⬦ **DOMAINE ANNE GROS** Another Vosne-Romanée domaine, another great wine. It's called Le Grand Maupertui after the informal name given to this section, just beneath Grands Echezeaux. The clay here is dense, and the wine has big, burly tannins undergirding a parade of gorgeous, plush dark berry and floral notes.

⬦ **DOMAINE MUGNERET-GIBOURG** This domaine is run by a pair of delightful sisters, Marie-Christine and Marie-Andrée. In their impressive portfolio, this wine is always a delight, capturing the breadth and fullness of Clos de Vougeot, while somehow remaining smooth and approachable with lots of bright, aromatic fruit.

Vosne-Romanée

Little is left to say of Vosne-Romanée that hasn't already been said. British wine writer Clive Coates called it "the greatest Pinot Noir village on earth." Allen Meadows, who rates Burgundy under the moniker Burghound, wrote an entire book about it called *The Pearl of the Côte*. And indeed it is: the most regal of villages with the most prestigious Grand Crus and an all-star lineup of elite producers, including DRC, Domaine Leroy, Anne Gros, Méo-Camuzet, Liger-Belair, and more.

At their best, the wines here magically bring together all of Burgundy's iconic, sometimes contradictory, qualities in one. They can be intellectual, yet at the same time hedonistic. They can be austere, yet also generous. They can be muscular, but also lithe. Aristocratic, but also appealing to the common palate. Mineral and fruity. Profound and joyful. The list goes on.

Particularly impressive is Vosne-Romanée's collection of Grand Crus, which total six (eight, if you throw in neighboring Flagey-Echezeaux, which really is adjunct to Vosne). They read like the roster of an all-star team: La Tâche, Richebourg, Romanée-Conti, Romanée-St-Vivant, La Romanée, Echezeaux, Grands-Echezeaux, and lastly La Grande Rue. Even the Premier Crus are tremendous: Malconsorts, Gaudichots, Cros Parantoux, Suchots, Beaux Monts, and Petits Monts. Anyway, you get the idea. This is some sacrosanct ground.

PARTICULARS OF PLACE

Why is this ground so hallowed? It's hard to say. Writers talk about the perfect blend of limestone soils and marl the gentle but intensifying slope of the Grand Crus. We've heard about the presence of montmorillonite, a special kind of clay mineral, with exceptional ability to nourish vines (montmorillonite shows up in many great wine places, including Pomerol in Bordeaux).

On the surface, Vosne doesn't look particularly different than other places, so perhaps the greatness is cultural. There is mediocre wine made here, which suggests that a great terroir is never enough to save an untalented vigneron. But perhaps because the general standard of achievement is so high here, the local community of vineyard owners has pushed each other to greater and greater heights. Or perhaps the care in vine selection—as noted in Aubert de Villaine's Pinot Fin project, which encourages vignerons to comb their vineyards to collect specimens of the highest quality individual vines—has been superior here for generations.

However, perfection can be boring, especially when most of us never even get to taste the Grand Crus, so let's focus on Vosne's strivers. The three Premier Crus above Richebourg are all supersonic in quality to price—Reignots (Liger-Belair), Petits Monts (Drouhin), and Cros Parantoux (Méo-Camuzet, Rouget). These are higher on the slope, but especially in warm years can make incredibly expressive wine, if slightly lighter than lower-slope wines. These vineyards are not in the slipstream of Vosne's combe, known as the Combe de Concoeur.

The south-facing vineyards influenced by the Combe de Concoeur do indeed produce wine of typical combelike elegance. Les Suchots is the lowest vineyard in this area and makes a rich, full-bodied wine that, in great winemaking hands like those of Leroy or Liger-Belair, can be almost Grand Cru quality. Climbing up the slope into the combe brings Aux Brulées, a magnificent spot that, despite its position in the wind, can make a wine of great meaty body with structure nonetheless (see Leroy, Méo-Camuzet). And, finally, Beaux Monts, a bit higher on the slope, makes an angular, slightly tannic wine much of the time, but in great years or with age, produces a beguiling wine of great verve, texture, and perfume.

And, of course, there's the Premier Cru many would consider at or just beneath the level of the Grand Crus: Malconsorts. Pressed between La Tâche and the border with Nuits-St-Georges, Malconsorts makes a voluptuous, deep, structured wine with opulent fruit that in many years stands just behind La Tâche in terms of nuance and complexity. In 2005, a prime part of it was sold, split between Dujac and de Montille. De Montille's part includes this odd section that protrudes from the rest of Malconsorts into one side of La Tâche. If La Tâche were a full pan of lasagna, de Montille's bite out of it would be a good three pieces. Étienne de Montille vinifies this section separately, calling it Cuvée Christiane, after his mother.

"It is the missing part of La Tâche!" de Montille joked to us at a tasting in 2016, but then pulled back. "I don't mean to dash your dreams; it is not La Tâche. But it is very good." After all, presumably, when the lines were drawn, this section was given to Malconsorts for a reason. That is, La Tâche was never a full pan of lasagna; it may have always been missing those pieces. Nevertheless, we tasted five vintages of de Montille Malconsorts next to the same five of Malconsorts "Cuvée Christiane" (alas, the budget didn't provide for the same years of La Tâche), and there was a difference that we likened to looking at the same photograph but in different resolutions. The image was the same, but the Christiane seemed to be presented in higher resolution—greater pixel density, more detail, more nuance.

QUESTION OF TASTE

Two divergent styles of winemaking exist in Vosne-Romanée: grapes can either be fermented whole cluster or destemmed. Which is better?

That is, do you remove the grapes from their stems at fermentation or ferment them with the stems in the vat? It can be a long and detailed discussion about fermentation dynamics, tannins, anthocyanins, and the like, but the proof is ever in the glass. On the whole cluster side, you have heavyweights like DRC, Domaine Leroy, and Domaine Dujac. Championing destemming you have the late Henri Jayer and his disciples at

Liger-Belair and Méo-Camuzet. This ongoing "discussion" plays over many vineyards, many wines, but for comparison's sake, take a look at Richebourg from Méo (destemmed) versus DRC (whole cluster). The DRC emphasizes the dark, savory side of Richebourg; the wine is somewhat thick and dense, yet with a rich, lacy texture. The Méo is a very different wine, looking more toward red fruits, spice, and an orange-peel brightness. In time, they will go to different places, too. The whole cluster wine will retain a savory element, melding with the fruit to creating flavors rich in earth and umami. The destemmed wine will go to more ethereal heights of pure fruit and flowers. Which is better? The answer is that there is no answer. Both styles are great.

RAJAT'S TOP PRODUCERS

◇ **DOMAINE DE LA ROMANÉE-CONTI (DRC)** There is not much to say here that isn't already known. Perhaps the greatest wine estate in the world, unmatched in quality, integrity, pedigree . . . and price. Single bottles are routinely priced in the several thousands of dollars.

◇ **DOMAINE DU COMTE LIGER-BELAIR** Since Louis-Michel Liger-Belair took over, this domaine has skyrocketed to the highest of echelons. Liger-Belair's unassailably great portfolio of vineyards—including Aux Reignots, Les Chaumes, and the incomparable La Romanée—gets the respect it deserves from his winemaking touch, which is extraordinary. He is a natural, as his wines capture the ebullient red fruit of Vosne-Romanée in a beautifully gentle manner that has both energy and grace.

◇ **DOMAINE LEROY** Perhaps the only domaine that can match or even exceed DRC in Burgundy when it comes to quality. Domaine Leroy is fascinating, beguiling, and maddening, thanks to the animating spirit of its founder, Lalou Bize-Leroy, one of Burgundy's greatest characters, who does things her own way—whether it's a unique style of training the vines, or audaciously pricing some of her wines even above those of DRC. That said, the wines often live up to their billing. They are invariably charming, full of typicity, and exceedingly digestible.

◇ **DOMAINE MÉO-CAMUZET** Jean-Nicolas Méo's wines are a credit to his mentor, the great Henri Jayer. They are true to the terroir of the vineyards, yet also carry an unmistakable grace and fluidity thanks to wonderful winegrowing.

◇ **DOMAINE GEORGES MUGNERET-GIBOURG** Run by the two sisters Mugneret, this domaine, besides having great holdings, makes wines of pure deliciousness. They are recognizable for their ebullient fruit, gentle texture, and joyful accessibility.

Nuits-St-Georges

Poor Nuits-St-Georges. In a gentrifying neighborhood, it's the humble, old working-class house next door to blingy Vosne-Romanée, where limos are pulling up 24/7, and the pool party never seems to end. Vosne-Romanée has a riot of Grand Crus, while Nuits-St-Georges has none. Vosne-Romanée has aristocrats, while Nuits-St-Georges has workers—all the more reason to love it.

A hub of the industry and business—equipment suppliers, distillers, coopers—Nuits-St-Georges has its own bustling energy and a DIY sensibility that comes through in the wines. The style here is defiantly rustic. The wines are not polished or slick and rarely worry about trying to please. Rather, they're earthy and soulful and a little suspicious—they will take some time to come around. But when they do, they're immensely satisfying and affordable (though, this being Burgundy, affordability is relative).

PARTICULARS OF PLACE

In the absence of Grand Crus, Nuits-St-Georges has twenty-seven Premier Crus. In contrast to, say, Chambolle, which is a tight little square, Nuits-St-Georges is a very long expanse with the village itself tucked into the center of the appellation. This length provides the wines a distinct range of character. There's not just one wine here, but two distinct options. The first is on the north end of the village, where it borders Vosne-Romanée with terrain generally of limestone and marl underneath a surface layer of smaller pebbles. Here, Nuits-St-Georges vineyards like Boudots and Chaignots give wines that possess clear shades of Vosne. The second choice is from the vineyards south of the village, like Vaucrains and Les Saint-George, where Nuits-St-Georges borders on Prémaux, with a heavier, craggier topography. Vineyards end here close to the big quarry of Prémaux until they pick up again at Beaune.

QUESTION OF TASTE

How to distinguish from the northern and southern ends of Nuits-St-Georges?

In this case, the wines of Robert Chevillon, a wonderfully classic producer, provide good instruction. Chevillon possesses both Premier Crus Chaignots and Vaucrains, which make for a good comparison, as they are on similar elevations. On finer-grained soils, the former wine possesses some of the elegance, as its polished tannins are tightly interwoven into the wine's larger fabric. It's burlier than most Vosne-Romanée, but the tight-knit integration is palpable. On the other side of the village, Vaucrains is muscular and coarse, with larger, jagged tannins that need time to come around. The ground here is quite rocky, rendering a wine that's fairly wild.

Over centuries, these mounds are made from rocks pushed up into the vineyard soils and removed by the vignerons.

◇ **DOMAINE HENRI GOUGES** Probably the most famous name in Nuits-St-Georges, the Gouges family has farmed grapes here for centuries. They were one of the first grape growers to create a domaine and bottle their own wines (in 1919). The style is true to the character of the village: direct, stalwart, tough in youth, built to flower in age. But there's also lots of pleasure here, as the wines have earthy intensity and blossom over time.

◇ **DOMAINE PRIEURÉ ROCH** Given that the Roch family is part owner of DRC, this domaine has some celebrity appeal. However, despite some glitzy holdings in other villages (e.g., Clos de Vougeot, Chambertin-Clos de Bèze) some of its heart lies in Nuits-St-Georges, where crus like Clos des Argillières and Clos des Corvées form the soulful bedrock of the portfolio. The vines here are farmed biodynamically and the wines are made with only a bare minimum of sulfur, making this domaine a darling of the natural wine movement. The wines are idiosyncratic, characterized by fresh, chewy fruit and a certain rawness that belies the typical polish of Burgundy.

◇ **DOMAINE ROBERT CHEVILLON** Chevillon is discussed above, but ranks with Gouges as a quintessential Nuits producer, making somewhat rustic wines that haven't changed much over the decades. The style is pure and direct, focusing on getting the raw material from the grapes into the bottle. Like Gouges, this may mean a minimum of processing and therefore somewhat stodgy wines in youth, but over a decade or more they blossom into gorgeous, full-throttle Burgundies.

Côte de Beaune

The southern half of the Côte d'Or reaches south from the namesake town of Beaune (or in fact, just above it in the appellation of Corton) through the villages of Pommard, Volnay, Meursault, Puligny-Montrachet, and Chassagne-Montrachet. While the Côte d'Or is celebrated as the home of the world's greatest Chardonnays, renowned reds are made here too.

Corton

The history here is well known, but bears retelling. Vines on the great hill that kicks off the southern drive through the Côte de Beaune go back to Roman times, as they do in so many parts of France. It is accepted that the wines of Corton were a favorite of the well-known oenophile, the HRE (Holy Roman Emperor) himself, Charlemagne. The (apocryphal, but fun) story goes that sometime in the middle of the eighth century, gazing high on the hill, Charlemagne noticed the snows melting in one location before the rest. He commanded that some vines be planted there, it was good and—lo!— Corton-Charlemagne. Later in life, the story continues, Charlie's wife, tired of his red-wine-stained beard, hinted (to put it gently) that maybe he should drink more white wine. White grapes were then planted in his favorite spot and, Corton-Charlemagne may have become the world's first cult Chardonnay.

It's strange to say that Corton, Burgundy's largest Grand Cru and one of its most historic, is a place in transition, given that most places of such stature are tended as carefully as bonsai trees. "It has not been defined correctly," says Etienne de Montille, as he drives us on the narrow and often vertiginous roads near the top of the Corton hill. "Too many Grand Crus, too widely granted. It started to mean very little." But Etienne sees a little hope. "I think that now there's some new domaines coming up here looking for opportunity," he said, "as there's so much pressure on the Grand Cru in the Côte de Nuits. So I think this is a new day for Corton."

Indeed, the new day has been dawning slowly but consistently for a while. Etienne bought his vines in 2005. In 2009, DRC made a surprising move to lease vines on the hill. And in 2017, Bonneau du Martray, one of the biggest producers of Corton, was sold to American billionaire Stan Kroenke (owner of such diverse pleasures as Screaming Eagle and the Los Angeles Rams). The influx of new money, new expertise, and new attention may be enough to snap Corton out of its long-lasting lethargy.

Or perhaps not. Corton's fall, as Etienne de Montille notes, was not simply due to indifferent producers. Far too much underserving land was classified Grand Cru. The result is a lot of boring, tannic, and hard red wines and rich, flabby white wines at exorbitant prices. The new wines from de Montille and DRC are excellent, but perhaps not enough to change the reputation of the site.

PARTICULARS OF PLACE

The hill of Corton is somewhat divided into its own terres blanches and terres rouges. The white soil is instantly noticeable in Corton-Charlemagne, where hard limestone and clay-dominant marls, as you might expect, are ideal for Chardonnay. Lower on the slope, the soils turn reddish with iron, and Pinot predominates. Vineyards surround the hill in most directions including northwest, the result of expansion in 1966 and 1978, aiding the region's decline.

Corton-Charlemagne, the mostly Chardonnay appellation, covers over 50 hectares, (123 acres) with the principal sites called en Charlemagne and le Charlemagne. The former faces west to northwest, ripens late, and makes a racy, mineral wine. The latter's brilliant west-southwest exposure creates a riper, more opulent showing. Chardonnay on pure south exposures can become plump, cloying, and tropical from over ripeness. Pinot Noir is permitted here.

Grand Cru Corton for red wine is a challenge to understand, given the size of it. But the named plots within it are what you need to remember. Les Bressandes has a strong mid-slope position, as do its cohort of Les Perrières, Les Pougets, Les Renardes, Le Corton, and, best of them all, Clos du Roi.

How to recognize red Corton in a blind tasting?

The reds do best mid-slope, where there's more clay. However, Corton is definitely a white wine terroir. Reds here are not lush and juicy, but bony and structured. They have power and concentration, but are angular and tannic.

How to recognize Corton-Charlemagne?

The producer is essential here, but when it's great it's mind-bending. Somehow it makes a very austere, mineral wine that yet has incredible presence and a regal bearing. It has the least amount of topsoil of any Grand Cru and is thus always stern with a chewy, resinous quality, like a white wine with tannin. Except in really warm vintages, you don't find soft, lush Corton-Charlemagne, because it faces mostly west and northwest. It's an unusual Grand Cru, as most others face south and east.

◇ **BONNEAU DU MARTRAY** Based in nearby Pernand-Vergelesses, this domaine is best known as Corton-Charlemagne specialist, making wines that capture the site's minerality and lean, stoic grace. These wines need time, usually ten years, before they start really opening up.

◇ **COCHE-DURY** The culty Meursault producer's cultiest, most expensive wine, Coche-Dury Corton-Charlemagne combines that lean and intense minerality with a ripeness and opulence unusual for the vineyard. This may be due to the famously perfectionist viticulture, allowing a higher level of ripeness.

◇ **PIERRE-YVES COLIN-MOREY** PYCM, as this wine's abbreviated in the industry, makes an excellent Corton-Charlemagne. It is intense in every way, including concentration and oak, and many years are needed before approaching.

Beaune

What are the defining characteristics of the wines from Beaune? "I don't think we can get a clear idea yet," says proprietor of Domaine des Croix David Croix, bespectacled and thoughtful, who is trying to answer that question for himself. "It's very hard to say, because Beaune is forty-two different crus, and most of them are still blended together into a cuvée by the big négociants or the Hospice de Beaune. So, even though it's a big appellation, the sample size is relatively small."

Small indeed. While gazing down at the appellation in a peaceful breeze high up above the vineyard of Bressandes, the young, ambitious Croix tells us that he recently tried to count the grower-producers who bottle Beaune wines. "I had trouble reaching ten producers," he says. "And seven of them you've never heard of, because they're mostly selling fruit or selling wine to friends.

"The copious vineyard land here—the third largest appellation in the Côte d'Or, behind Gevrey and Meursault—doesn't seem too different from the other villages, but for the fact that it springs up immediately on the outskirts of Beaune, the thriving, busy, personable hub of the whole region. This town is the stronghold of the négociants, and they have likewise claimed its vineyard as their dominion. So long has this village been dominated by large property holders, that the ubiquitous Beaune wine is just a blend—a Premier Cru cuvée, for instance—that does little to generate interest or character for the village. Small growers, the engines of personality, are hard to find.

"For a lot of people, Beaune is just a pretty wine, a smiley wine," Croix said. "You don't have to think about it. Lunch wine. But for me there are areas in Beaune that don't make smiley wines. Where the wines are just as serious as anywhere." Croix himself makes more than lunch wine, but that requires the time and experience to figure out what each of his different parcels has to contribute.

We start by looking at Croix's nod to smiley wine: his village blend. Down at the base of Beaune's large, monolithic slope, the soil is gravel—alluvium washed in through the gaping valley that holds a buzzing highway toward Savigny. This village-level wine is bright, fruity, and easy to drink—*smiley* is indeed a good word for it.

Beaune's more interesting soils are up on the hill, and their differences are measured from north to south. In these appellations we find strong Premier Crus like Marconnets, Clos du Roi, and Bressandes. Croix is particularly enamored with the latter, and he shows us its thin, gravelly soils, mixed with limestone and clay. It's high up and east facing, a cool site that's reflected in the wines from this part of the appellation—structured, strict tannins underneath crisp, somewhat dark fruit.

The midsection of the appellation is dominated by Beaune-Grèves, smack in the middle of which is Bouchard's famous wine, Vigne de L'Enfant Jesus (unsurprisingly referred to by sommeliers as "Baby Jesus"). This middle area sees a bit more clay added to the gravels for a more supple, rounded, and juicy wine. Moving south from here, we come to a collection of largely undistinguished Premier Crus on sand- and clay-rich soils that often get blended into one of those large Premier Cru cuvées from négociants like Jadot, Drouhin, and Bouchard.

In the south of Beaune, at its border with Pommard, lie Clos des Mouches and Vignes Franches, sources of two other iconic négociant wines: Drouhin's Clos des Mouches and Jadot's Clos des Ursules, respectively. The soils change as you head down the slope from very stony and hard, to more exposed limestone, to deeper red clay at the bottom. The best of these wines combine aspects attributed to both soils, rendering a supple, fruit-forward wine with a strong spine of minerality.

What's the profile of Beaune?

Tasting a wine blind and knowing it's from Beaune is almost a feat of luck. You call it a Beaune mostly because it doesn't specifically cry out that it's from somewhere with a stronger signature. In general, Beaune's fruit profile tends toward more black than red—almost blue fruit, really—with a notable earthiness underneath. Texturally the wines are fairly lush and fleshy, with medium acidity and moderate, often grainy tannins.

◇ **DOMAINE DES CROIX** The aforementioned David Croix made his name as the very young vigneron behind Camille Giroud, an old domaine revitalized in 2002 when it was bought by Americans. He recently stepped down from that post to focus all his time on his own domaine, which, aside from its mission to revive the name of small-grower Beaune wines, has a nice set of Corton offerings. He now also works as a winemaker for Jean-Marc Roulot (see Meursault).

◇ **DOMAINE DROUHIN** Veronique Drouhin is an icon of Burgundy, a wonderful winemaker who has taken a lead role in guiding her family's négociant to admirable heights. One of the crown jewels of the domaine is their large plot in Clos des Mouches, which produces a very serious wine indeed, replete with high tones, taut red fruit, and an abiding minerality.

◇ **NICOLAS POTEL** Son of the late Gerard Potel, the legendary winemaker of Volnay's Pousse d'Or, Nicolas Potel has created an admirable career as a négociant making excellent small-lot cuvées from all over the Côte d'Or, but with great bottlings from Beaune Premier Crus.

Pommard

Like Beaune to its immediate north, Pommard has for various reasons gotten a bit lost in the churn of Burgundy's recent history. But, unlike Beaune, Pommard's history includes a more precipitous fall from grace. One of the best-known appellations in the eighteenth and nineteenth centuries, Pommard prices were more or less on par with wines of the Côte de Nuits. Pommard was known as a masculine, rustic, earthy wine that was also durable; it could stand up to travel, in those days an important consideration. As such, explains Etienne de Montille, as we rumble through the lower slopes of the village, the négociants of the day sold bottles labeled Pommard, whether the actual wine was from there or not. "The name Pommard became synonymous with a type of wine," he says, "not so much the place."

Of course, that didn't help the local growers of Pommard. And in 1935, when the growers won the fight against the négociants that resulted in the modern appellation system, Pommard didn't ascend as much as other villages, in part because the négociants were buying most of the production. "And so it went a bit to sleep," Etienne notes, suggesting that even today, it is only beginning to open its eyes.

DAVID CROIX
Domaine des Croix, Beaune

CLOS DES DUCS
Volnay

SAVIGNY-LÈS-BEAUNE

VINEYARD FOCUS

We are big fans of this little village just 4 miles northwest of Beaune, just off the main slope of the Côte d'Or. It's a quiet little town, but oversees a large chunk of vineyard—over 380 hectares (930 acres). The Premier Cru vineyards are divided by a small valley, with a northeast-facing slope underneath the ever-present whooshing of the A6 auto-route and, opposite, south-facing vines sloping down from a forested cap. They both give different wines, the highway side being the tougher, grittier reds from such vineyards as Marconnets, Narbantons, and Dominode. The slopes on the north side tend to offer wines that are more elegant and better integrated, with familiar vineyards being Fourneaux, Vergelesses, and Serpentières.

Some very good producers offer Savigny, including Chandon de Briailles (known especially for Corton) and Domaine Leroy, but it's impossible nowadays to mention the town without a bow of respect for the great Domaine Simon Bize. A Savigny stalwart, Bize made a name for itself under the brilliance and perfectionism of Patrick Bize, the fourth generation of Bizes on the property, who sadly died in 2013. Patrick proved that Savigny's wildness could be tamed again to produce expressive, graceful wines that spoke of place and person. And these wines, which can age well for at least a decade, continue to be bargains, as Bize's wife Chisa and the rest of the family have managed to uphold the tradition of quality.

The other reason Pommard hasn't enjoyed the upward mobility of other Côte d'Or appellations since 1935 (like Volnay) is right underfoot. Or rather on our feet, as our shoes sink into some of the fairly heavy clay for which Pommard's lower half is known. Iron-rich and dense, these clay-laden soils make for the dark-colored, rustic wines that are a hallmark of Pommard. These wines were fashionable in a day when such wines were harder to come by. But in today's sunny new world, color and weight are less valued. "People want Musigny, Volnay, perfume, refined tannins," Etienne says. "So I think the renaissance of Pommard will be probably more difficult than the renaissance of Volnay, which has these qualities that please the market. It's as with Corton: something's going to happen, but the new generation will have to find out the way to render those wines more palatable and more attractive. It's a question of farming, of winemaking, and extraction."

But of course, this is only part of the Pommard story. Higher on the slopes sit some exceptional vineyards, headlined by Rugiens, which lies on the southern half of the appellation, near the border with Volnay. The name comes from the color red (*rouge*), owing to a good dose of iron in the soils. There is a qualitative division between the upper and lower parts (Rugiens-Hauts and Rugiens-Bas, respectively), however, with the latter being seen as far superior, the source of Rugiens's reputation for intense, long-aging wines. There's been talk of elevating Rugiens to Grand Cru status, though Etienne says, "if that's the case, we will probably oppose the project if they include Rugiens-Hauts. About a third of it was village wine until 1981, when it was upgraded. You cannot respect historical terroir and see a plot upgraded from village to Grand Cru!"

The other frequent player in upgrade talk is on the other end of Pommard, the north side next to Beaune: Epenots. Subdivided into two parts, Grands Epenots and Petits Epenots, many producers just call their wines Epenots. The soil is not red, but runs from a more classic whitish marl on the Beaune border (Petits Epenots) toward a gravelly mix nearer the village (Grands Epenots). Petits Epenots is more lithe and elegant, while Grands Epenots is more robust and structured. In between the two lies the great Clos des Epeneaux, a monopole of the Comte Armand since 1826 and a purveyor of silkiness that belies the village's reputation for coarseness. These few great sites represent Pommard's ceiling, but make us no less grateful for the hearty fare supplied by the rest of the zone.

QUESTIONS OF TASTE

What is the profile of Pommard?

Classic, generic Pommard is dark, rustic wine that can be quite chunky with rustic tannins, dark fruit flavors, and an earthy grit. However, there's a lot of expression, and good producers can do well enough here. In certain vintages, the fruit will emerge in a supple, graceful wine, but in others it reverts to its tougher, more muscular form.

How to tell the difference between Premier Crus Rugiens-Bas and Clos des Epeneaux?

The wines are very different. From one end of the spectrum entirely, Rugiens-Bas is a robust, powerful wine with long ability to age. Rich and ripe, it fills the mouth, but buoyant acidity prevents it from being weighed down. Conversely, Clos des Epeneaux, a massive 5-hectare (12.3-acre) monopole, also has intensity, but it's more linear and smooth, an elegant wine at its core. Depending on vintage, both wines are best with at least a decade of aging.

RAJAT'S TOP PRODUCERS

◇ **DOMAINE DE MONTILLE** Pommard has long been a staple of de Montille, even if it's not their most famous wine. In recent years, however, bottles of Rugiens from vintages like 1978 and 1971 have been nothing less than astonishing, a testament to the power of Pommard when placed in good hands.

◇ **COMTE ARMAND** This storied producer's name really rests on the Clos des Epeneaux. But it also rests on the winemakers who helped pull it from a long torpor—first Pascal Marchand in 1985 and, since 1999, the phenom Benjamin Leroux, who first worked at the domaine at the age of fifteen.

Volnay

Next time you're in Burgundy, don't be content to only visit the vineyards at the bottom of the hill. A trip to the top of Volnay's slopes renders a different worldview, as you realize how high into the sky the Côte d'Or truly ascends and how steep the slopes can be. The climate feels different up here, as we stand in a gusty wind atop Volnay Taillepieds with Guillaume d'Angerville, the whole Saône river valley spread beneath us. "We have a little saying here that 'Volnay will always be higher than Pommard and Meursault'" the proprietor of Domaine Marquis d'Angerville says. Burgundians never miss a chance to take a dig at their neighbors. "It's important to note," he continues, "that Volnay sits at a greater altitude and has a more dramatic slope than most villages."

For centuries, Volnay's wines have been famous for their delicacy—an ethereal, lacy quality that captures Pinot Noir's nimbleness. Volnay can seem light and airy, yet it also manages to have power, intensity, and longevity. In many vintages, the fruit tends toward the red spectrum. The village is also gifted to have two of the greatest producers within its borders, both representing a different facet. Domaine Marquis d'Angerville represents the regal side, beautifully embodied in the polite, learned elegance of d'Angerville himself. And the other epic producer is Domaine Lafarge, which channels a more classic Burgundian farmer persona—more robust and forward—into brilliant wines of great soul and depth.

GUILLAUME D'ANGERVILLE
Domaine d'Angerville, Volnay

In another contrast to Pommard, Volnay is rich in active limestone as opposed to heavy clay, making for the signature style of graceful, balanced wines, especially on the slope. In the middle of the appellation, Taillepieds, with its white marl, makes for a more austere, reserved wine that blossoms with age. Downslope, Champans, with more ferrous, brown soils, makes a rounder, stouter wine that's ever chewy and satisfying. On the southern edge of Volnay, Clos des Chênes beautifully marries Volnay's potential for grace and power. Just below, Caillerets, with its small stones of limestone and marl, is often held up as the archetypal Volnay, blending that lacy raspberry and cherry fruit with a distinctly mineral texture. North of town, toward Pommard, the wines become, as you'd expect, more muscular, lacking some of Volnay's classic grace, in vineyards like Les Angles and Fremiets.

QUESTIONS OF TASTE

What's the classical expression of Volnay?

Volnay is well loved as the Côte de Beaune's embodiment of elegance in Pinot Noir. It tends toward red fruits in most (but not all vintages). Yet sometimes this elegance can have an austere, hard-edged frame. While some vineyards can produce wines of great tannin and power, when it all comes together, the wines seamlessly blend fruit and minerality in medium-bodied wine with a lacy, delightful texture and vibrancy and freshness.

Volnay is often compared to Chambolle-Musigny in the Côte de Nuits—are there similarities?

We put this notion to the test on a panel at well-known sommelier and importer Daniel Johnnes's famous Burgundy event, La Paulée, in 2017. The similarities are that both villages produce atypically elegant, airy wines, begging the question of whether the soils are the same. Both villages are at high altitude too, which could contribute to a lighter profile. But, in fact, they are otherwise not very similar, according to geologist Françoise Vannier, who said, definitively, "Volnay is more white soil, less limestone, not the same kind of limestone. In my opinion it is not possible for the soils and subsoils to have a parallel." And, indeed, as our tasting—which compared d'Angerville Volnay and Roumier Chambolle—determined, the two villages have a very different feel. Volnay really did have a very light, airy sense to it above a lacy minerality. Chambolle, while nimble and graceful in its own way, had a stronger, more powerful core, typical of the Côte de Nuits.

◇ **DOMAINE MARQUIS D'ANGERVILLE** Pure and precise, elegant and pristine. What else is there to say except that the monopole Clos des Ducs is one of the greatest vineyards in Burgundy? According to Guillaume d'Angerville, in 1507, when Clos des Ducs was inventoried for the brand-new kings of France (who, strangely, left it in the name of its former owners, the Dukes of Burgundy, instead of changing it, as was standard practice, to Clos du Roi), its size was measured at 52 *ouvrées* (2.15 hectares, 5.3 acres)—exactly its size today. It hasn't changed in more than five hundred years. "It makes us feel very small," he says. Only slightly less humbling are d'Angerville's other exquisite Volnay wines: Champans, Caillerets, Taillepieds, Mitans, Clos des Angles, and Fremiet.

◇ **DOMAINE LAFARGE** The spirit of Burgundy personified. Great farmers. Great winemakers. Great people. Humble and convivial, the Lafarges make powerful, soulful Volnay in a style somewhat more full than d'Angerville's. But it's incredibly compelling and ages beautifully for decades. Lafarge makes several Volnays, all beautiful, but best after a few years: Caillerets, Clos des Chênes, Clos du Château des Ducs, and Mitans.

◇ **DOMAINE DE MONTILLE** Historically very much associated with Volnay, the domaine's reawakening began with patriarch Hubert de Montille and has continued under his children, Etienne and Alix. Hubert's Volnays were more tannic and darker, while Etienne's are more elegant and floral, but both are true to the nature of Volnay.

Meursault

It's time to rewrite the book on Meursault. All the old books hold the same line: Meursault is the roundest and richest of the three great villages for white Burgundy, with flavors of rich butter and toasted hazelnuts. These simply do not apply today as they once did. The premox (premature oxidation) scandal of the 1990s and 2000s basically ended the practice of the long aging of white Burgundy, as trust has not returned that these expensive wines will not turn brown in the bottle while sitting in the cellar. At the same time, wine tastes have evolved in the last twenty to thirty years, favoring cut and precision over luxuriance and flesh. Responding to both changing tastes and a preference for earlier drinking, producers have adopted the more fashionable, racy, leaner approach we see in many regions. The upshot is that buttery, nutty Meursault is now a relic. The new style is stony and lemony, fresh and bright. Wait, you say, doesn't the terroir dictate the nature of the wines? Indeed, though style is always present in the interpretation of terroir. And the fact remains that Meursault's terroir is much more oriented toward the current style than most people would suspect.

This all seems strikingly clear when spending an afternoon with Jean-Marc Roulot, the leading light of the new Meursault. His wines are all the rage right now, and rightly so, as they run the gamut from great Premier Crus to distinctive village wines. First we drive out into the extended flats east of the village to see the vineyards of his excellent Bourgogne Blanc. It's his most humble wine, but that doesn't mean it lacks attention. "I'm very motivated with Bourgogne Blanc," he says. "It's nice to have the high wines, but I love to produce a good bottle at a lower price." He notes that his farming practice and cost for Bourgogne Blanc are the same as for Meursault Perrières, which fetches ten times the price (if you can find them, the BB sells for around $80 and the Perrières anywhere from $500 to $1,000).

Next we drive high up into Meursault's lofty hillside vineyards, one of the village's great strengths. Though only village rated, in the new Meursault paradigm of leaner, racier wines, many produce at near Premier Cru level, a notion strengthened by the fact that so many are now familiar names to wine lovers: Rougeots, Tessons, Narvaux, Luchets, Chevalières, Tillets, and Grands Charrons. At their high altitudes, in (increasingly common) warmer years, these vineyards excel. The soils are thin and more complex than what gets reported, says Jean-Marc. He offers his famous *lieu-dit* (unclassified single vineyard) Les Tessons as an example. "In 260 feet the soil changes from white to yellow to dark and red. We are still learning about it every year." The grapes are all harvested and vinified together, so the nuances of these soil differences are hard to quantify. But Roulot, like most great vintners, strives for precision and wants to know every detail of his vineyard.

And then, finally, to the great vineyards in the middle of the slope: Perrières, Charmes, Genevrières, each with its own personality: Perrières—the eternal Grand Cru in waiting, with its epic fusion of body and minerality, frame and physique; Charmes—full-bodied and physical, but deep and engaging; and Genevrières—crystalline in structure, at once gossamer and formidable.

QUESTION OF TASTE

What are the signature characteristics of Meursault?

As we note above, the style in Meursault has changed in recent years, from a rich, round, and buttery emphasis to something more lean and cut. However, the richness that allowed Meursault to achieve those sizable wines can still be coaxed from the soil. The best of today's Meursault wines evince this depth and unctuousness, but still manage to find precision and tautness in the structure. It's a beautiful thing, well demonstrated in the current wines of Comtes Lafon, Roulot, and Ente.

ST-AUBIN

VINEYARD FOCUS

Hailed quite frequently these days as a "hidden gem" or "unknown terroir," St-Aubin is indeed an excellent and often good-value source of white Burgundy. Sellers of St-Aubin love to point out that a couple of its vineyards—En Remilly and Les Murgers des Dents de Chien—lie only a measure of feet away from Puligny's epic Grand Crus of Montrachet and Chevalier-Montrachet, but make wines at only a fraction of the price.

This is all true, and we are big fans of St-Aubin, but there is more to say here. First, it's not really one terroir, but two, as detailed below. Second, En Remilly is great, but it's not Montrachet. Three, for all those who think a warming climate may vault St-Aubin into the ranks of the top village: it's not climate that holds it back, but soil. Let's address these in order.

St-Aubin is not on the Côte d'Or. The appellation begins in the gaping combe that cuts through the Côte d'Or between Puligny and Chassagne. This combe takes a 90-degree left turn at the town of Gamay, opening into a small valley behind Chassagne. St-Aubin's first major Premier Cru vineyard area lies in the combe, reaching down to almost touch Montrachet. This is the best part. The vineyards here have some shockingly steep slopes, reach high elevations of 1,200 feet, and sport a pure marl-heavy limestone that produces high-acid, mineral-laden whites. The vineyards to know are En Remilly, Les Murgers des Dents de Chien ("wall of dog's teeth," referring to old jagged stone walls), and La Chatenière. It is cool up there, and in warm vintages (2009, 2015), these wines can be amazing. They're largely the same soils as the great Grand Crus of Puligny, but thinner and more exposed.

The second valley, the left turn at Gamay, produces weaker wines. The soils are bonier and less interesting, and thus the wines produced here—both reds and whites—don't have the same nuance or thrill as the wines from the hill above Montrachet. It's cool and windy here too, but mostly it's the thinness of the soils that holdsback the wines.

The best producers in St-Aubin are Pierre-Yves Colin-Morey and Domaine Hubert Lamy. Both make excellent wines. But know that St-Aubin is indeed good value compared to Puligny-Montrachet, but En Remilly in a good vintage can still be a pricey wine.

◇ **DOMAINE GUY ROULOT** A working actor and writer, Jean-Marc Roulot has talents and interests beyond Meursault. Perhaps those inspirations help him improve the wine, though his commitment to his vineyards and cellar is never in question. His wines are Meursault's most poetic and human. There's a pureness and limpidity that gives them elemental status. All are excellent, but Roulot's is the quintessentially great Bourgogne Blanc, and his collection of lieux dits are unmatched: Tessons (Clos de Mon Plaisir), Tillets, Meix Chavaux, Vireuils, and Luchets.

◇ **DOMAINE DES COMTE LAFON** Dominique Lafon is a true legend in his own time, producing some of the greatest Meursault. He's also a vision of the new Meursault, as his leap to the new, racy, acid-driven style has been one of the prime indicators of the village's general shift. Lafon makes a number of Côte de Beaune wines (including a lot of Volnay), but his Meursault offerings are storied, particularly Clos de la Barre, Charmes, Genevrières, and Perrières.

◇ **DOMAIN COCHE-DURY** Does the rarefied, insular house of Coche still deserve its cult status? It does on the basis that only a tiny club of very wealthy people get to taste it. The wines are still very, very good. But the flash of sulfury matchstick that used to captivate some of us is more rare than it used to be. Still, in their fusion of power, minerality, and streamlined grace, the wines are some of the most defining of Meursault: Chevalières, Rougeots, Caillerets, and Perrières.

◇ **ARNAUD ENTE** One of the rising winemakers of Meursault, Ente has the resume (he worked at Coche-Dury during its heyday) and the drive to be consistently listed among the village's top producers. In the 1990s, he partook in the rich, luxuriant style, but, like Lafon, has moved away from it in the last decade and a half, finding a great citric bite, as well as intense stoniness. In particular, seek out these wines: Meursault Clos des Ambres, La Goutte d'Or, and Le Petits Charrons.

Puligny

The classical thinking on Puligny is as Burgundy critic Clive Coates wrote: "Puligny-Montrachet is the greatest white-wine commune on earth." Everyone kneels at the altar of the Grand Crus. If Burgundy is poker, Puligny got dealt a royal (Grand Cru) flush: Montrachet, Bâtard, Bienvenues, and Chevalier. Nothing beats those kingly vineyards in terms of complexity, richness, expression, and price. But what if you're not playing poker anymore?

Welcome to the new reality. It's hard to have conversations about Puligny's great Grand Crus anymore when so few people get to drink them. Accessible only to the extremely wealthy and the sommeliers who serve them, these are beasts now very rarely seen in the field. The same goes for Puligny's great Premier Crus—Cailleret,

Clavoillon, Folatieres, Combettes. What's left to taste is Puligny village, a rather sparse set of wines that lacks the affordability and accessibility of wines from neighboring Meursault and Chassagne. This is not to disparage Puligny. Times have simply changed . . . for now.

PARTICULARS OF PLACE

Puligny-Montrachet is a wonderfully tight, compact appellation that's easy to understand. The great vineyards start on a gradual slope that sharpens on its way up. The straw that stirs the drink is Montrachet. The Hope diamond of Chardonnay vineyards is set like the crown jewel amidst a coterie of other beautiful Grand Cru jewels. If Montrachet is the perfect combination of factors—active (but not too active) limestone, a preponderance of stone to ensure great drainage, enough clay to round the form without becoming corpulent, an ideal exposure—well, then, its cohort makes perfect sense. Chevalier, on thinner soils higher on the slope on more active limestone, is the more edgy, mineral one. Bâtard, on more clay, is a bit rounder and richer, more golden. Bienvenue-Montrachet and Criots-Bâtard-Montrachet are round and regal, but slightly less complex and less compelling.

The Premier Crus are all north of and in line with the Grand Crus: Caillerets, Pucelles, Folatiers, Combettes. They too are excellent spots, if not producing at the weight and complexity of the Grand Crus.

It's telling, however, that there's no transitional area between Grand Cru Bâtard-Montrachet and basic village-rated vineyards. The terroir jumps from high-born to humble in a matter of feet. That's because Puligny's water table is so high; shortly after the slope ends, the ground becomes too moist to make great wine. To wit, houses in the village of Meursault have underground cellars. In Puligny, cellars must be above ground. This moist, rich soil ensures that good village-level Puligny is highly limited and tough to produce.

QUESTION OF TASTE

How do you distinguish Puligny from Meursault?

In the past, Meursault was the plump one and Puligny the lean, mineral one. That seems to have shifted; today, Meursault is the vision of straight-line minerality with lemon cream. Puligny now seems more opulent, with more body and more flesh. There's still a sense of stoniness, but it's a thicker band of stone compared to Meursault's more elegant contour. Puligny's fruit character runs riper, from lemon curd to peach and pear to slightly underripe pineapple. The texture of minerals is always at the core, but Puligny is a richer wine than Meursault.

JEAN-MARC ROULOT
Domaine Roulot, Meursault

◇ **DOMAINE LEFLAIVE** One of the great domaines in the world, it has not skipped a beat since the death of its guiding spiritual and oenological force, Anne-Claude Leflaive, in 2015. Her nephew, Brice de la Morandière, was chosen to succeed her and appears only intent on maintaining her high standards in farming and wine production. These wines remain Puligny of the old school, intensely mineral and powerful. From a resplendent collection of Grand Crus (including Montrachet, Chevalier-Montrachet, and the others) to wonderful Premier Crus (Pucelles, Folatières, Combettes, and Clavoillon), no other domaine so defines the village of Puligny.

◇ **DOMAINE FRANÇOIS CARILLON AND DOMAINE JACQUES CARILLON** Two Carillon brothers, François and Jacques, ran the Domaine Louis Carillon until 2010, when they split into separate domaines. Before the split, these were delicious wines, capturing a lovely vision of Puligny—generously ripe, approachable Chardonnay, not too mineral or austere. Separately, the brothers appear to be continuing in the original family style, but now as two domaines with separate importers and chains of distribution, it's much harder to find the wines. Both domaines make village and the Premier Cru Les Perrières, and you'll find the wines to be more similar than not.

◇ **DOMAINE ETIENNE SAUZET** Though affectionately known (by us, anyway) as "Keyser" Sauzet, this house has nothing in common with that nefarious character. Rather, it's a revered old domaine with a flush of great Puligny holdings from Montrachet and most of the Premier Crus. The style tends toward the opulent with big, bold flavors and a palpable dose of new oak.

Chassagne-Montrachet

Chassagne is relatively unknown to many wine drinkers, and even a bit of a mystery to other residents of the Côte de Beaune. As the most southern of the Côte d'Or's major villages, it keeps to itself. That insularity is on display by the sheer frequency with which the same names—Colin, Morey, and Pillot in particular—recur on the town's signage, representing a handful of powerful and sprawling families who have consolidated in the village.

But Chassagne is also an enigma wine-wise. Yes, it has a share of two Grand Crus—Montrachet and Bâtard-Montrachet, which cross the border between Puligny and Chassagne—but most of the wine it produces has little to do with those two celebrities, who may have a foot in Chassagne, but primarily reside in Puligny. Criots-Bâtard-Montrachet is all Chassagne, but considered the least of the Grand Cru suite.

Though it's known for its white wine today, Chassagne's vineyards produced mostly red in the nineteenth century, and even local vintners agree that the bulk of its soils may be better for red. But now, even if half of Chassagne's production is in red, that percentage is dwindling as Chassagne's Chardonnay is in greater demand and fetches far better prices than its Pinot Noir. "Many vineyards that were red, people are now putting in white," Pierre-Yves Colin tells us. "But these places were never really great in red. And they will not be really great in white," he says, insinuating that his village possesses a lot of middling soils that lack the perfect balance of clay and limestone. In the best vineyards, though, the best color orientation is clear, and it's always for white wine.

Pierre-Yves represents a changing of the guard in Chassagne. The 1970s to the 1990s was the heyday of producers like Ramonet, Niellon, and Gagnard, who pushed a rich, sometimes unctuous and unapologetically oaky style of Chassagne. The wines were mineral, but often lacked the posture of Puligny and the mellifluous modulations of Meursault. Today, the new wave, led by younger producers like Pierre-Yves, Alex Moreau (Domaine Bernard Moreau), and Vincent Dancer, are tapping Chassagne's mineral reserves for racy, razor-sharp wines.

ALEX MOREAU
Domaine Bernard Moreau, Chassagne Montrachet

"Chassagne is quite simple to understand," says Alex Moreau as we drive in his truck south down the D113A toward Santenay. "Village vineyards to your left. Premier Cru to your right on the hill. You can see the difference."

He's right—the difference is clear. The village vineyards are flat, drab, and featureless, whereas the vineyards passing on our right side start to climb the giant mound of rock that produces the famous pink Chassagne limestone, polished to a glassy sheen, used to build the Louvre in Paris. (It can only be used indoors, as it's prone to fracturing during frosts, a fact that also explains the massive amounts of sharp limestone shards we see littering some vineyard floors.)

But Chassagne is not *that* simple, as Moreau is about to demonstrate. Soon enough, we are in a Premier Cru zone on both sides of the road. He's taken us to a large district called Morgeot, containing 58 hectares (142 acres) with twenty-one separate vineyards. Morgeot is defined by a visible fault, a break in the hillside, signaled by a sheer rock face, where the lower terraces lie maybe 10 or 12 feet below the upper ones. That which is not Morgeot sits above the fault—vineyards like La Romanée, Grandes Ruchottes, and En Cailleret. These vineyards have but a bare minimum of topsoil and produce intensely lean, strict, mineral wines.

The land beneath the fault is the Morgeot district. It has the same bedrock as up above, but is buried under many feet of runoff from up above and alluvial deposits from out of the Combe of St-Aubin. Vines from down here, usually just called Morgeot, make a rounder, fleshier wine.

Closer to the village, red and white soils are intermixed. Clos St-Jean, just beneath the quarry, is a well-known red wine terroir. Directly north of it, Chaumées and Vergers have more rock and produce classic whites. Chenevottes, just in the mouth of the combe, has light soils and makes a warmer, fruitier white with tropical overtones.

QUESTION OF TASTE

How is Chassagne different from both Puligny and Meursault?

These days, with top producers seeking a racy style, Chassagne can produce some of the most raw, mineral wines on the Côte de Beaune. The wines don't always knit together in the sleek, professional package you find in other villages—that is, they may often seem unbalanced in the fruit direction, or overly acid and stony—but the raw material is compelling. Chassagne's higher vineyards, planted on the slopes of a big quarry, make wines that crackle with acid and power. Wines from Morgeot wrap that core minerality in a sheath of lemon to apricot flesh. Except in its vineyards right on the border with Puligny—Chenevottes, Blanchot Dessus, and Enseignères— Chassagne doesn't have Puligny's fruit and robustness, or its sleek contours. Nor does it have Meursault's polished, elemental flash.

DOMAINE LOUIS MICHEL
Chablis

◇ **PAUL PILLOT** This multi-generation domaine is now in the hands of young vigneron Thierry Pillot, who by all accounts is obsessed with improving his farming, a quality that shows in the vibrance and freshness of the wines, which aim for an impressively focused, linear, high-energy style. Be on the lookout for Chassagnes like Clos St-Jean, La Montagne, and Grandes Ruchottes.

◇ **PIERRE-YVES COLIN-MOREY** This domaine, run by Pierre-Yves Colin (known as PYC) and his wife, Caroline Morey, is one of the most impressive new domaines of the Côte de Beaune. PYC is a tireless farmer and, the quality of his raw material shows in his wines' energy and drive. A lack of judiciousness with new oak in the past has evolved into a more considered, integrated approach. However, these wines, even the Bourgogne Blanc, can often benefit from a little bottle age (from two to ten years).

◇ **DOMAINE BERNARD MOREAU** Alex and Benoit Moreau have taken over from their father, but continue his style, which depends on pristine fruit from a number of great vineyards, aged in barrel (a minority percentage of which are new), to find a path down the middle between racy and rocky and fruity and fleshy. Their Chassagnes are top-notch, especially Enseignères, Chenevottes, Maltroie, and Caillerets.

Chablis

Chablis's ubiquity makes it easy to forget what's amazing about it—namely, that it's one of the greatest demonstrations of terroir on the planet. How do we know this? Because it's one of the few places where Chardonnay, with basic winemaking techniques, produces a complete wine of uncommon distinction. It's not difficult to pull the Chablis out of a flight of blind wines.

By contrast, in the new world, Chardonnay is considered "the winemaker's grape." A grape without a lot of inherent character, Chardonnay makes a fairly bland wine unless the winemaker tricks it up with winemaking techniques and barrels. Chablis happens to be a place, the only place, where Chardonnay needs nothing—no bubbles, no lees stirring, no new oak, no TLR (see page 155)—to be captivating.

Even in the hands of average producers, Chablis declares itself in a way that comforts us with its cool, brisk familiarity. It has that distinctive acidity, that suggestion of minerality, that vaguely earthy note lurking under a mélange of citrus flavors. In the hands of above-average producers, it becomes something altogether magnificent.

We see three producers as being the iconic representations of Chablis: the wines of Domaine Raveneau and Vincent Dauvissat are Chablis's cultiest. Raveneau's wines not only carry the stamp of site, but a unique flavor that's hard to describe (somewhere between ripe fruit, cheese, and honey) and idiosyncratically appealing. Dauvissat's wines are more straightforward, reticent in youth, with a sort of purity and sense of transparency being the calling card. It is only after years in the cellar that they begin to show a greater and more expressive character, such as the 2007s today. The approach of the third producer, Domaine Louis Michel, is self-effacement. Its extreme transparency and lack of imprint become its signature.

Beyond these, there's a roster of high-quality producers, whose wines are available and, more important, affordable (like Patrick Piuze, Domaine Collet, William Fèvre, Alice and Olivier de Moor, and Château de Béru, to name a few). The latter remains one of Chablis's underappreciated qualities. It's still a great value, considering the quality level of many domaines. Chablis also ages better than whites from the Côte d'Or.

If there's a reason Chablis lacks the glamour and glitz of the rest of white Burgundy, it's probably Chablis's own fault. It's a small town, remote from the hubbub of the Côte d'Or, filled with old-school producers who don't court attention. The town's inhabitants and merchants rarely project a sense of welcome and warmth. But, then, this is a cold, rural village, the most northern place to produce still Chardonnay. If there's a lack of charm in Chablis, it's perhaps because they save it for the wines.

PARTICULARS OF PLACE

If you visit Chablis, drive to the top of Grand Cru Les Clos. A little forest path behind the great hill opens onto a gorgeous vista, where young Guillaume Michel of Domaine Louis Michel gestures theatrically. "Here it is! All of Chablis!" Indeed, almost everything is visible from here—the village, the river, and all the surrounding hills containing the vineyards of Grand Crus, Premier Crus, village wines, and Petit Chablis. A mounted map helps you discern which is which. Even on a blustery day, the secret of Chablis's feng shui is clear: it's all about the sun.

Chablis sits roughly halfway between Paris and Beaune in the far northern reach of Burgundy. Emanating outward from the town of Chablis, the region is bisected by the Serein river, which, though small, helped carve these important, low valleys. It's a widespread area, with 5,500 hectares (13,475 acres) under vine (almost three times the size of the Jura). Of that massive vineyard area, 64 percent is rated village level, 16 percent Premier Cru, and just 2 percent Grand Cru, the highest rating. The rest is rated Petit Chablis, the lowest designation of Chablis. The Grand Cru appellation is really just one privileged 1.2-mile slope on the Serein's right bank. It's divided into seven named parts that everyone refers to as vineyards, though they're all contiguous. It's a cold place and the vantage point Guillaume has brought us to affirms the openness and exposure to which these low hills are subject.

The defining characteristic of Grand Cru and Premier Cru Chablis compared to other still Chardonnays is what the wine grows on: slopes of marl formed during the Kimmeridgian age, between 152 and 157 million years ago. A marl is defined as some combination of 35 to 65 percent clay, with the balance in limestone. In Chablis, the Kimmeridgian hills are capped by a younger formation known as Portlandian limestone, which is harder and contains less clay. Thanks to its relatively high clay content, Kimmeridgian marl (which also famously occurs in the Aube of Champagne and Chavignol in Sancerre) is thought to have better water retention. It also occurs mid-slope in Chablis, giving it an ideal drainage situation. Wines grown in Kimmeridgian have always been acknowledged to be Chablis's best—the richest, fleshiest, most powerful, and longest-lived. Harder and drier, Portlandian limestone lies atop the hills, where the climate is colder and windier, and its soils become the basis of Petit Chablis.

On the hillsides, plenty of Portlandian has fractured and tumbled down onto the Kimmeridgian slopes. We are told that in Chablis, the secret may not be in one soil or the other, but in the way they interact. Dense, rich Kimmeridgian marl provides the water and the nutrition for the vines' roots, while hard, fractious Portlandian stone penetrates the marl, allowing good aeration, an important factor in vine nutrition.

If these soils are what distinguish Chardonnay from Chablis from other places, what distinguishes Chablis vineyards from each other? Given the general consistency of soils, the most salient differences come from exposure and slope. Of course, there are subtle differences in soil, but these are hard to quantify. The larger point is: in such a small area growing one variety, even minor differences in slope and soil can be magnified in the resulting wines.

Since they exist on both sides of the Serein, Premier Cru vineyards show more extreme differences. On the right bank, the Premier Crus flank the Grand Cru slope to the north and south, with different exposures. On the Serein's left bank the vineyards, which line the fingerlike extensions of the plateau, always face south and southeast. In addition, the slopes on the right bank tend to be steeper and more convex (indicating better drainage and perhaps more ripeness) compared to the left bank slopes, which are gentler and vaguely concave.

We should note that there are varying approaches to vinifying Chablis, which have an impact on the wines. Louis Michel ferments and ages everything in steel tanks, preferring an inert, hermetic vessel to age the wines and preserve vineyard character and vitality. Many other producers use at least some wood barrels, usually old and neutral (not imparting flavor). Dauvissat, for instance, ferments in both vats and woods, but ages everything in old, neutral barrels. He believes wood aging is important to soften the wines. Raveneau ages in wood, with a small portion of it being new, which is sometimes detectable. Predictably, Louis Michel wines have a bright clang from the steel tanks, while the edges of Dauvissat and Raveneau are softer, though their wines' interiors are perhaps even more dense.

What are the different characteristics of the most important Grand Crus and Premier Crus?

Here's the Grand Cru rundown, from northwest to southeast:

Bougros South-facing and low-sloping, this is a fantastic Grand Cru, one often overlooked. The wine is full-bodied and supple, with mineral depths couched in a ripe, fruity skin. Often rustic in nature, Bougros lacks the precision and nuance of the other Grand Crus.

Preuses A sunny and warm section, high on the slope over Bougros and Vaudésir with a southern exposure. Very stony soils and a gentle slope yield forward, assertive wines that are more approachable in youth, but lack the steel of other crus.

Vaudésir Occupying the high and mid-slope area just east of Preuses, Vaudésir is complicated, but belongs in the top tier of the Grand Cru hierarchy (along with Les Clos and Valmur). It stretches across a bend in the slope to form two main sides with different exposures. One face looks south-southeast and produces rich, floral, voluptuous wines that can be a bit ponderous. The other major section faces more south and west to produce very tight, mineral, austere wines. Louis Michel's Vaudésir (about $60), for instance, comes from a slight north-facing sliver and performs best in hot vintages like 2015.

Grenouilles The lowest Grand Cru on the slope, with a great, but cool situation, produces a very delicate, perfumed wine that needs time. Seven of the nine hectares are owned by the co-op, and only a handful of producers—including Jean-Paul and Benoit Droin, Domaine Testut, and Daniel-Etienne Defaix—have the rest, so it's a wine rarely seen.

Valmur High on the slope, Valmur is a very mineral, firm wine with a lot of poise and restraint. It is shy in its youth and needs years in the bottle to properly open, but when it does, it approaches Les Clos in quality, but in a more structured, steely wine that feels slightly less complete.

Les Clos The king. The biggest cru, occupying a massive swath of the hill facing just between due south and southwest, Les Clos is rocky and extremely well draining. It produces a hyper-mineral wine of enormous depth. Usually somewhat shut down and brooding for its first decade, it emerges with time to be something wonderfully complete, complex, and generous. Its wines always have notable power, length, and breadth.

Blanchots With its southeast exposure and well-draining capacity, the last of the Grand Crus makes floral and finessed wines that are accessible when fairly young. It simply lacks the steel and power of its Grand Cru brethren.

Here are the major Premier Crus on the right bank of the Serein:

Fourchaume At almost 3 miles long, Fourchaume is a huge Premier Cru, so it's hard to characterize. It's all the more complicated (and odd) given that a portion of it, called Vaulorent, is separated from the rest by a swath of unplanted, unauthorized land in the hill. Fourchaume has a cool, floral nose, and a round palate. In the hands of a good producer it can approach Grand Cru depth, but without the forcefulness and aging potential. Vaulorent is an interesting case, as it's the only Premier Cru on the same slope as the Grand Crus. It borders Preuses, but can't be called Grand Cru because it doesn't lie within the official boundaries of the town of Chablis. Vaulorent is not well known in the States, but highly appreciated in France, as many think it approaches the level of Grand Cru. It makes an austere, powerful wine with a lot of density that usually requires a few years of bottle age to begin expressing itself. Buy it if you see it; Patrick Piuze, Louis Michel, and William Fèvre produce it well.

Montée de Tonnerre A favorite Premier Cru, as many think it produces at Grand Cru status, but still goes for Premier Cru prices. Powerful and dense with a profoundly rocky texture, it's a full wine, but never rounded or voluptuous. Historically, Montée de Tonnerre refers to the top section of the vineyard, while the larger lower slope goes by the name Chapelot. Some, like Raveneau, still bottle a separate Chapelot.

And these are the major left bank Premier Crus:

Vaillons One of the five extending fingers of Premier Crus on the Left Bank of the Serein, Vaillons is one of the largest and most important. Guillaume Michel calls it a "solar" vineyard, meaning it's warm, amply collecting the sun's heat. It's one of the first places harvested, achieving a deep, full ripeness and a soft, voluptuous texture. Inside it is another wonderful Premier Cru called Sécher. Some bottle it separately (look for Dauvissat's, who spells it "Séchet"), while some just bottle it as Vaillons. Sécher is fantastic, sharing the tropical ripeness of Vaillons, but with a more acidic, mineral bearing.

Montmains The next finger over from Vaillons is Montmains, which is divided into three separate Premier Crus, any of which can take the name Montmains. The eponymous section lies closest to the Serein where Montmains is a cool locale, producing a very fresh, crisp, floral wine with a hint of sea breeze. Next to that section is Forêt, most famously vinified by Dauvissat (who spells it "Forest"— Chablis producers have the unusual habit of employing many spelling variations). Forêt's topsoil is very thin, containing less clay and therefore exposing the vines more quickly to the bedrock to produce a more linear, elegant, mineral wine. Last is Butteaux, which is the opposite. Deeper clay produces a fleshier wine, though big chunks of marl are said to give the wine its somewhat coarse, unwieldy texture. "It's a connoisseur's wine," Guillaume says, noting that some people don't love its slightly grizzled nature. But others adore its personality and rusticity.

◇ **DOMAINE RENÉ & VINCENT DAUVISSAT** The greatest Chablis producer of our time. Vincent (his father is René) Dauvissat's farming uses biodynamic methods (though not certified) and is meticulous. The wine style, like the man, is so self-effacing that these quiet wines express themselves subtly at first and then by action as they mature, expand, and blossom. They make you pause and ponder. For the quality, the prices (typically ranging from $70–$150) are actually quite reasonable. All of his wines are worth seeking out, particularly Petit Chablis, Chablis, La Forest, Séchet, Vaillons, Preuses, and Les Clos.

◇ **DOMAINE RAVENEAU** The other pillar of Chablis, these wines are as singular and unique an expression as can be found anywhere in the world. They are funky, visceral, and eccentric, and sometimes seem at odds with this quiet, austere place. Raj's epiphany wine, tasted in 1996, was 1986 Raveau Clos, and he calls it "still one of the greatest wines of my life." The roster is amazing, from wonderful village wine to the iconic Montée de Tonnerre, as well as Butteaux, Valmur, Blanchot, and Les Clos.

◇ **DOMAINE LOUIS MICHEL** The sashimi of Chablis—pure, clean, elemental. Never any oak, this is as energetic and pure as Chablis can get. The wines are steely and bright when young, but age gorgeously for years and decades. The holdings are phenomenal, from Grand Crus Grenouilles, Vaudésir, and Les Clos to expressive Premier Crus like Montée de Tonnerre, Forêt, and Montmains.

◇ **CHRISTIAN MOREAU** A top producer, making crisp, mineral wines with extraordinary precision. He splits the difference between tank and barrel aging, doing portions of each wine in each vessel. The wines are all spot-on, but look out for the Vs: Valmur, Vaudésir, and Vaillons.

◇ **DOMAINE PATTES LOUP** Young Thomas Pico is an upstart, taking the conventionally farmed, underperforming vineyards he inherited and converting them to organics and quality production. The result has been phenomenal. Using a mix of old barrels, steel tanks, and concrete, egg-shaped fermenters (that may have some impact on mouthfeel), he makes a deliciously chewy, fleshy style that still has minerals at its core. The Vaillons and Butteaux are great, but don't overlook his excellent village Chablis.

BEAUJOLAIS

One of the most beautiful wines of the world, Beaujolais couldn't catch a break. From the humiliation it must have suffered in 1395 when its grape, Gamay, got unceremoniously booted from Burgundy by Philip the Bold, to the summers of 2016 and 2017, when brutal hailstorms destroyed the crop in many of its best vineyards, the hits have kept coming. Add in the fact that its one claim to fame, Beaujolais Nouveau, which brought international fame and tons of cash, was based on an iffy wine that would obscure the existence of the good Beaujolais and ultimately contribute to an economic tailspin lasting decades, and you've got a major crash on your hands. Even the heavily hyped vintages of late—2009, 2010, and 2015—all of which prompted forecasts of a "Beaujolais turnaround," were not magic bullets.

Quick fixes, however, were never what Beaujolais needed. The region's people and its wines have always been regarded in France as sort of charming, convivial country bumpkins, providing simple bucolic pleasure if never profundity. And while there is a jovial, outgoing spirit here, Beaujolais is also home to many extremely talented, driven vignerons. And it's in these men and women that lies the region's reclamation, which is being powered by quality, site-driven wines, not magic bullets or marketing gimmicks.

You've probably heard the Beaujolais Nouveau story before. If you haven't, it's a useful case study in dodgy business strategy. It's complex, but in a simplified telling, postwar Beaujolais (as the rest of France) was in a bad state. Beaujolais wine was well loved in France, but only as a country wine that was not taken as seriously as its two prestigious neighbors, Burgundy and the Rhône. In the 1950s, the idea was hit on to promote a local tradition of celebrating the new vintage by selling a young, simple fresh wine just weeks after it was harvested and fermented. November 15 was originally specified as the release date (now it's the third Thursday of November), and promoters successfully made an event out of the Beaujolais Nouveau, racing it to Paris to be opened at the stroke of midnight. Like the Macarena, it somehow caught on and in the seventies and eighties took the world by storm, making Beaujolais a household name. Good, artisanal Beaujolais Nouveau can be delicious (try Foillard's), but global demand and exploitation by large négociants ended up degrading the wine and it became thin, insipid, and candied. Add in widespread industrial farming (to produce heavy crops) and poor grapes, and quality in the region took a downward spiral.

See a problem with that business strategy? Sure enough, Beaujolais developed a reputation for exactly what it was marketing—bad wine to be consumed only once a year. Internally and externally, as Beaujolais became solely associated with Nouveau, the négociants dominated the local economy and prices plummeted. With no ability to make better money, most producers succumbed to the lassitude of industrial production: chemical fertilizers to raise yields, early picking of grapes that aren't fully ripe (to avoid any bad weather), fermenting with cultured yeasts instead of natural, adding sugar to the fermentations to compensate for underripe grapes, employing lots of sulfur dioxide as an antioxidant and disinfectant, and sterile filtering the wines to avoid potential spoilage. The wines, like the soils, were dead.

However, there was a resistance. In the early 1980s a small group of young producers in Morgon, dubbed by importer Kermit Lynch the Gang of Four (Jean-Paul Thévenet, Guy Breton, Jean Foillard, and Marcel Lapierre), fell under the influence of an elderly, brilliant sage named Jules Chauvet. Chauvet and his assistant Jacques Néauport preached traditional winemaking—use old vines in vineyards farmed without chemicals, harvest fully ripe grapes, ferment with natural yeasts, age the wines in barrel, and bottle without fining or filtration. Chauvet also proved that this could be done without adding sulfur dioxide, wine's universal protector. The Gang of Four adopted these methods and essentially gave birth to the natural wine movement, countering the rise of industrial winemaking and preserving Beaujolais's soul.

Today, Beaujolais is well on its way out of the pit into which Nouveau cast it. Just as the attention of modern young wine drinkers is finding the previously obscure wines of the Loire and the Jura, Beaujolais too has been recognized for the complex and thought-provoking, yet utterly delightful, wines it can make. In a beneficial feedback loop, the opportunity Beaujolais currently presents—cheap land, high-quality and historical terroirs, newfound cachet—is attracting both young, aspiring vintners and even some famous names from Burgundy (Lafarge and Thibault Liger-Belair, to name a couple) who help raise the profile even higher.

Beaujolais's governing bodies are also finally acting in the name of quality. In recent years, the regional wine authorities have launched aggressive marketing of Beaujolais abroad. They've also realized that Beaujolais's failure to present itself seriously as a complex terroir had caused it to lag far behind other regions in reputation. Thus, a few years ago an ambitious program was begun to map villages according to soil and *climat* (vineyard plot). The idea is that the ten named villages should not simply be known as Crus of Beaujolais, as they are, but rather possess as much a sense of identity and resonance—a brand, if you will—as Meursault or Chambolle-Musigny enjoy in Burgundy. Eventually, the hope is to create a classification that will see some climats within the villages promoted to Premier Cru status (by French law, Beaujolais can have no Grand Crus, as Gamay is not considered a noble grape).

All of this amounts to a great act of Beaujolais becoming modern and, in a way, coming to terms with itself. Over the generations, it's almost as if Beaujolais internalized a sense of inferiority. The fact that many growers never expressed much interest in promoting the specificity of their own terroir suggests that they didn't see it as something worth understanding or promoting.

To finally see this shift is gratifying to those of us who love Beaujolais. Today, demand is rising, as are prices. For instance, Lapierre and Foillard used to be readily available for sommeliers at all times throughout the year; they've now become allocated wines. Beaujolais deserves to have its terroir studied and plotted and printed on large, saturated, official topographic maps. It deserves Premier Crus. We, in turn, promise to stay up late into the night with our friends, half drunk on the dark, sapid wine of Morgon, arguing about the details of the classification.

We know the greatness of Beaujolais. We've had Moulin-à-Vent from 1929 that was indistinguishable from any great Burgundy of the same vintage. And we've also quaffed bottles of Fleurie and Morgon so quickly we didn't even see them go. The quality of extreme deliciousness is a gift not mutually exclusive with depth, complexity, or profundity. Great Beaujolais inherently invokes the beautiful in life, but that doesn't mean it can't be taken seriously.

PARTICULARS OF PLACE

Given that the Beaujolais region is finally making strides toward better defining and identifying its own terroir, based on its ten great villages, we're going to briefly look at each village individually to describe the salient features of its terroir, as we understand it, and the general style of wine we've tasted from each. Before we get to that, however, we'd be remiss not to address the subject of winemaking. Beaujolais is particularly associated with a vinification method known as carbonic maceration, which produces wines that tend to be light in color and body, low in acid, and sporting signature flavors of bright, sometimes candied, red fruit. Full carbonic produces a wine like Beaujolais Nouveau, which fits all of those characteristics, whereas semi-carbonic can make wines that are darker and richer, but still have some element of those signature bright, fruity aromas.

Carbonic (and semi-carbonic) maceration's role in producing serious Beaujolais is becoming a hotly debated topic in the region. The technique has become popular all over the world to produce fruity, easy drinking wines. This signature flavor, delightful as it is, becomes rote when you taste it over and over. To wit, it doesn't convey a sense of place, but rather of method, and a method that makes charming, easy wines at that. Many producers in Beaujolais think carbonic maceration is holding them back and, consequently, are experimenting with more traditional methods that avoid the carbonic fruit signature. They see this as the path to more sophisticated, site-oriented wines that will be taken more seriously. These non-carbonic Beaujolais instead show the darker, more savory and earthy side of Gamay and possess higher acid and more tannin. Some producers, such as Jean-Paul Brun, have been making wine like this for a long time. And as more and more experiment with non-carbonic winemaking, we may begin to see a shift in the nature of Beaujolais.

Eschewing the fruity carbonic signature may cause Beaujolais to be taken more seriously. But this is still only a question of winemaking. Beaujolais's road to higher prices and respect has always been there: its terroir. The Beaujolais Crus, the ten named villages, have long been recognized for their unique characters. The act of better marketing these villages while fostering an even more granular understanding of their respective terroirs is truly Beaujolais' path forward.

Here's our understanding of the ten villages' salient characteristics and tastes, from north to south.

St-Amour

In this, the most northern of all the Beaujolais Crus, the soils are complex and varied, making the wine somewhat hard to pin down. There's clay, flint, and granite, but slate also plays a big role. Most crucial, though, is the slope, which is steep and has little topsoil. That and the relatively high altitude (1,050 feet) results in the wine being a bit lighter in body than other Crus, with gentle red fruit and a slightly coarse, unrefined edge.

Juliénas

Winegrowing here goes back at least two thousand years; the village is named for Julius Caesar. One of the most rugged of the Crus, Juliénas shares St-Amour's soil variations, but stretches higher into the foothills (up to 1,300 feet) and has similarly steep slopes. Soils are deeper here than in St-Amour, and the wines are consequently more powerful and dense, with bigger tannins.

Chénas

As the smallest of all the Crus at just 240 hectares (about 600 acres), Chénas is the least known. That's a shame, as the wines can be utterly delicious. On the eastern side the soils dip into the heavier alluvial deposits of the Saône. In the western—and best—locations, the soils are derived from pink granite, with red sand and ground-up quartz. Low in organic matter and high in minerals, they yield fleshy and powerful wines with black fruits and a peppery snap that suggests the Rhône.

Moulin-à-Vent

We could probably write an entire book about the cultural and vinous nature of Moulin-à-Vent, but we'll try to keep things brief. Forever, and with good reason, Moulin-à-Vent has been considered the greatest of the Beaujolais Crus. In old wine lists (from the early 1900s) it's often the only Beaujolais Cru listed, and then at prices equal to or just beneath Burgundy. It's the village with the aristocratic château, as opposed to the down-home, farmer-producers who populate the other Crus. This chasm has fostered a cultural divide between Moulin-à-Vent and the rest of Beaujolais. Though it's but a tiny village tucked into the same foothills that contain the other Crus, the people of Moulin-à-Vent, we heard, generally keep to themselves. That said, there is a unique typicity in the wines. They are tannic and powerful, though still drinkable when young. Yet these tannins are fine-grained, intricately woven into the fabric of the wine. Indeed, the structure here is just more complete, more dimensional than other Beaujolais, resulting in solid and powerful, though elegant, wines. Flavors tend toward dark fruit and florals in youth, turning red with age. What makes it so special here? That's hard to say. The soils are composed of sandy and rocky pink granite distributed over shallow, low-set hills. Some attribute the fine structure and ageability to the preponderance of manganese in the soil (there was an adjacent manganese mine), as well as iron. Some point to the heavy winds (the town is named for its famous windmill, after all) that slightly dehydrate and concentrate the grapes. It's hard to say why the wines have their certain majesty, but it's a case where quality doesn't lie.

Fleurie

Just southwest of and higher on the hill than Moulin-à-Vent, Fleurie shares its pink granite soils. This is one of the larger Crus, famous for its seductive wines and talented producers. While flatter sections exist, a good amount of Fleurie spreads over steep hills that provide concentrated wines. Fleurie has thirteen different climats, which hopefully over time will become better known. A couple are already gaining recognition, thanks to the producers who make vineyard-designated wines, notably the majestic, Burgundy-like bottlings made by Jean-Louis Dutraive of Domaine de la Grand'Cour, from the terroirs called La Chapelle des Bois and Champagne, as well as his monopole of Clos de la Grand'Cour. Fleurie's flavors tend toward dark, red fruit adorned with a high-toned violet perfume, making it one of the most beguiling of all the Crus. At its best, the texture is juicy and lavish, atop a full structure. The roster of great producers is long: Dutraive, Métras, Sunier, and Baligny, to name a few. One of our favorites is the uber-traditional Clos de la Roilette, whose powerful wines age like a Moulin-à-Vent.

Chiroubles

Not nearly as well known as it should be, Chiroubles, more than any other village, captures the beautiful, lilting side of Beaujolais. It's got the highest altitudes and some of the steepest slopes in the region, as well very thin soils of granitic sand over granite bedrock. These factors conspire to yield a lighter wine, but full of bright, juicy fruit and beautiful floral flourishes. But don't be fooled into thinking the wine insubstantial. It too has a stony, mineral spine that ensures good posture and length. It ages better than you'd think: we drank an amazing one-off made by Guy Breton (he got the fruit for just one year) from 2009, and the wine had barely begun to age. Keep an eye out for this Cru.

Morgon

In many ways, Morgon is the heart of modern Beaujolais, at least to wine drinkers in America, where the village is well known. In general, its wines are dark-hued and savory, with powerful flavors, a rich texture, and moderate tannins. If Moulin-à-Vent is the most established, aristocratic place, then Morgon is the home of its rebels and artists. With over 1,000 hectares (2,470 acres), it's the second largest of all the Crus and therefore stretches out over a number of distinct terroirs. More and more, these areas are being vinified separately and appearing on wines' front labels, as Jean Foillard has done for years. The Côte du Py is already the most famous subzone. Schist, remember, makes powerful wines, and Côte du Py is a giant mound of brittle, fractured schist, rich in iron and manganese. The Côte du Py makes deeply structured, tannic, long-aging wines notable for smoky dark fruit and a savory wild side. By contrast is Corcelette, where the soils are made of a light, granitic sand, producing a silky and elegant red with light tannins and an easy-drinking juiciness. Another climat is Grand Cras, a lower vineyard with deeper granitic soils and alluvium. It produces a classically dark, savory Morgon, but with a little more flesh. Douby is a popular zone with deeper, sandy, granite-based soils, making elegant, smoothly textured wines that still have great length and powerful structure. Another important place is Les Charmes, the highest climat of Morgon at around 1,200 feet of elevation. Its granitic soil mixes sand and stones to produce wines of a silky elegance without sacrificing structure.

Régnié

Only promoted to Cru status in 1988, Régnié is often looked upon as the least of the ten villages, as it abuts a large section of vineyard land only qualified as Beaujolais-Villages. The soil here is a light, shallow pink granitic sand that produces red-fruited wines that are generally light. The best of them, though, such as Guy Breton's, have a firm core of minerality that gives them backbone and textural complexity.

Brouilly

The largest of the Crus, Brouilly is the hilly expanse surrounding the towering Mont Brouilly. The appellation spreads out over 1,000 hectares (2,470 acres) and across several soil types. Most famous of these soils are the hills of sandy pink granite, but half of it is also given to alluvial stones, deeper clays, and even some limestone. Most winemakers blend vineyards from different soils to come up with a pleasing cuvée that represents Brouilly style as much as terroir. And that style is a friendly, accessible, all-purpose wine, more dense in substance than Chiroubles or Régnié, but not nearly as powerful or deep as Morgon. The wines can have grippy tannins, and sometimes don't seem to have the breadth of structure to carry them, but in general are quite vibrant and dark-fruited.

BEAUJOLAIS'S NEW GENERATION

Any region experiencing as lively a regeneration as Beaujolais attracts its share of new producers, particularly young ones who are more likely to be able to afford grapes or land in a region that's depressed than one that's booming (like, say, Burgundy). Hence, we find a plethora of exciting young producers making delicious wines in Beaujolais. (However, it should also be noted that in many cases these youth are the exceptions, and not the rule. An entire generation of children has also left Beaujolais, and many domaines, albeit not the most famous ones, will experience secession problems in years to come.)

In Juliénas, Fleurie, and Chiroubles, look out for Domaine Chapel, which is producing some of the most graceful and irresistible new wines around. Yann Bertrand of Famille Bertrand came back from university and travels to find himself drawn into winegrowing with his family's vines that age from thirty to over a hundred years old. He developed his reputation for his ebullient Cuvée du Chaos from Fleurie, made in the natural style from biodynamically farmed century-old vines. Also in Fleurie, Anne-Sophie Dubois has made a name for herself with graceful, savory, complex wines. She trained in Burgundy and has brought that style of vinification to Beaujolais (instead of carbonic fermentation). Indeed, she even breaks convention by labeling her Paso Doble wine as Bourgogne, as she's allowed, even though it's made from Gamay in Beaujolais. In Chiroubles, Jules Métras, son of his famous winemaker dad, Yvon, is producing gorgeously juicy, red-fruited Beaujolais. Brouilly is home to Pierre Cotton, another young upstart making wines without sulfur. Vibrant and juicy, the wines are dangerously easy to drink. Another agent of the newest generation, Alex Foillard (son of Jean) produces Brouilly and Côte de Brouilly with the same freshness and verve as his father.

Côte de Brouilly

The volcanic tower of Mont Brouilly looms large (1,600 feet) in the middle of the Brouilly appellation, making Côte de Brouilly very special indeed. The stone that composes the peak and the Côte is a famously hard, blue-tinged rock called diorite that survived for millions of years, as the volcano that once surrounded it eroded into the sands and gravels below. This kind of rock is so hard that stonemasons in ancient Egypt used it to carve granite. Somehow, vines have found purchase in the thin soils that manage to grip the hill's steep slopes. The wine from here is impressive. Look for deep, very pure blue and black fruits and a spicy, peppery nose. But it's the structure that's most telling. Firm, but with rounded edges, the wines show a deep minerality, not only in the sense of a dense structural core, but also texturally, with a fine-grained stoniness.

QUESTIONS OF TASTE

How do wines from Morgon's Côte du Py area taste different from straight-up Morgon?

Morgon bottlings are generally blends from a variety of sites around the appellation, and the wine is made to be accessible young, and easy-drinking. It still may be recognizably Morgon, with dark cherry on the nose, savory flavors, and a medium body with density, fine tannins, and only moderate acidity. Côte du Py (which the French pronounce as the letter "P") wines amp up the structure with more tannin, a more robust body, and bigger mouthfeel. In addition, they may give the impression of higher acidity and the flavors become less overtly fruity and more in the realm of pepper, earth, and a little gaminess. There are many very serious bottlings of Côte du Py, but most famous are Jean Foillard's Côte du Py and his famous Cuvée 3.14 (from hundred-year-old vines, bottled only in great years). Contrast the two of these with his regular Morgon to see the full range.

What are the sensory differences between Brouilly and Côte de Brouilly wines?

With a similar dynamic as that between Morgon and Côte du Py, here the Brouilly is the more approachable wine, while the Côte de Brouilly is the showstopping wine of profundity and power. People tend to talk about minerality being a more obvious quality of white wine, as there's less in the wine to obscure it. Thus it's exciting when minerality appears starkly in red wines, as it does in Côte de Brouilly, providing a deep, firm core and a stony texture that beautifully contrasts the wine's outer, plush layers of dark, juicy fruit. Look for bottlings from the great Claude Geoffray of Château Thivin as well as the beautiful version from Nicole Chanrion.

⬦ **LAPIERRE** Marcel Lapierre became a pivotal figure in Beaujolais's history, helping to found the movement of natural winemaking that would counter the region's descent into industrial production. He died unexpectedly in 2010, but his legacy is large and the estate is carried on by his exceptionally able children Matthieu and Camille. Lapierre's wines are still as warm, generous, and vibrant as Marcel himself was. Morgon and Côte du Py are the great reliables. But don't pass over the more powerful, old-vine Cuvée Marcel Lapierre and Cuvée Camille.

⬦ **JEAN FOILLARD** Indisputably one of the greatest Beaujolais producers, Foillard, an original Gang of Four member, makes wines that beautifully blend power and structure with a lush, flowing grace. In that way, they exemplify Beaujolais's ability to be both serious and playful in the same sip. He's known for Morgon, but also makes a serious Fleurie. His Morgon Cuvée Corcelette is smooth and round, while his Côte du Py is firmer and more muscular. Recently he introduced a Beaujolais-Villages from somewhat younger vines, which, priced in the mid-$20s, is a great deal.

⬦ **GUY BRETON** Everyone in Beaujolais knows Gang of Four member Guy Breton as Petit Max, for some reason, but that doesn't obscure his excellent wines. It's a small domaine, and the wines have a uniquely personal style that creates a little more structure and angularity than some other Morgon producers. High acidity makes the wines long agers, as evinced by a recent, brilliantly youthful bottle of 15-year-old Morgon. His plots are principally in a high-elevation Morgon locale called St-Joseph, which likely won't have its own official Cru because of the conflict with the Rhône appellation of the same name. The Morgon P'tit Max from 90- to 100-year old vines is his top cuvée, but he also has a terrific Vieilles Vignes (old vines—just 80 years old), and his Chiroubles is one of the best.

⬦ **DOMAINE DE LA GRAND'COUR (JEAN-LOUIS DUTRAIVE)** Somehow this great producer from Fleurie flew under the radar for years, but the secret is out now. No one in Beaujolais makes more fluid, artful, and ravishing wines. They have depth, seriousness, and concentration, but simply can't escape the same sense of warmth, humor, and generosity that animates their creator. The Fleuries (village and the single parcel "Champagne") are epic works of grace and beauty, while the Brouilly shows a slightly firmer cast.

CAMILLE AND MATTHIEU LAPIERRE
Domaine Lapierre, Morgon

THE JURA

With its pristine green hillsides, spectacular limestone bluffs, and cow-filled meadows worthy of a von Trapp family reunion, the Jura looks almost too lush and bucolic to make world-class wine. Of course, as with everywhere in France, despite the abundant beauty, there's plenty of past struggle in this little corner of eastern France, which is one reason the Jura has remained, until the last decade, unknown territory for most wine lovers.

When enthusiasts began to explore Jura wines and even visit the region for themselves, they found plenty to reward their curiosity: appealing varieties and peculiar wine styles from a place they knew nothing about. The grapes in question were just familiar enough (Chardonnay) to be understood and exotic enough (Savagnin, Poulsard, and Trousseau) to be intriguing. They discovered a sort of bizarro Burgundy. A correspondence between the two regions is implied, as the Jura sits just 50 miles across the Saône river valley, facing the Côte d'Or. Indeed, geologically, the two regions used to be one, but tectonic forces split them apart, creating the valley of the Saône river between them. But if they think they're gazing into a mirror, it's a carnival mirror, as some major distortions blur the symmetry.

A century ago Jura wine almost disappeared, which would have been not only a terrible loss to the culture of wine but also a collapse of epic proportions. In the early nineteeth century, the Jura was an enormous engine of French wine, sporting nearly 20,000 hectares (49,000 acres) under vine, even rivaling Burgundy's production. But a series of devastating events—including the advent of railways that allowed the burgeoning Languedoc to replace Jura as a source of wine for northern France, terrible afflictions of mildew and rot, the decimation of vines caused by phylloxera, and then World Wars I and II—brought the wine industry to its knees. According to Wink Lorch's *Jura Wine*, after the famous frost of 1956, vineyards eligible to produce Jura appellation wines declined to only 800 hectares (1,960 acres). In the ensuing sixty years, it's rebounded, but not that much. Today, just 2,000 hectares (4,900 acres) are under vine (in contrast, Burgundy's at around 28,000 hectares [68,600 acres]), and the region's high slopes have never been replanted.

Wine production today may be small—it's no longer the dominant industry, which is cheese, specifically Comté, the magnificent cow's milk product that's arguably the greatest cheese of France (amazing with Chardonnay from Jura or Burgundy)—but it punches above its weight class thanks to both high-quality indigenous varieties and vignerons.

Jura is primarily a white wine region, with two great grapes in its arsenal. One is Chardonnay, which Jura can produce at the level of very good white Burgundy (from the best producers it can be hard to distinguish). But, even more exciting is Savagnin, a variety unique to the Jura, with quasi-mystical status as a "founder variety." That means it's a progenitor, its genes dominant enough to breed several other, world-beating grapes: Sauvignon Blanc, Chenin Blanc, and Grüner Veltliner. It's funny that we should know the offspring better than the parent. Savagnin is like some superior physical specimen from the prehistoric times. It can achieve high ripeness, to the tune of 14 to 15 percent alcohol, yet simultaneously be bone-dry, with ripping high acidity, like Champagne or Riesling. In short, Savagnin is incredibly intense and impressive as a dry white table wine. But the grapes's freakishness also provides its wine the mettle to age for six years in barrel under a sherrylike veil of yeast to produce a semi-oxidized wine called *Vin Jaune.* The flavors are reminiscent of sherry, but Vin Jaune isn't fortified (who needs fortification when you're built like Savagnin?), and it's not aged in solera. A great Vin Jaune (notably from the appellation Château Chalon) is a memorable experience—powerful, broad-shouldered, buttery, salty, and dry. It's also great with a hunk of crystal-crunchy, well-aged Comté.

Surprisingly, Jura's red grapes make lighter wines than the whites. Pinot Noir grows here, but since oceans of that exist just across the Saône, we're far more interested in two native reds: Poulsard (known as Ploussard in the important wine village of Pupillon) and Trousseau (the same grape as Spain and Portugal's Bastardo). Both make red wines on the lighter end of the spectrum, oh-so-fashionable today. We apparently take these reds much more seriously than Jura natives do, as the wines (especially Poulsard) are often derided as nothing but mindless rosé over there, thanks to their light hue, perfume, and delicate, fruity flavors.

Jura's current fame has also been stoked by the fact that it is home to a couple of winemakers who have achieved cultlike status in the occasionally cultlike natural wine movement. First on the list is the now-retired Pierre Overnoy, an influential pioneer of sulfur-free winemaking. Overnoy's mercurial Jura wines are treasures, embodying all of the pleasures and maddening inconsistencies of the natural wine movement. Occasionally you can find a bottle overwhelmed by volatile acidity or some other off-putting flaw. But usually the wines are dazzlingly vibrant, pure, and alive. Mostly, they are soulful and modest, speaking to the place (Pupillon) and the gentle people who farm assiduously to make a product that's as close to nature as wine gets.

Another superstar, living at the other end of Jura, is Jean-François Ganevat, likewise producing wines with no (or very little) sulfur, and farming biodynamically. He makes a wide range of cuvées, but is especially revered for his range of Chardonnays and Savagnin (though his Pinot Noirs and Trousseau are very good indeed). Beyond these two icons, a few other fantastic producers deserve mention. Stéphane Tissot is not only one of the great winemakers of France, but he is the Jura's most visible ambassador, tirelessly educating the world about this little gem of a region. And our man in Volnay, Guillaume d'Angerville, turned heads in 2014 by buying the vineyards of celebrated winemaker Jacques Puffeney upon his retirement, creating Domaine du Pélican, a house committed to producing classic Jura wines.

Jura's rebound from near dissolution just sixty years ago has a long way to go. If it continues, it will be slowly, as raising dairy cows is currently a more popular occupation than raising grapes. But the potential here is undeniable; it just requires a hardy temperament to bring it about.

PARTICULARS OF PLACE

We're trying to follow Stéphane Tissot up the rocky slopes above his vineyard Les Bruyères. Tissot doesn't move quite as fast as he talks, but it's still quick—we clamber over jagged rocks while trying to absorb the story he's narrating about the Jura's creation. "It's perfect from the top of Les Bruyères," he says, "because you can see all the features of the Jura from the first plateau down to the Saône Valley, 50 miles wide. And we see how all the vineyards live in the small hills between the Saône and the first plateau."

Understanding a little of the geological story of the Jura helps to understand its particular soils, which in turn help to understand its wines. So imagine the soils of this part of France like a layer cake. The top layer is Bajocian limestone, just like in Burgundy. Below that is a layer of bluish-gray, clayey marl called Lias (for Lower Jurassic era). Beneath that is a different version of clayey marl, dark in color, called Trias (for Triassic). When the Côte d'Or of Burgundy and Jura got stretched apart during the Jurassic to the Oligocene, it bared the top layer of limestone, which is still exposed in Burgundy, as the Côte d'Or.

The difference is that in the Jura, the lower layers got pushed up during the creation of the Alps. And then they got pushed outward toward the west, creating the steppe-like first and second plateaus before the high mountains. The upshot is these layers of older clayey marls—Lias and Trias—became exposed and formed the slope (along with some of the limestone) where Jura vineyards grow. (Burgundy too has the Lias and Trias marls, but they're well buried under hundreds of feet of limestone.)

Still today, the clayey marls are generally at lower altitudes, while a preponderance of limestone remains higher up. As Wink Lorch writes in her book, *Burgundy and the Jura*, "Both have limestone and marls in abundance, but in the Côte d'Or around 80 percent of the base rock is limestone and 20 percent marl; in the Jura it is the other way around."

The Jura weather is slightly different than Burgundy's, as well. It's also a continental climate—cold winters, warm summers—but the winters are much colder. More significant for the winegrower, the Jura receives about 50 percent more rain than Burgundy. Clouds come mostly from the west, and they may breeze past Burgundy, but get hung up against the Jura mountains and Alps and then drop all their moisture. This rainfall helps explain the area's afflictions with mildew and rot. Finally, the major exposures of the Jura are to the west, promoting warmer afternoon sun, while Burgundy largely faces the cool morning sun of the east.

STÉPHANE TISSOT
Domaine Tissot, Arbois

TLR

In our first book, *Secrets of the Sommeliers,* we noted a quality in some Chardonnays we love. Known technically as reduction, we called it the Coche-Dury effect, as it was most reliably encountered in the wines of this most reticent of Meursault producers. The aroma is described in various ways, but the most accurate is probably the vaguely acrid, smoky crackle of a recently struck match. Some call it flinty, which drives the geologists crazy, because flint is inert and has no smell, but they are being pedantic—the term "flinty" is clearly shorthand for the use of flint to create a spark in fire-starting, and its aroma.

Over the years we came to understand more about reduction, and began to refer to it (in private, to each other) as CLR, which stood for both Coche-Like Reduction and Curry Leaf Reduction, as Raj had correctly noted that the struck-match scent was very similar to fresh curry leaf. We should also note that reduction can be good or bad, and should always be in moderation. Too little and it's just simply fruity; too much and it can smell like rotten eggs (its aromas come from various sulfur-containing compounds). Proper CLR requires only mild reduction, and it's not a game everyone can play.

We're now retiring CLR for a couple of reasons. One, since the transition to a new generation of vigneron at Coche-Dury, the wines don't display reduction as often as they used to. Two, the wines are now so expensive and hard to come by that very few people (not us!) ever get to taste them anymore.

Instead, we're happy to introduce a new acronym: TLR (Tissot-Like Reduction). Yes, we're happy to celebrate Stéphane Tissot's Chardonnays as, often enough, being joyfully reduced, they provide us that matchstick note we so love. Here, we must interject that not all people thrill to TLR as much as we do. In 2015, British critic Jancis Robinson wrote, "But wines in which the reductive character completely obliterates the natural fruit can be both wearying and boring to taste—and if overdone, it can lead to bitterness. It is not enough for a wine simply to smell of struck matches; there has to be something interesting underneath." We wholeheartedly concur. Matchstick alone is not the point; it must be accompanied by a wine of substance. Indeed, it's not the smoky element alone that makes the wine, but the way it contrasts with Chardonnay's often mild flavors of cream and lemon curd.

In Stéphane Tissot's wonderful wines, this is always the case when they display reduction. The matchstick overlays Chardonnays of incredible body and intensity. Furthermore, he has taught us that it is clay more than limestone that seems to influence reduction, as his Chardonnays with the most profound expressions of TLR come from the dark-colored Trias clays. And, with age, the smokiness fades, becoming one with the wine and making it more complex. So, all we can say is: Thank you, CLR; it was great knowing you. Long live TLR!

Amphorae at Domaine Tissot

COMTÉ CHEESE

Naming one single cheese as the greatest in the world is an impossible task. But naming the greatest cheese to pair with wine is easy. That cheese comes from the Jura and only the Jura: Comté.

This golden-colored, nutty, creamy, complex, buttery godsend of a cow's milk cheese is a friend to all wines. Naturally, white wine is the best choice. The native Jura wines from Savagnin all work incredibly well, especially the famous partially oxidized wines called Vin Jaune and Château Chalon. However, Chardonnay is also a champion of Comté—from the Jura, of course, but also white Burgundy (especially a creamy Meursault Premier Cru or Puligny). These wines have the richness to match Comté's exquisite creaminess, but also enough acidity to balance out the fat. Red wines also work well, especially ones that are soft and feature red fruit. Red Burgundy is a natural, as is Beaujolais, or any Jura red.

Few cheeses are made with the integrity of Comté. It must come predominantly (95 percent) from a breed of cow called Montbéliarde, and each cow's yield cannot exceed 4,600 liters of milk per year, a far cry from the range of 10,000 liters supplied by most U.S. dairy cows. This is a mountain cheese—the cows spend their summers and falls high in the green pastures of the Jurassic Mountains, eating a diverse diet of grasses, flowers, weeds, and thistles. Production centers around small, local dairies called *fruitières* to which local farmers bring their milk every morning. The milk used at each fruitière must come from within a 16-mile circle, rendering a certain regard for terroir in its cheeses. Aging can run between four months and several years, though the sweet spot for complexity, power, and texture tends to be between 16 and 30 months. Due to the richness of the cows' diets, summer cheeses are more golden in color compared to winter cheeses, when the animals are fed on hay. But summer, winter, young, old—it doesn't matter. Comté should be a fixture of every cheese plate when you're trying to show wine at its best.

How do these details manifest in the wines? Strongly. That clay soil is the engine behind Jura's powerful white wine Savagnin. As Tissot explains, "Savagnin needs the muscle of the clay to give it the acidity and alcohol to age long enough to become Vin Jaune." Poulsard also grows best on clay. Trousseau and Pinot Noir are at their best on limestone. And Chardonnay is just happy to be there: it grows well on each soil, making it the perfect vehicle to demonstrate Jura's soil-based differences. Obsessively, Tissot makes many different Chardonnays, each from unique soils. We taste many of them, all from the 2013 vintage.

Les Bruyères Chardonnay is from the dark, Trias clay, and shows classic characteristics of that soil. It's mouth-filling and powerful, electrified by a current of humming acidity, and flavored with a dose of smoky reduction (TLR—see page 155) and spice, with a mildly bitter finish. By contrast, his Chardonnay from Les Graviers comes from vineyards of limestone and displays classic calcareous traits. Compared to the dense onslaught of the Trias clay, it's open and fresh, salty with slightly less acidity, and has a more grainy, mineral texture. Next we taste a wine called Sursis—the word *sursis* means "reprieve" or "suspended sentence" in French. Sursis is a small block of Chardonnay on Lias soils in a Savagnin vineyard located in the generally Trias soils of Château Chalon, Jura's premier spot for Vin Jaune. Savagnin is the only grape allowed to make Château Chalon, so the Chardonnay is technically a waste of this land, and Tissot's wife wanted to graft it over to Savagnin. But he was intrigued to see what Chardonnay tasted like on pure Lias soils, so he gave the vines a reprieve and made the wine. It's quite different than the Trias wine—much more fresh and bright, with a citrus character and high acidity. It falls somewhere between Les Bruyères and Les Graviers, just as the Lias soil layer sits between Trias and limestone. Finally, we taste La Mailloche, yet another variation. This is from Lias soils, Tissot says, but a special variation from which all the limestone has leached out. It's pure clay, he says, and it's a monster, channeling that power from the clay. Huge in body and mouth-filling, its nose is spicy and smoky with matchstick. We go back and taste a 2005 La Mailloche, and, from that warm vintage, it's a more exaggerated version of the 2014: TLR for days.

If you like great Chardonnay, we recommend filling your cellar with Tissot. His are remarkable wines that stand shoulder to shoulder with many of the greatest Chardonnays of the Côte de Beaune and, best of all, can be had for a fraction of the price. If you love TLR, buy the wines from clay soils. Ganevat also makes incredible Chardonnay, though his natural winemaking inclinations can lead to less consistency. And by all means, don't just focus on Chardonnay in the Jura. Try all the wines. Savagnin—whether vinified as an unoxidized table wine or allowed to oxidize for Vin Jaune—is a mind-blowing grape. And Poulsard and Trousseau are delicious, refreshing reds.

QUESTIONS OF TASTE

How do you distinguish Savagnin from other white grapes?

When it's made in the non-oxidative style, the one thing Savagnin lacks that its famous offspring have is a signature flavor. Grüner Veltliner has lentil, Sauvignon Blanc has green grass, and Chenin has lanolin. Savagnin's flavors are less distinctive. They're savory and salty, dwelling in the constellation of underripe pear, green herbs, meadow flowers, and lemon zest. What sets Savagnin apart is its electric acidity matched up against its big, broad-shouldered form. Often heavier wines produce less acidity, but not in this case. Savagnin is raw power. Ganevat's Les Vignes de Mon Père, which ages ten years in barrel, is one of the best wines in the Jura—in the world, actually—and it's pure, austere Savagnin with just a hint of oxidation.

How do you tell Jura Chardonnay from white Burgundy?

Discerning between the two can be difficult, especially on Jura from limestone soils, which are a match with the fresh, citrusy, mineral style of Burgundy. But from Lias and Trias marls, Chardonnay becomes heavier and more powerful, without the lilt of limestone. The fruit qualities can edge into more tropical, hinting at pineapple and mango.

How to tell Poulsard from Trousseau?

Both are light red wines, but if anything Poulsard is even lighter, especially in color, thanks to its thin skin. Locals often blow it off as "rosé." A great Poulsard, however, can be deceptively potent for a light-bodied wine. Since it grows on clay marls, it too can be prone to reduction (the bad, stinky kind) that can take hours in a decanter to recede. So, don't be afraid to open it an hour before serving to see if it needs some air. When showing well, look for a light color, sweet aromas of cherries and strawberries, and a smooth, easy mouthfeel that lacks tannins.

Trousseau, on the other hand, has a thicker skin and therefore more tannins and color. Locals consider it the superior grape. Compared to Poulsard, its acidity is lower, and the wine will be a little darker and more structured, with similar flavors that edge toward black cherry and blueberry.

RAJAT'S TOP PRODUCERS

◇ **PIERRE OVERNOY/EMMANUEL HOUILLON** From the area of Arbois-Pulillon, these wines from the domaine of now-retired Overnoy and his former disciple Houillon (who now runs the show) capture the magic of truth, purity, simplicity, and beauty. In these bottles you find life itself, in all of its unpredictable beauty and grandeur. These are some of the hardest wines to find nowadays, but they turn up sometimes in the oddest places—a small, unheralded bistro in an outskirt of Paris or the cellar of one of your friends whom you didn't think cared about Jura wines—and must be ordered immediately.

◇ **JEAN-FRANÇOIS GANEVAT** One of the great winemakers of the Jura, Ganevat's wines are biodynamic, natural marvels. Daunting in variety (over thirty different cuvées in any given year) and idiosyncratic in style, the genius of these wines is in their purity and concentration and their mastery of all the Jura's styles, from oxidized to crisp and fresh. From old vines, the Chardonnays—Marguerite, Florine, and Chamois du Paradis—are beautifully fluid and full, yet have shape and prickly acid. And don't sleep on the reds; Ganevat's Pinot Noirs are very good, and his Poulsard and Trousseau are crunchy, spirited, and light.

- ◆ **DOMAINE DU PÉLICAN** Guillaume D'Angerville's fascination with Jura began with a glass of Chardonnay poured for him by a sommelier in Paris. And when he bought into the region, he started with a fantastic boost: the vineyards of retiring Jacques Puffeney, so-called "pope of Arbois." Just a few vintages in, the wines are already showing the Volnay domaine's penchant for precision and clarity with Chardonnay and Pinot Noir as well as Jura varieties Savagnin, Trousseau, and Poulsard.

- ◆ **STÉPHANE TISSOT** A master vigneron, Tissot's wines are icons of the non-oxidative style, captured with power and poise in his epic sparkling wines, Chardonnays, and reds. (His oxidative Vin Jaune is a powerhouse, too.) His "natural" credentials are in good order—biodynamic farming meets low-sulfur winemaking—and his wines have the purity and concentration to age gracefully in the cellar for decades. In particular, seek out his Chardonnay and Poulsard from Les Bruyères and his Savagnin.

CHAMPAGNE

What can the shape of the glass tell you about the wine inside it? When it comes to Champagne these days, the glass says a great deal. People everywhere are ditching Champagne's signature vessel, the flute, in favor of the standard wine glass. And this simple change tells you all you need to know about what's been happening in the Champagne region, which has amounted to a taste revolution.

The Champagne flute's long, lean shape evinces a dedication to one thing and one thing only: showing off that which separates Champagne from other wines—the bubbles. "Look at the fine robe streaming up the glass," you'd be instructed in Champagne tastings. In fact, the base of a high-end flute is often etched with microscopic scratches to agitate the wine and release that mesmerizing torrent of bubbles. The drawback of a flute is that its narrow aperture hinders our ability to enjoy a wine's aromas. Inversely, the narrow mouth also prevents us from being as aware of a wine's flaws. By contrast, a standard white wine glass or even a rounded Burgundy bulb for Champagne is now a common sight in fine restaurants. The difference between a wider glass and a thin one is like listening to music through large, warm speakers versus the tinny rattle of a transistor radio.

The flute is wonderful if you care foremost about the way your wine looks. It says: Champagne. The broader glass emphasizes flavor and aroma, de-emphasizing bubbles and allowing them to escape. It says: Wine. This distinction is indicative of a seismic shift in the region.

Economically, Champagne is still dominated by the Grandes Marques, the big négociant houses—Moët et Chandon, Veuve-Clicquot, Deutz, and the like. Many of them still make excellent products. This was their model all along, to make Champagne into a product—a brand, a very powerful thing. And for most of the last century, the Grandes Marques alone embodied Champagne to the rest of the world. This is no longer true.

One thing the Champenois like to point out is that their region has always been a battleground, its soils bloodied by war, as centuries worth of invaders from the north and east used it as their road to Paris. But over the twentieth century, an internal battle raged as well, between the big houses and the more than nineteen thousand small growers and landowners who supply almost 90 percent of the region's grapes. The two factions haggled endlessly over prices and contracts, over who deserved a bigger piece of the ever-increasing pie. The big houses hated being dependent on all these small families and wished they could more directly control the means of production. Meanwhile, growers often derived little satisfaction from their lives. Many had no connection to their property or the wines their grapes produced, thanks to the cold, harmful efficiencies of chemical farming, or because they had contracted out their vineyards. They just cashed checks because their families were lucky enough to own land in Champagne. It was in this environment that Champagne became no longer a wine, but a product.

But in the last twenty years, a rising tide of grape growers decided to take matters into their own hands. Many of them had long vinified some of their own grapes into personal labels, but these "grower Champagnes" were hardly seen outside France or even the Champagne region. Starting quietly in the 1970s and 1980s, the American importer Kermit Lynch brought in a couple of grower Champagnes (J. Lassalle and Paul Bara), a trend that received a boost when Terry Thiese, a magnetic proselytizer for wines of terroir, began a grower Champagne portfolio in the late nineties. These importers helped teach generations of new wine drinkers that place is the most salient feature of wine (along with a good dose of character and narrative). None of those things had entered into discussions of Champagne for decades. If you appreciate the notion of terroir in Burgundy or the Rhône or Barolo, why not in the historic region of Champagne?

The early wave of grower Champagne incited a revolution that's ongoing today. Not only did it excite consumers all over the world by offering new perspective on Champagne as a serious wine and a place full of actual people, but it also activated and empowered thousands of small growers in the region to explore their own territory in a way many had never considered—as vignerons. It was a liberation, with Moseslike figures such as the great Anselme Selosse inspiring and empowering a generation of young people to literally take back their land (from long-term contracts or négociants), to connect with it through farming, and to find meaning in life through the craft of turning their grapes into wine.

CHAMPAGNE'S GREAT NÉGOCIANTS

Even though we focus on grower-producers here, it's wrong to give the impression that négociant producers are at all inferior or even fail to make wines of terroir. Indeed, it's the négociants who have driven the region—and still do—making possible the success of today's small growers. One need look no further than Salon to see a négociant making terroir-driven wines from the Grand Cru village of Mesnil at the highest level. Krug makes wines to its own style, but the skill and sophistication needed to make such powerful wines so consistently is undeniable. And greatest of all perhaps is Roederer, the very model of the modern négociant, insisting on organic fruit to make wonderfully complex, nuanced wines, and keeping Cristal at the top with biodynamic viticulture.

As you might imagine, it's been a very powerful process that has impacted more than just the people of the region. The salvaging of Champagne from the domineering grip of corporations has injected a level of soulfulness, touch, and character that has profoundly changed the wines. Once taboo topics that would make standard conversation in other wine regions—organic farming, single-site expression, full maturity, no chaptalization (the addition of conventional sugar to ferments in order to prolong the ferments and raise the alcohol), indigenous fermentations, dryness, wood aging—are more and more common in Champagne.

This shift has also given Champagne a refreshing new mood. Before, visiting Champagne was a buttoned-up affair, dominated by formal staterooms and serious men in suits. For a place supposedly devoted to the world's most pleasurable beverage, Champagne could be a dour, drab experience. Today, it is bursting with personality. More often than not, our visits took place in small cellars and were very personal. For example, two hours in the backyard barn of a winery with birds loudly chirping outside, while inside we stood around an upturned barrel in philosophical conversation with the ruminative Jérôme Prévost of La Closerie. Or romping through the vines of a terroir called Mont Benoit with the rambunctious former soccer player Fred Savart before returning to his little home cellar and draining a couple bottles of his exquisite productions. In the old corporate-dominated Champagne, you were rarely taken to see vineyards, but in today's world of grower-producers, it's the first place they want you to see. And see it you must, as the new generation of growers is proving that the taste of Champagne too varies widely between villages, soils, and sites.

JÉRÔME PRÉVOST
Champagne La Closerie, Gueux

Champagne is a place, as its growers and producers would like us to remember. And as they push more and more to have Champagne received not just as a brand but as a wine, deserving of all the reverence and contemplation we reserve for other wines—it's important to know a little about the geography of Champagne. Technically, it's divided into five subregions, each with a different specialty or character: the Côte des Blancs (Chardonnay), the Montagne de Reims (Pinot Noir), the Vallée de la Marne (Pinot Meunier), the Aube (Chardonnay and Pinot Noir), and the Côte de Sézanne (the smallest and least developed of the regions is mostly Chardonnay). Some wines are specific to a region, a village, or even a vineyard within a region, while others may be blends across several of them. While the overall climate of Champagne is fairly consistent, there are soil and exposure differences that make one region better for, say, Pinot Noir or Pinot Meunier than Chardonnay, and vice versa.

Like most wine regions in France, each Champagne region is subdivided by its villages, which give their names to the surrounding vineyard areas. Each of the 318 villages in Champagne is classified with a rating on a 100-point scale (though the scale doesn't go below 80). The 17 Grand Cru villages all have perfect 100-point ratings, while the 44 villages rated between 90 and 99 are Premier Crus, and the 257 rated between 80 and 89 receive no special designation. The rating is somewhat controversial, as it's rare and imprecise to see entire villages rated. Even Grand Cru villages will contain some spots that are considered far inferior to others, yet still are entitled to the 100-point rating. Nevertheless, this becomes less and less important, as talented vignerons (like Alexandre Chartogne of Chartogne-Taillet) have shown that world-class wines can be made from even low-rated villages (his, Merfy, scores but an 84).

In the following sections, we look at the four major subregions of Champagne, as well as the less-developed Côte de Sézanne, and briefly discuss some of the most important villages within them, giving a sense of the distinctiveness of each place both in terms of terrain and typicity of wine.

Côte des Blancs

A spine of exposed, active limestone, the Côte des Blancs stretches along the ridge of a highly eroded plateau south of Épernay. Not known is whether the name refers to the often exposed bright-white chalk slopes or the fact that the Côte des Blancs almost exclusively produces white wines. No matter; its four Grand Cru villages offer iconic expressions of Chardonnay that every Champagne lover should know.

There's no better person with whom to discuss the Côte des Blancs than Rodolphe Péters of Champagne Pierre Péters, as his family, who has been involved in wine here for just under two hundred years, owns vineyards in all the important villages.

RODOLPHE PÉTERS
Champagne Pierre Péters, Le Mesnil-sur-Oger

While the extremely white, chalky soil is key to the region's razor-sharp, mineral expressions, Péters cites another, overlooked reason: eastern exposure. "If you check the Champagne map," he notes one winter morning, "you will see that the three main locations for Chardonnay—the Côte des Blancs, the Côtes de Sézanne, and the beginning of the Aube—all have eastern exposure." (He even points out that the "island of Chardonnay amidst the Pinot Noir" in the Pinot-heavy Montagne de Reims also faces east.) Of Champagne's three major grapes, Chardonnay blooms the earliest, he says, and is thus most vulnerable to early-season frost. The early-morning eastern sun, therefore, helps protect it on cold days.

The four major Grand Cru villages neighbor each other and roughly pair off. Wines from Cramant and Avize, the northern two, tend to show more richness (thanks to a bit more clay in the soil), while the southern pair of Oger and Le Mesnil-sur-Oger are more austere and precise.

Cramant

Is it because of the sound of its name that Cramant is often described as the creamiest of the Côte des Blancs Grand Crus? Perhaps not. The village makes a powerful style in which the chalk is not as pointed as in neighboring villages, but rather seamlessly couched in a rich bouquet of fruit and spice. The fruit is lemon, but candied lemon with a tinge of orange, ginger, and other tealike spice. The most poignant expressions of Cramant are found in Larmandier-Bernier's Vieille Vigne du Levant, and Jacques Selosse's Cramant Chemin de Châlons. And don't forget about Diebolt-Vallois, a terrific Blanc de Blancs specialist.

Avize

Just south of Cramant is the village of Avize, home to the transformative figure of Anselme Selosse and his transformative boutique hotel and restaurant Les Avisés. There are two parts to the vineyard. One is a steep planted slope that Péters assures us is too cold to ripen fruit consistently; consequently, no one in the village really loves the wine from there. Rather, the warmer, flatter land is where Avize's greatness comes, as these soils ripen fruit perfectly and are the source of Avize's signature generosity. Here the wines are relatively full-bodied and exuberant, with ripe, juicy lemon and grapefruit, and a prominent, precise minerality. Get a sense of this village via Agrapart's Venus bottling or Selosse's famous cuvée Initial.

Oger

The slopes framing Oger open to the east like a giant, gaping shark's mouth. These slopes ingest the eastern sun, forming an amphitheater-like enclave that concentrates warmth and heightens ripeness. The result is a bounty of flowery fruit, which matures beyond juicy and ripe citrus into flavors of pear and apple. Oger is prized because this richness of flavor is juxtaposed with an equally potent sense of upfront minerality. While Oger is the anchor site for many houses' Blanc de Blancs blend, its nature is on great display in Jean Milan's Terres de Noël.

Le Mesnil-sur-Oger

Firm, mineral-driven, austere, and elegant, wines from Le Mesnil-sur-Oger are described by hometown boy Rodolphe Péters as "wintry." The character here is cold, he says. "Cold citrus and cold stone." It's a good description, as these wines just have the cool precision of a surgeon, and a scalpellike sharpness. While going under the knife may not sound appealing, Mesnil wines are indeed thrilling in their single-minded, brilliant pursuit of minerality. The warmth and complexity of expression comes with time in the bottle. Ironically, Mesnil wasn't promoted to a Grand Cru until 1985, despite being the source of two of the most prestigious of all Champagnes, Salon and Krug's Clos du Mesnil. Salon is made from parcels around the village, while Krug's is a single site and a true clos (walled-in vineyard). Not as widely known (because it's less blingy and much more reasonably priced), but equal in quality, is Pierre Péters' Les Chetillons.

Montagne de Reims

Surrounding the region's capital and largest city of Reims (like the Loire village of Bourgueil, one of France's most difficult wine names to pronounce—say *rance,* as in "rancid" with a French "r" and minus the "id"), the Montagne de Reims includes a series of slopes on roughly a 180-degree arc, curving northwest to southeast. The *montagne* in question is hardly mountainous, but rather a broad, flat plateau with hilly slopes and a bountiful forest on top. Vineyard sites are tucked against its slopes, then spread onto the extensive plain around Reims. This massive area is known for Pinot Noir, the featured variety in each of its nine Grand Cru villages. However, a great and growing renaissance of Pinot Meunier is also occurring (see page 179), and there's even some insurgent Chardonnay on the far eastern slopes. All in all, the region shows diversity, but its heart is in Pinot Noir, and the dynamic here is based on the tensions between body and acidity, richness and minerality, red fruit and citrus. Exploration of this happens in many styles, from deep and dense to lighter and more fluid styles, but power and intensity are always part of the equation.

Merfy

Located in the northwestern subdistrict of Massif de St-Thierry, Merfy does not rate high on Champagne's controversial village rating scale, as we noted, but it bears inclusion here as a historic terroir for many centuries and, more recently, as the home of one of Champagne's bright lights, Alexandre Chartogne of Chartogne-Taillet. The soils here cover a wide range of profiles, but are somewhat unique for Champagne with fairly deep sand and clay above the classic limestone basement. Since taking over in 2006, Alexandre has mounted an ambitious program of single-site bottlings, while experimenting with different vinification styles, including oak aging, concrete egg fermenting, and stainless steel. He's asking questions that begin to redefine what Champagne can be. Merfy's Pinot Noir and Pinot Meunier wines tend to be rich and round, with a broader palate and a prominent suggestion of red fruit.

Ambonnay and Bouzy

On the south side of the Montagne de Reims, these two Grand Cru villages are south-facing powerhouses of Pinot Noir. If there's a detectable difference between the two, it's that Bouzy's exposition is more fully south, producing warmer sites and richer wines. Bouzy Rouge, as its still red wine is called, is perhaps Champagne's most famous still red Pinot Noir. Ambonnay has slightly thinner, chalkier soils and produces a wine of marginally less density and power. A few growers in these villages are exceptional: Marie-Noelle Ledru makes luscious, robust wines by hand (each bottle is hand-riddled, a laborious process of tilting each bottle gently in the cellar as preparation for expelling the fine lees, so the wine will be crystal clear), while Egly-Ouriet makes powerful, vinous styles rich in red fruit. Grower Jean Vesselle is another exponent of Bouzy, with gorgeous, vinous Champagnes that make the most of the region's ripe red fruit.

The Southwest Villages

The towns south and west of Reims, Premier Crus, don't get the press of the Grand Crus to the east. Village ratings be damned, some of the most compelling Champagne is coming from this area, emphasizing that there's still much to be learned in Champagne. For instance, the site called Mont Benoit is really but a mound in the center of a large expanse of vines just outside of Reims's sprawl, yet Emmanuel Brochet and Fred Savart are both crafting incredible detailed, precise wines off of its gentle slopes. Savart's work continues nearby in Écueil, where, despite his rambunctious personality, he makes wines of exquisite grace and poise. Up north in Gueux is where the incomparable Jérôme Prévost fashions his two wines from a single vineyard, Les Beguines, which he inherited as a young man. All three of these producers work a number of micro-terroirs to produce dry wines that are indistinguishable in quality from any Grand Cru site in quality and in cost. These wines showcase how maniacally great vineyard work can achieve the maturity needed to make rounded, rich, racy wines.

Vallée de la Marne

As the name implies, this region follows the slopes of the Marne river as it flows off to meet the Seine in Paris. By far Champagne's largest region, the Vallée de la Marne is also the least associated with high quality, bearing just one Grand Cru, Aÿ, and a handful of Premier Crus. In cold weather, the fairly deep river valley can be prone to frost, which sinks into its trench. In warm weather, botrytis is an issue, as warm, humid air gets trapped. Also, the famous chalk of Champagne is buried deeper underground here, meaning the soils support more clay, sand, and river-borne alluvium. Pinot Meunier, long cast as Champagne's ignoble workhorse, is the dominant grape here, as it is more impervious to frost. Despite all these supposed strikes against it, the region is rife with incredible producers making dazzling wines. And given the redemption of Pinot Meunier (see page 179), the Vallée de la Marne may have yet a new tale to tell.

Aÿ

This is a powerhouse Grand Cru village in many ways, including its size (over four thousand people, big for a Champagne wine village) and its wine, 90 percent of which is Pinot Noir. The vineyards here are generally south facing and lower on the hillside than nearby Pinot Noir Grand Crus Bouzy and Ambonnay, meaning warmer temperatures and riper wines. But Aÿ is also a powerhouse for the scale of the Grandes Marques that call it home: Bollinger, Moet et Chandon, Ayala, Deutz, and Gosset, to name a few. The Aÿ expression of Pinot Noir is one of ripeness and strength. For great expressions of Aÿ, think of Bollinger's Vieilles Vignes Françaises or Gatinois's Brut Réserve.

Mareuil-sur-Aÿ

Just east of Aÿ, Mareuil-sur-Aÿ is also known for its powerful Pinot Noir. But it must be mentioned as the home to Champagne Philopponnat and its truly awesome vineyard Clos des Goisses, Champagne's first single-vineyard wine, dating to 1935. This stunning hill, rising from the bank of the Marne at a dauntingly steep pace, was the lone carrier of terroir's banner for generations. It's a wine of finely wrought power with the ability to age for decades. But, as the wines of the area show in general, Mareuil-sur-Aÿ's nature is not to challenge Aÿ for muscle, as it is often a little bit lighter on its feet, gliding rather than stomping. In addition to Philipponnat, the popular Billecart-Salmon is based here, as are the excellent grower houses Marc Hébrart and R. Pouillon & Fils.

Other Great Growers

Given its size, it should be no surprise that the Vallée de la Marne is home to a great number of other producers, who offer fascinating takes on its terroirs. Dizy-based Gaston Chiquet enjoys a wonderful presence in the United States with his wide range of wines, including a rare Blanc de Blancs from Pinot-specializing Aÿ, an especially forceful, ripe Chardonnay. In recent years, the wines of Champagne Georges Laval, based in the tiny hamlet of Cumières on the Marne's right bank, have gained a strong following among sommeliers. The orthodoxy of vigneron Vincent Laval deserves admiration, as his vineyards are worked by horse and winemaking is done by hand without any chaptalization, dosage, or filtration, but it's the vinous complexity and purity of his wines that win him fans.

The Aube

A fascinating subplot of the grower revolution in Champagne has been the recent uprising of the Aube. Even if the wines from here were not so compelling, the narrative is irresistible. The Aube, aka the Côte des Bar, is remote, sitting about 70 miles south of Epernay, near the city of Troyes, which was Champagne's capital until the French Revolution. Though Troyes is no longer the capital, the region is still important, as it holds 20 percent of Champagne's planted vineyards. However,

FRED SAVART
Champagne Savart, Écueil

it's not been treated by the mainstream Champagne industry with much respect. Rather, the powers behind Big Champagne have happily employed all this wine from the Aube, blending it into their cuvées without giving credit or respect (a savvy move if you want to keep prices low). Indeed, in the 1920s, Reims tried to exclude the Aube from the official appellation, and, when that failed, they granted zero Grand Cru or Premier Cru vineyards and classified the whole area as a secondary zone. Essentially, Big Champagne wanted to pretend the Aube didn't exist. That's a lot harder now, however, as the Aube has issued something of an unofficial declaration of independence, in the form of a cadre of top-quality producers who, by way of distinctive wines from radical sites, have captured the fancy of Champagne lovers around the world.

The Aube terroir is radical for Champagne, but not for Chablis. Indeed, the heart of the Aube is closer to Chablis than to Reims and largely shares the same soil formation—Kimmeridgian marl topped by a hard cap of Portlandian limestone. Given the proximity, the Burgundian impulse is strong here, though the Aube producers continue to make Champagne. Yet a process of self-discovery is clearly under way.

"I wanted to know the taste of my area," explains Bertrand Gautherot about the 2001 founding of his label, Vouette et Sorbée, on land he largely inherited from his family. "That's why I farm biodynamically. I never blend the different vintages. I never blend varieties. I never use sugar. And it's always natural yeast fermentation. It's very simple wine. But it's not like this to be fashionable; it's to discover."

If that sounds like an austere form of discovery, it is. A touch of austerity seems appropriate, though, when you're in the Aube and considered second-class by the rest of Champagne. Austere is also an apt descriptor for many of the wines from here. Though they're sparkling, Aube Champagnes (from both Chardonnay and Pinot Noir) carry an unmistakable Kimmeridgian signature, a deep, rumbling energy beneath a taut surface of lemon and flower notes with just a little hint of smoky earth. It's lovely and profound, but unflinchingly dry. Several of the other famous domaines from here also show it: Marie Courtin, Pierre Gerbais, Dosnon & Lepage, Cédric Bouchard. Like Chablis, the wines are dry, racy, complex, and pure. You think of them as wines first before Champagnes. This is intentional. Bouchard, for instance, has said he doesn't love the bubbles in Champagne, and recommends decanting his wines for an hour or two.

The Aube has other quirks. There's the idiosyncratic Emmanuel Lassaigne of Domaine Jacques Lassaigne in Montgueux. In this unique region, just west of Troyes, an odd outcropping of chalk in the form of a massive hill in the middle of a flatland led to the planting of Chardonnay in the 1960s. Perhaps due to the more southern position and exposure of the hill, Lassaigne's wines have the elegant, mineral finesse of the Côte des Blancs, but with a riper, almost tropical character that makes them unique.

There's the town of Les Riceys, whose sparkling wines are less renowned than its still wines, particularly rosé. The standout here is Olivier Horiot, who farms biodynamically. His sparkling wine is delicious, but thankfully most of his production is in still wine, as his rosé wines from two vineyards—En Barmont and En Valingrain—are two of the more profound rosés on the planet. They age beautifully (unusual for this kind of wine), coming into their own only after several years in the bottle.

Even with its newfound fame—these wines are some of the hardest to come by in all of Champagne—it's hard to think the Aube will ever be overrun. It is far out of the way of everything. The towns are small and desolate. There is nowhere to eat (we looked), and very little to do but drive to a more happening area. Yet the wines are something found all too rarely in France these days: new and original. We discovered something we hadn't considered before. And for that, we will always keep coming back.

The Côte de Sézanne

South of the Côte des Blancs, just below the St-Gond marsh (whose swampy expanses figured strongly into the muddy World War I Battle of the Marne that's credited with saving Paris and turning the war), lies another series of slopes in the vicinity of the town of Sézanne. Known as the Côte de Sézanne or the Sézannais, the region wasn't really planted extensively until the 1960s, but is emerging today as a unique terroir that can provide another perspective on Champagne, much like the Aube, 60 miles to the south. While it is often looked at as a continuation of the Côte des Blancs, the Sézannais has its own identity. Chardonnay predominates, but because the soils contain chalk but also clay and silex, dense and ripe Pinots can also emerge.

The producer who has brought the most attention to the Côte de Sézanne in recent years is Olivier Collin of Domaine Ulysse Collin. A 2001 stage with Anselme Selosse inspired Collin to work to retrieve his family's vineyards from contractual obligation to some large négociant houses. His first wine came from the 2004 vintage from Les Perrières, a Chardonnay vineyard with chalky subsoils and scattered pieces of silex. When it came out in 2007, the wine made an instant stir, with its rich, powerfully vinous quality that was more reminiscent of a white Burgundy than a Champagne from the Côte des Blancs. By contrast, Collin's Pinot Noir from the Maillons vineyard has an ethereal elegance. He works in a natural, non-interventionist style and his wines show full maturity of the grapes, balanced by surging minerality and an austerely dry palate. Collin is but one standout producer working in a relatively unknown region, but given the quality and distinctiveness his wines show, we have no doubt there will be more.

What does it mean when a Champagne is described as *vinous*?

The quality of being vinous—or wine-like—is somewhat odd, but you find it more and more being used to describe Champagne, which is, after all, a wine. So what does it mean? The use of the word gets at the contemporary push, especially by the grower-producers, to have their Champagnes seen more as wines and not simply as brands (Veuve, Bolly, etc.) to be quaffed mindlessly at parties. Hence, they farm more meticulously, harvest by hand, vinify in small vats, and treat the wines basically as small-lot Burgundies or fine wines from any region. The result is a Champagne that drinks with the force, nuance, and presence of a wine, despite the bubbles. For most producers, it is a compliment to hear their wines described as "vinous."

How to distinguish Champagnes made from Chardonnay, Pinot Noir, and Pinot Meunier?

Given that Champagnes, even those made from red grapes, are fermented without the skins (except in the case of a few rosés, whose juice sees a modicum of skin contact for color), it can sometimes be difficult to determine which might be a Chardonnay from the Côte des Blancs, which a Pinot Meunier from the Vallée de la Marne, and which a Pinot Noir from the Montagne de Reims. The trick is to look for the subtle clues you'd expect from these grapes anyway. If you taste lemony citrus and the wine has a more delicate, lacy structure, a good bet is that it's Chardonnay. If it's powerful and full and structured, maybe even smelling of fresh raspberry or cherries, likely it's Pinot Noir. And if it suggests red fruit along the lines of strawberry or cherry, but is more supple, rounded, and soft than a Pinot Noir, it may be Pinot Meunier dominant.

RAJAT'S TOP PRODUCERS NORAH - 95

◇ **JACQUES SELOSSE** The great terroirist of Champagne, who convinced so many that it could be treated like wine, and both inspired and mentored an entire generation of ambitious grower producers. Of course, he continues to make great wine in the often rich, slightly oxidized, terroir-sensitive, and entirely idiosyncratic manner he's famous for. Expensive, but worth getting to know.

◇ **CHARTOGNE-TAILLET** This was already a terrific house before young Alexandre Chartogne took over from his parents, and now he's turned the family domaine into one of the iconic wines of the modern Champagne movement. A disciple of Selosse, Chartogne follows the same non-interventionist ways to produce exceedingly vinous Champagnes from his home village of Merfy.

◇ **CHAMPAGNE SAVART** Fred Savart has a beautiful touch with wine, making Champagnes of grace and purity from Chardonnay and Pinot Noir grown around the small villages of Écueil and Villers-aux-Noeuds. L'Ouverture is his entry-level wine, made from Pinot Noir. It shows his style well, wrapping ripe, round fruit in a delicate skin of acid and bubbles.

◇ **PIERRE PÉTERS** This Chardonnay specialist from Mesnil-sur-Oger, one of the great Chardonnay-growing villages on the planet, never disappoints with fresh, zingy Champagne that nevertheless has great nuance, stoniness, and complexity. The Cuvée Reserve is the basic Champagne and is always satisfying, while the single-vineyard Les Chétillons is a stunner.

◇ **CHAMPAGNE LA CLOSERIE (JÉRÔME PRÉVOST)** Working with just 2 hectares (5 acres) of vines inherited from his grandmother, Prevost makes one of the lowest production and most compelling of all Champagnes. Eschewing Champagne's tendencies to blend sites and years, his focus is truly wine-like—a single vineyard, a single grape (Pinot Meunier), and a single vintage. The result is a powerful but supple Champagne that gets better with time in the bottle.

◇ **BÉRÊCHE ET FILS** Brothers Raphael and Vincent Bérêche have made the family domaine, which dates back to 1847, into one of Champagne's bright lights with an emphasis on organic and biodynamic farming and structure-building winemaking that leads to wines of power and substance held together by a fine balance.

◇ **BENOIT LAHAYE** Based in the Grand Cru village Bouzy, Lahaye is a purist's purist: farming with biodynamic principles and plowing his vineyards with a horse. Wines are made in barrel with natural yeasts and minimal sulfur. His super-dry rosé from Pinot Noir is a standout, as is his fruity, vivacious, sulfur-free cuvée Violaine.

◇ **EGLY-OURIET** Francis Egly was an early progenitor of the grower-producer movement, and his wines still show the energy and verve that powered them in those early days. The Champagnes, from Pinot Noir and Pinot Meunier, are powerful, intense, and exceedingly vinous.

◇ **VOUETTE ET SORBÉE** One of the great producers of the Aube, Bertrand Gautherot farms his vineyards biodynamically, preserving the intensity of the fruit grown on his steep, cool hillside. Indeed, his cuvée Fidèle, made from Pinot Noir on Kimmeridgian soil, may remind as much of Chablis as of Champagne.

◇ **JACQUES LASSAIGNE** In the village of Montgueux in the Aube, Lassaigne is making impressively original wines in a place never historically known for them. Chalk and clay mix to form a base for powerful wines, especially Chardonnay, as in his Blanc de Blancs de Montgueux.

RAPHAEL BÉRÊCHE
of Champagne Bérêche at the lieu-dit Le Craon de Ludes, Vallée de la Marne

THE MEUNIER RESURGENCE

In Champagne's not-too-distant past, when the region was ruled by the mighty négociants, an innocent question about Pinot Meunier—which is listed, after all, as one of the triumvirate of important varieties—would beget a dismissive answer. "It's rustic, a mere blending grape," you'd hear. "But it accounts for 30 percent of the vineyards," you'd press, "that seems kind of like a lot." "Ah, it's just for fruitiness," meaning it's not to be taken seriously. In a classic brut blend, Pinot Noir provides the power and structure, Chardonnay the elegance and energy. Meunier? Well, some fruit and bulk.

Fast-forward fifteen years, and Pinot Meunier's in a different place, thanks to the rise of the grower-producer. Since the growers' focus is usually to express place, not region-wide blends, it's understand-able that they would use whatever's at hand, and some of the time that means featuring Pinot Meunier. Along the way, several iconic 100-percent Pinot Meunier wines started to change the perception of the grape. Egly-Ouriet's Les Vignes de Vrigny, made from a plot of forty-year-old vines in the small Premier Cru village of Vrigny, is not an epic wine. But it is absolutely delicious, upholding the characterization of Meunier as fruity and lighthearted, but also proving that it can have structure and intensity and can carry a wine on its own. Even more notable are the wines of Jérôme Prévost's La Closerie, which is composed of just one 2.2-hectare (5.5-acre) vineyard of Pinot Meunier in the village of Gueux. Prévost makes just two wines, a brut nature and a rosé, both dry. He produces tiny quantities and therefore they are rare and expensive (around $100–$150), when and if you can find them. However, they show Pinot Meunier's serious side, as they are precisely made and very intense, needing years in the bottle to attain their peak. Yet they never lose the playful, red-fruited charm one expects from the variety. Also long on charm are the wines of Vallée de la Marne grower Christophe Mignon, whose all-Meunier brut and brut rosé are incredibly winning, yet also con-centrated. In 2006, Alexandre Chartogne (Chartogne-Taillet) started bottling a truly epic single-site Meunier from sixty-year-old vines in Merfy. All these wines capture a depth, richness, and power few knew Pinot Meunier possessed. In some ways, you can say that Pinot Meunier is a totem of the grower's redemption—proof that the disrespected can rise to a place of dignity and importance.

ALEXANDRE CHARTOGNE
Champagne Chartogne-Taillet, Merfy

BORDEAUX

So, even Raj, famous Burgundy palate and Rhône lover, admits that many of the greatest wines he's ever tasted were old Bordeaux. Of course, this was long ago and some of these vintages begin with an 18, but still, the reality cannot be denied. In any conversation about the world's greatest wines, it's impossible to overlook Bordeaux, much as sommeliers of the current generation might want to do so. It simply is (or was) the world's greatest, most respected, and scrutinized wine. So, why has it fallen from favor? Well, that's a longer analysis, but it probably starts with the fact that Bordeaux's major varieties are Cabernet Sauvignon and Merlot, two grapes it made so famous that they spread across the globe, becoming the world's two most ubiquitous. And we know how sommeliers pride themselves on finding more obscure wines. In this case, Bordeaux was a victim of its own success. Younger sommeliers didn't want it because it was too popular with an earlier generation.

Bordeaux's path toward greater acceptance with this newest generation of American wine drinkers remains an uphill climb. A conservative place that's been the center of the wine world for several hundred years, Bordeaux was happy to recline passively in its châteaux while the world came knocking on its door with the hope of being invited in. It's not accustomed to hustling through a wine market like Los Angeles, trying to connect vividly enough with some twenty-four-year-old sommelier that she might buy the wine. American sommeliers (and wine drinkers in general) love family-run properties, vignerons "with dirt under their fingernails," and a good story—anything that promotes a more intimate relationship with a place and a wine. Unfortunately, Bordeaux can't project that kind of image. Its most famous estates are largely owned by corporations, banks, and insurance companies. The ones that aren't belong to wealthy, aristocratic families who don't represent their wines personally. Since they rarely venture into the market and instead rely on agents and distributors, there's no hope of a personal touch. Bordeaux tastings are often suited, formal affairs that run more like business meetings than friendly exchanges.

So, with little personal connection, sommeliers haven't visited the region much, preferring to taste in a damp cave in Burgundy or trace the lava trails on Mount Etna. And those who did visit often came back with horror stories ("no one ever even took us to see a vineyard!"). Therefore, they haven't engaged the wines, which have likewise obliged by being unengaging—a never-ending procession of nearly identical bottles of Château Blah-Blah. The world's Cabernet/Merlot fatigue hasn't helped.

Good reasons to connect with Bordeaux, of course, exist—hundreds of years of them. First on the list, naturally, is the wine. This is an awkward (for those who don't find Bordeaux "cool") but incontrovertible truth: very few wines are as delicious as mature Bordeaux. The savory, umami-rich perfume of old Bordeaux—

mushrooms, tobacco, forest floor, soy—is enchanting and irresistible, evocative of something between the luminous, antique-filled attic of a fascinating great-uncle and one of the greatest meals you ever had but just can't quite remember. The best part is that these beguiling flavors are hardly exclusive to the best growths. Even cheap bottles of properly aged Bordeaux develop that burnished complexity in a way few other Cabernet-based wines can. Second on the list is the place: southwest France. Let us not forget that Bordeaux, nestled between duck and goose territory and Basque country, is hallowed ground for gastronomy. A region with a beautiful oyster and fish culture, Bordeaux is also a gorgeous place, crisscrossed by rivers and canals with stately châteaux popping up amidst rolling, vine-combed expanses.

Best of all, Bordeaux's formal iciness appears to be melting. Perhaps increased competition driven by dozens of hungry wine regions around the world has shaken it from complacency. The new generation running Bordeaux appears to prefer an open collar instead of a fastidious Windsor knot. Filled with youthful energy, Bordeaux, the town, has been spiffed up and now routinely rates as one of the more lively cities in France.

When we head to Bordeaux, we rent an Airbnb in the city to experience some of this vibrant town. In the morning we drive out an hour (traffic's bad) to the wine country. Our first stop is Château Palmer. There's a great history there (dating to 1814), but under the leadership of CEO Thomas Duroux since 2004, Palmer has been one of Bordeaux's most innovative estates.

Duroux playfully celebrates Bordeaux's heritage, as with his Historical Nineteenth Century wine (which includes 15 percent Rhône Syrah in the blend, a common practice back then to strengthen the wine). But mostly, he's forward-looking. He provides Palmer a youthful, dynamic public face. And he's converted it to biodynamic farming, making Palmer one of the very few estates to undertake that challenging practice in humid, mildew-prone Bordeaux.

"I think it's the only way," he says, as we meet in the vineyard. "Sooner or later everyone here will have to be organic—their customers and the world will demand it. The other way is just no longer acceptable for wines like these." With a flock of eighty sheep to chew the grass cover crop in the winter, to an ever-expanding herd of cattle to supply all the fertilization the estate's soils might need, to planting over a thousand new trees and other flora to expand biological diversity, Palmer is teeming with life. Not only is organic farming morally and environmentally the right thing to do, the hope is that it also promotes the wine's expression of typicity, or its ability to express the commune of Margaux and Palmer's own estate.

The world's most famous and most examined wine is challenging to define by taste these days. Pinpointing its various communes in blind tastings used to be much easier. Thanks to a warming climate, wholesale advances in winemaking and vineyard techniques, and a desire to appeal to a global market, Bordeaux's wines have no doubt "improved" across the board, but the cost of this improvement has been the detectable signatures of place knowledgeable tasters used to savor. At best, today's Bordeaux instead asks wine drinkers to recognize its nuances by house style—or the way a particular château shapes and determines the wine through the winemaking process. Nevertheless, we hold that an understanding of the landscape both above and below ground might still give clues to how the wines may taste and at least provide compelling narratives to a place that often seems to lack them.

PARTICULARS OF PLACE

For those new to Bordeaux—this includes many sommeliers and American wine drinkers under forty—it might be tempting to view the famous 1855 Classification of the Médoc, Bordeaux's premier region, which created the famous First Growths and their first-name celebrities (Lafite, Mouton, Latour, etc.) as functioning like Burgundy's classification of Grand Cru vineyards. That would be a mistake, as Bordeaux's classification was based on the prices fetched by the wines of the sixty-one estates that were classified. By contrast, Burgundy's vineyards—which anyone could own a piece of—were rated, giving primacy to terroir. Bordeaux's an entirely different way of thinking, with the determiner of quality placed on the estate, not solely the land. It vexes the Burgundy-conditioned mind to know that if Château Latour buys a new vineyard, no matter where in Bordeaux it might be, those vines become eligible to produce First Growth wine (the highest classified level, which runs from first to fifth growth and then to a few even more broad, less elevated ratings).

Since the classification, much has changed. Indeed, in 1855, Carménère and Malbec were still popular in the region, while Cabernet Sauvignon had just begun to gain its foothold. Only around 10 percent alcohol, Bordeaux wines were so light-colored (hence the still-in-use Britishism "claret" to refer to them as a whole) that darker, heavier wines were added to make them more potent and transportable (most famously, Hermitage—see page 204). The amount of land covered by the classified estates has increased by over 50 percent. Today, many classified châteaux on the list don't belong anymore (or have changed hands and names), and some châteaux obviously deserve promotion.

So compared to Burgundy's focus on terroir, the whole thing sounds like a joke, right? Well, in large part it is, despite the fact that in 150 years much of the price hierarchy has held up—the First Growths still do fetch higher prices than those on down the list. And many critics will say that the highest-rated growths still make the best wines. This could be a self-fulfilling prophecy: they're spurred to make better wines because of their high expectations. But possibly location—okay, terroir—does have something to do with these estates of the Médoc.

To help us understand the bigger picture of the Bordeaux landscape and to see if indeed some generalities of taste can be found in the region's geography, Duroux arranges a visit with David Pernet, a well-known vineyard consultant. Pernet takes us through a quick tour of Bordeaux's geologic history, which impacts everything that goes on today. Even if the flattish landscape is hardly thrilling, the subterranean narrative is compelling.

First, let's get situated and establish a few terms in case you're new to Bordeaux. The whole region is defined by the confluence of two rivers, the Garonne and the Dordogne, which forms a large estuary known as the Gironde (confusingly, it's often referred to as a river) that flows into the nearby Atlantic. You'll always hear Bordeaux spoken of in terms of Left Bank and Right Bank. The Left Bank speaks to the sides west of the Garonne and west of the Gironde. It includes the Médoc (whose name may come from the Latin *in medio aqua*, meaning "between two waters," as it sits between the estuary and the Atlantic) and beneath it, Graves (pronounced *grahv*). The Right Bank lies to the east of the Gironde estuary and the Dordogne river. It includes the famous districts of Pomerol, St-Émilion, and many other appellations.

Left Bank

From north to south within the Médoc are the famous sub-appellations of St-Estèphe, St-Julien, Pauillac, and Margaux. At the southern end of the Médoc is the city of Bordeaux. To its south (still on the Left Bank) is the famous region of Graves (which contains Pessac-Léognan and Sauternes). The oldest wines of the region, from Roman times, came from Graves and St-Émilion, since the Médoc, Bordeaux's most celebrated area, didn't even exist. It came into existence in the 1600s, when Dutch engineers, in the most consequential act of terroir creation the world has ever known, emptied the marshland that would become it. European vignerons chide the New World for its dependence on irrigation; this was the opposite of irrigation. The Dutch, literally, drained the swamp.

Being on lowlands next to the sea, in Bordeaux the concern is always water. The Bordelais worry about too much water from the sky (wet vintages are disasters), too much water in the air (mold, mildew, and fungus pressures), and too much water in the soil. This last one—the amount of water in the soil—is the principal factor in distinguishing the great vineyard land from the mediocre and the shabby. Thus, the soil's ability to deal with water is the key.

Wine people love to trumpet the age of the rocks in their region—"our soils are 400 million years old!"—with the implication that more ancient stones produce more profound wines. This is nonsense. At least in Bordeaux they confront the truth head-on. "In the Médoc," Duroux says, "all the key terroirs are recent: between a million and 100,000 years old. Geologically speaking, very young."

These "key terroirs" of the Médoc were formed by ice-age glaciation recurring over the last five million years. The freezing of glaciers and subsequent melting during warming periods caused intense erosion and runoff, resulting in the depositing of incalculable amounts of rocks and gravel. Every few hundred thousand years, massive rivers would spill into the Bordeaux lowlands, spreading the broken rocks of nearby mountain ranges into and around the estuary. As the glaciers froze and melted, the sea level would rise and fall. Thus, as gravels, clays, and silts moved and re-deposited on top of each other over the millennia, the landscape of Bordeaux grew and shrank.

The gravel deposits of each epoch have been mapped and categorized into six different "terraces" spread out over the Left Bank. Gravel is of special interest because it drains water very quickly. But you can't have only gravel, or there would be no water retention. And therefore clay, nature's great sponge, comes into play.

In Burgundy, the soil dynamic lies in the interaction between clay and limestone; in the Médoc, it's between clay and gravel. Gravel, which has big grains, holds no water. Clay, on the other hand, "is made up of tiny particles, below two micrometers in size," Pernet says. "It's so small that when you have only clay, you will have no free water, because the clay is so fine and dense, it absorbs it all. Even if the clay is

THOMAS DUROUX
Château Palmer, Margaux

full of water, you won't see the water, which is so fixed by the clay that it's hard for the vine roots to uptake. So they do it only slowly in very small amounts. Clay can produce some moderate hydric stress, but not as much as gravel. That's why the tannin ripens faster on gravel than on clay."

To be suitable for viticulture, every gravel terrace must have a certain amount of clay, and the best of the terraces have the most perfect balance. They possess enough gravel to drain the water, but contain enough clay to hold water when the summer heats up. The vine's roots reach into this clay and are able to extract just enough water to function. The effect produced by the vine's water deficit—which Pernet calls "hydric stress"—is the most important factor in a Bordeaux vineyard. When the vines have access to water, they ripen tannins slowly and lazily. When the water supply is constrained, tannins ripen quickly. Bringing those tannins to full maturity before autumn rains arrive is the goal. So it's all about finding enough natural hydric stress to convince vines to ripen their tannins enthusiastically, but not too much that they give up and assume the fetal position.

The geologic age of the gravel terraces does in fact come into play—for the amount of clay they contain, not for the composition of the gravel. The younger gravel terraces (the fifth and sixth) contain relatively large amounts of clay—too much. In the first and second terraces, the oldest gravels, most of the clay has washed out over the eons, making them too gravelly and well-draining. The third and fourth terraces have just the right balance. Had Goldilocks been a vintner, she would have planted vineyards there. Not coincidentally, the third and fourth terraces run up and down the Left Bank more or less in correlation with most of the best estates.

Of course, there is far more, er, granularity to the discussion of soils than is possible here. Palmer, a third growth (that fetches both praise and prices more in line with first growths) is mostly located on the fourth terrace, but Duroux has identified eighteen different types of terrain on the property. And it's not the gravels themselves that are essential, he says. "The gravel just takes up space. It creates structure. What's important is everything around it. So the permutations are endless."

Pernet adds another wrinkle. "There's another differentiation between south and north that's not so well known on the geological aspect," he says, pointing at a map of the distribution of the terraces. "On the top of the gravels, you can also find some very recent clay, like you can find in a swamp. This clay is more present above the gravel in St-Estèphe [in the north] than in Margaux [farther south]. There's a gradient between St-Estèphe and Margaux of clay in the top layers of the soil."

To sum it up: The greatest differences across the Médoc run from east to west, determined by the various terraces. And there's a more subtle difference from north to south, because of clay deposits that are thicker in the north at St-Estèphe, thinning gradually as you get down to Margaux, where Palmer is. How does this manifest in the wines? Roughly, the Médoc's best wines come from estates situated on the

GUILLAUME THIENPONT
Vieux Château Certan

narrow band of the third and fourth terraces (much wine is made on the other gravels, it's just less consequential). And the wines in the north are more muscular and tannic, becoming somewhat more elegant moving south.

"The identity of Palmer," says Duroux, "comes from 80 percent of vineyard parcels having moderate to strong water stress. It leads to some very soft, elegant tannins. Every year they have enough stress. Cos d'Estournel, in St-Estèphe, has more than a third of its vineyards on clay, which leads to stronger structure, and tannins which are mainly not so soft. That's part of the identity of the estate—elements linked to terroir and the soil." You can see that this makes vintage in Bordeaux so important. In a poor year, Palmer's wine might be (and has been) accused of being too thin. Likewise, Cos, in a tough year, can have gnarly tannins. Ironically, given the hype surrounding great vintages, it's the difficult ones that reveal the best terroirs: these wines maintain consistency of quality and typicity despite challenging conditions.

Pg. 195

As its name suggests, Graves, the region south of the Médoc, is also based on gravels. In its northern reaches, just touching the city of Bordeaux, a new appellation inside Graves was created in 1987: Pessac-Léognan. It's home to Graves's two greatest estates, Château Haut-Brion (First Growth) and La Mission Haut-Brion (Second), as well as a slew of other well-respected estates. The Haut-Brions are strange in that they have been completely subsumed by urban sprawl and are fenced off in the middle of a busy, ordinary cityscape. We literally gaze at the stately mansion of Haut-Brion from a gas station across the street while refilling our rental car. According to Pernet, geologists have found the fourth and third terraces in Graves, as well as the second. Pessac-Léognan is structurally similar to the Médoc, but in the rest of Graves more of the subsoil has been eroded and the dominant elements are gravel and sand. Consequently, the red wines are a bit lighter. And white wine comes into the picture in Graves; it doesn't figure meaningfully in the Médoc. Graves whites, based on Sauvignon Blanc and Semillon, are rightfully considered among the greatest white wines in the world. And certainly the celestial sweet wines of Sauternes and Barsac, grown near the Garonne, whose humid mists allow the development of "noble rot" (botrytis, which concentrates grapes' sugars), are iconic themselves.

Right Bank

Another story altogether is the Right Bank, the eastern side of the Dordogne river, which flows down from the Massif Central. (The huge area in between the two rivers, Dordogne and Garonne, is called Entre-Deux-Mers, and is covered with vines producing loads of inexpensive wines that, if well chosen, can be a source of great value. We visited Château Biac, a wonderful little property there just on the east side of the Garonne, and found huge potential at $50 and under.) Wine-wise, the Right Bank includes the famous appellations of St-Émilion and Pomerol, as well as the more rustic, but rising, regions of Bourg and Blaye.

Contrasts between the Left and Right Banks are as much cultural as geographical. Whereas Cabernet Sauvignon rules the Left Bank (with rare exceptions, such as Palmer, which is around 40 percent Merlot), the Right is mostly given to Merlot and Cabernet Franc. Whereas the Médoc is organized by sweeping estates watched over by grand châteaux, the Right Bank's properties are much more modest and, in most cases, more humble. Even some of the most elite—Pétrus, for instance—have no château, just a cellar and offices. The structural difference is not merely window-dressing. The Left Bank is more corporate and bears a somewhat impersonal vibe and a sense that the levers of control are pulled elsewhere. On the Right Bank, even top houses are more likely to belong to families, and the average producer is a vigneron. Even some of the most famous families of the Right Bank are relative newcomers—Moueix (Château Lafleur-Pétrus, Château Trotanoy, Château Hosanna) and Thienpont (different branches own Vieux Château Certan, Le Pin, and run several more châteaux)—having risen from only the merchant class in the first half of the twentieth century. Indeed, though they occupy some of the most ancient vineyard land in the region, Pomerol and St-Émilion only began achieving their current renown in the 1950s.

Pomerol has risen to notoriety thanks mostly to acclaim for wines like Pétrus, L'Évangile, Vieux Château Certan, and La Conseillante. Scarcity only helps the reputation: Pomerol's vineyard covers only 800 hectares (1,960 acres), seven times less than neighboring St-Émilion. One cloudy autumn afternoon, we climb the famous hill of Pétrus with its director, young Olivier Berrouet, and laugh. This is because it's not recognizable at all as a hill, but rather feels like a continuation of the flatland that stretches for miles around you. But Berrouet assures us that it is indeed a hill, just a gradual one. And this hill is the key to the wines. Most of Pomerol is covered by gravel and sand. But this shallow hill is formed of a circular bulge of distinctive, forty-million-year-old, blue, iron-rich clay. Our feet crunch on gravel here, but there's less than 2 feet of it before you hit clay. And this is a form of montmorillonite clay, prized in viticulture. Its incredibly fine, microscopically layered structure turns it into "swelling clay" that dilates with moisture to the point it becomes essentially watertight. "When it rains," Olivier says, "we absorb one tenth of the precipitation. Then our clay expands and becomes impermeable. Ninety percent of the water drains off."

Pétrus, which is planted to 100 percent Merlot, is truly king of the hill and enjoys the fact that most of its holdings reside on this unique clay terrain. Its neighboring estates— L'Évangile, Vieux Château Certan, Gazin, and La Conseillante—also have a purchase on the hill, but not as centrally as Pétrus, as their vines slope off into the gravel-rich areas. It can happen suddenly. Olivier points at Château Lafleur, just on the opposite side of the road. "To cross the street is to make a jump in time of thirty-nine million years," he says, "because the gravel deposits [there] are just one million years old." (To be clear, we don't think he's bragging about the elderliness of the forty-million-year-old clay; that would be absurd. He's merely stating the suddenness of the shift.)

The upshot in terms of taste is that the clay of Pétrus, as expressed by Merlot, brings a density and unique structure you don't get with other soils. It results in lush, hedonistic wines somewhat low in acid, but rich in texture and mouthfeel. Lots of tannin, but ripened until it covers the mouth like a soft, plush carpet. Flavors run from dark black and blueberry fruit to notes of smoky rocks and dark flowers. Pétrus and its neighbors make up the elite of Pomerol—particularly Vieux Château Certain, L'Evangile, and Lafleur—share many of these qualities, but not to the same degree. It's a different sort of structure than the Cabernet and gravel wines from the Left Bank, which are more linear, like railroad tracks running off into the horizon. Pétrus (and its clay confrères) is more expansive, dense, and mouth-filling, like floating in the vast, black void of space. And while it may seem lacking the architecture to age, that's not the case; it ages majestically.

Pétrus's irresistibility and stratospheric price drive sales for the rest of Pomerol. Unfortunately, not many share Pétrus's terrain. "A lot of people say, 'We have the same subsoil as Pétrus,'" Olivier points out over lunch (and a lip-smacking bottle of 1996 Pétrus). "Yes, but their clay is covered with 6½ feet of sand. For us, the clay is there after 20 inches. The few parts of our vineyard with sand are never used in the final blend."

For many estates, the final blend depends all too much on sandy soils. Consequently, the wines of Pomerol differ considerably depending on where the vineyard is, and there's no easy way to know exactly what you're getting. Pomerol has no classification (likely due to the fact that it also has no grand châteaux and was considered a bit of a backwater until just the last few decades), and estates often exaggerate the quality of their soils. The most effective way of judging a Pomerol without tasting it might, sadly, be price, though of course that leaves us all vulnerable to gouging, in which a wine worth $40 may go on sale for $240, thanks to its zip code.

The Right Bank's other major player is, of course, St-Émilion, just south and east of Pomerol, which simultaneously is the most pristine and touristed town in Bordeaux, and also a large wine region 5,400 hectares (13,230 acres) in area. St-Émilion can be hard to get a handle on, as it has three distinct types of terroir. There's the top of the plateau, with its limestone substrate and thin, clay-loam topsoils. The soils are drier here, but it's cooler. The second type of wine comes from the slopes, which lead down from the plateau to the river basin. The soils are a deeper clay limestone and a dense blend of clay, sand, and limestone called *molasse du Fronsadais*. The aspect is largely south, so there's protection from northernly winds and heat from direct sunlight. These soils have high water retention and they drain the water from the plateau, so they can be very cold. This is why Merlot dominates here, as it ripens earlier than Cabernet Sauvignon, which is barely found. Cabernet Franc is also popular for structure and aromatics, as it does well on limestone, but ripens a bit after Merlot. Wines from the slopes are less meaty and broad-shouldered as the wines from the top, but the tannins can be hard to get ripe. That said, the slopes are the greatest part of St-Émilion, confirmed by the fact that the greatest number of famous estates are situated there: Angélus, Ausone, Beauséjour, Larcis Ducasse, Pavie, Pavie Macquin, and Troplong Mondot. Wines from both the plateau and the slopes can be quite big and tannic, but we repeatedly find greater muscle in the wines from above, and a little more finesse in the wines from the slopes.

Far beneath the slopes is the third type of terrain: plenty of uninteresting sandy soils that make very average St-Émilion wine. However, there's also the part bordering Pomerol, where you find Pomerol- and Médoc-styled gravels. The wines from here are also famous—Cheval Blanc, Figeac, and Dominique—though one producer tells us that "Cheval Blanc is much more a part of Pomerol than limestone St-Émilion. It is in St-Émilion only for administrative reasons, I think."

The Right Bank has its confusions, to be sure. But not confusing is that this has been the most dynamic region of Bordeaux for some time now. And, thanks to the dependence on Merlot and, to a lesser extent, Cabernet Franc, its wines are also the easiest to drink when young.

Why is it harder to blind taste Bordeaux today than it used to be?

In earlier decades, the wines of Bordeaux châteaux were recognizably distinctive, defined by place. Now with so much advancement in vineyard and cellar work, the emphasis is more on the wine itself than the place. Benchmarks don't come from the other producers in the commune, but from all over Bordeaux and the world, with critics as the arbiters of taste. We are reminded of something Jean-Louis Chave, wise man of Hermitage, said to us about wine in general:

> You should be driven by your place, not by your idea of quality. What is quality? If you have no defects, by definition you only have quality, but that doesn't mean it's a great wine. I think a problem in wine today is that now people are so driven by this idea of quality. You must have fruit! But why not animal? Why not vegetable? It must be soft and round! But why not acid? Why not structure? When you're in your vineyard, let it speak to you. Let it tell you what it's about. This is the problem when the Grand Vin becomes a luxury good. A luxury good like a Hermès scarf can be endlessly and easily reproduced. Wine cannot and should not. It's why the mind-set must be different in wine, because wine is at its best when it has character—not defect, but character.

Sometimes you can get to a sense of place in Bordeaux, but not every vintage. Cooler vintages when the wines were less ripe—2011 and 2014 come to mind—may show identity more than warm vintages, perhaps because the stamp of character the vintage brings cannot be hidden. So, it's difficult to blind taste these Bordeaux luxury goods based on the old notions of place, but sometimes the old notions still hold up.

How to distinguish a Right Bank from a Left Bank?

Left Bank wines are almost always Cabernet Sauvignon–based. Look for classic Bordeaux Cab indicators—cassis, black and blue fruit, a leafy quality, and a tannic and austere profile in youth, narrower on the palate. Right Bank wines are Merlot, mostly, with some Cabernet Franc. Some may have black fruit, but look for more deep, plummy notes and more chocolate. Younger wines usually have softer, more chewy tannins than Left Bank wines.

What are the taste profiles of the major Médoc communes?

St-Estèphe Because of a greater proportion of clay in the soil, St-Estèphe wines are the Haut Médoc's most burly. Dark, full-bodied, rich, tannic, and energetic with acidity, these are sturdy agers. Cos d'Estournel is the king of St-Estèphe, but many great estates are here: Montrose, Calon-Ségur, Phélan Ségur, and the oft-overlooked Sociando-Mallet.

Pauillac This village is the heaviest hitter, what with three of the five First Growths (Latour, Lafite, and Mouton). These wines are therefore archetypal Médoc. Look for the classic combinations of fresh, vibrant fruit—not usually as dark as St-Estèphe—plenty of cigar box and oak spice, and dry tannins. In the mouth, look for energy and a forceful but fine-grained structure. Don't get hung up on the top growths. Also here you have the two excellent Pichons (Lalande & Baron) as well as Pontet-Canet and the ever-popular Lynch-Bages.

St-Julien The Médoc's smallest village lacks a First Growth, but has the highest proportion of classified estates of the Médoc, suggesting its terroir is very good indeed. The gravels here are not as deep as in Pauillac, so the wines are considered to lack exactly that heft. However, they do have a certain grace. Look for fruit that edges a little toward the red spectrum with age, and a fine note of graphite. While gritty and tannic in its youth (as they all are), St-Julien often softens into a graceful, fine wine. The big names here are ever the Léovilles: Las Cases, which is considered just under the top level, Barton, and Poyferré. They and the other popular Second Growth, Ducru-Beaucaillou, price over $100 a bottle in an average vintage, but Gruaud-Larose, another excellent Second Growth, can still be found for under that ceiling.

Margaux The village with the least amount of clay (and therefore the most gravel) is known to produce the most elegant of Médoc wines. Certainly these are tannic in youth, but relatively supple when compared to the villages to the north. And truly, with age, these wines can show the ethereal grace and exhilarating perfume that makes the Médoc such an entrenched place for wine. Château Margaux is obviously the big name here, but many could see Third Growth Palmer elevated to top level, if a new classification were ever to happen (it won't). Other good châteaux include Brane-Cantenac, Rauzan-Ségla, Cantemerle, and d'Issan.

Graves In Graves and Pessac-Léognan wines, look for a slightly lighter, less dense body than you generally find in the Médoc, and grainy but fine tannins. Aromatic and taste signals are hot rocks and peaty, smoky notes atop classic Cabernet Sauvignon flavors.

How to tell Pomerol from St-Émilion?

Pomerol—at least from the clay-based plateau—is viscous and thick, rich with dark, sweet blackberry fruit. There's less tannin and lower acidity. Pomerol and St-Émilion from the gravels will speak to higher Cabernet Franc percentage and show it with more leafy Cab notes than the plummy Merlot of Pomerol. Wines from the plateau and slopes of St-Émilion will be mostly Merlot-based, but have much more linear structure than those from Pomerol.

◇ **CHÂTEAU PALMER** This venerable château is one of the leading lights of Bordeaux thanks in large part to the visionary leadership of director Thomas Duroux. Leading the region into organic and biodynamic farming was a big step. The wines are better now than they have ever been—powerful and long-lasting, but without giving up that Margaux finesse.

◇ **CHÂTEAU PICHON LONGUEVILLE COMTESSE DE LALANDE** Also known as Pichon Lalande for short, this Second Growth of Pauillac is ever pleasing, showing beautiful balance between ripe fruit, a firm tannic structure, and explosive perfume. While it ages incredibly, it can sometimes be accessible within five years of the vintage date.

◇ **DOMAINE DU JAUGARET** A throwback to an earlier era of Bordeaux, Jaugaret is not owned by a corporation or made by a winemaking team. Rather, it's more like a Burgundian operation, with proprietor and vigneron Jean-François Fillastre handling all the duties. With their suppleness and extreme openness and digestibility, the wines reflect the intimacy of the domaine.

◇ **CLOS DU JAUGUEYRON** Another handmade Bordeaux throwback, Clos du Jaugueyron is a small domaine produced by Michel Théron, who farms organically, ferments whole cluster (a rarity in Bordeaux), and uses only a little new oak. The wines respond by being incredibly open and accessible in their youths, while displaying beautiful aromatics and supple tannins.

◇ **CHÂTEAU PÉTRUS** It's hard not to love Pétrus, one of the most hedonistic wines in existence. Crafted painstakingly from a blessed piece of clay in the middle of Pomerol, the wine lacks many of the things prized by wine lovers today (aggressive acidity, angular structure), but more than makes up for it with fruit so opulent and texture so lush as to almost defy belief.

◇ **VIEUX CHÂTEAU CERTAN** Another Pomerol gem, this venerable estate offers much of the luxuriant pleasures and similarly lush, blackberry and blueberry fruit of Pétrus, but in a slightly more modest, structured, and down-to-earth fashion that is anything but disappointing (and rather a welcome reminder of more tempered forms of beauty).

THE ASSEILY FAMILY
Château Biac

RHÔNE VALLEY

The Rhône Valley is divided into two parts so different they hardly seem to belong in the same thought. However divergent, the Northern and Southern Rhône are unified by a common denominator, the Rhône river, and consequently we always talk about them together. And, no, it's not a contest. But if it were, say, a game of sport, the score wouldn't even be close; it's a rout in every statistic. Number of significant red grape varieties: Southern Rhône, 5–1. Appellations: Southern Rhône, 15–8. Percentage of total Rhône wine production: Southern Rhône, 95–5.

However, everyone loves the underdog, the Cinderella story. The Southern Rhône may kick ass in terms of numbers, but the greatest wines are never about numbers, and most of those gaudy stats the SR puts up are thanks to oceans of perfectly okay wine that no one wants to talk about. So, for the purposes of this chapter, the Northern Rhône wins the only competition we truly care about—number of appellations we discuss: Northern Rhône, 4–1.

The Oxford Companion to Wine describes Syrah as "one of the noblest and most fashionable red wine grapes," offering as proof of said fashionability the surge of interest that carried it around the world over the past century, making it the icon of Australian wine, providing a strong foothold in America, and even seeing it blossom in the south of France.

But it's hard not to chuckle at the word "fashionable" when you visit the Northern Rhône, Syrah's homeland. Given Syrah's immense popularity, when planning a visit here you could reasonably anticipate the Northern Rhône to be lined with glistening hotels, jam-packed restaurants, and wine bars clamoring with beautiful people who have come to bask in the nobility and fashionability of Syrah. You might hope to glimpse one of the great Syrah producers, if only he would slow his Ferrari. You could probably imagine Northern Rhône roads clogged with map-clutching tourists in search of famous Syrah vineyard plots, like visitors to Hollywood stalking celebrity homes.

Well, we are the tourists driving Rhône roads in search of Syrah's legendary vineyards and we can tell you firsthand: the hordes worshipping at the altar of fashionable Syrah are nowhere to be found. There is no celebrity map; no stylish hotels, restaurants, or wine bars. Quite the opposite, in fact. It would be nice to say that we find even quaint old towns that capture the rustic beauty of rural France. (Another score for the Southern Rhône on that one.) The Northern Rhône is hardscrabble and relatively desolate, squeezed into a narrow valley along the Rhône river where the vines climb the soaring hillsides; but increasingly fewer and fewer people are willing to climb with them. It feels the opposite of a place profiting from Syrah's success, but rather a place where vignerons are barely making ends meet while working their bodies into tatters.

However, Northern Rhône Syrah is undeniably fashionable among sommeliers, wine hipsters, and aficionados, because it's the world's most compelling, confounding, and mysterious wine. Its inky blue-black color and wild flavors have an undeniable power and resonance. Syrah's shrouded, savory aromas stir long-buried primal memories of feral origins: the glory of coming across a patch of sweet, juicy, ripe wild berries; the smell of running through a thicket of untamed, flowering herbs and stands of pine and cypress; the scent of blood, fur, and bone, the taste of flesh, and a whiff of smoke from the fire that cooked it.

Growing grapes in the Northern Rhône's best spots—steep hillsides, always—is ridiculously hard work. Its most complete, most compelling, and epic wines are made by small vignerons working in old-school, traditional ways—laboring by hand in the vineyards, fermenting in old vats, aging in large casks. These challenges lead to a tenuous situation these days. Fewer and fewer small growers are around to do this work properly and able to make a good living at it. That's understandable, as working those steep rugged slopes by hand isn't for everybody. When they come up for sale, vineyards are gobbled up by the region's large négociants, leading to fewer and fewer active vignerons. And the next generation of vignerons are ever less willing to take over their parents' vines, understandably dissuaded from life of devilishly hard work for wines that, though expensive, rarely fetch prices worth the trouble. It's much easier to make apps or balance spreadsheets.

It's not all bad news, though. Interest in the great wines of the region has likely never been higher. And if this continues, it may lure growers back to the hills, as we're seeing in Beaujolais. And the Northern Rhône's ceiling is just that much higher.

Côte-Rôtie

"Côte-Rôtie is all about finesse and sometimes people don't seem to understand this," says Stéphane Ogier, arguably the most ambitious young producer in Côte-Rôtie, at whose slopes we gaze through the panoramic windows of his new winery's tasting room. A gifted vigneron with seemingly boundless energy and enthusiasm for Côte-Rôtie, Stéphane comes by his love of finesse honestly, having studied and worked for several years in Burgundy.

Freshness, acidity, and verve have always defined the wines from here. Especially when compared to its eternal downriver foil, Côte-Rôtie's wines are lighter, sharper, and more agile. In the past that was deemed a weakness, and Côte-Rôtie's prices lagged far behind Hermitage's. But today, when muscular, powerful, manly wines are a dime a dozen, Côte-Rôtie's talent for finesse is far more appreciated.

Ogier's ambition and rise mirrors that of the appellation as a whole. Just fifty years ago, it was still suffering a lingering postwar decline. The vineyard surface covered just 70 hectares (172 acres), and wines sold for a pittance—tragic, considering the death-defying skill needed to farm many of the steeper slopes. Around this time, the ambitious négociant producer Guigal made a dramatic bid for the limelight by introducing the first of what, over twenty years, would be three single-vineyard wines (the "La Las": La Mouline in 1966, La Landonne in 1978, and La Turque in 1985) made in modern style (extracted, new oak) that put them in stark relief to the rustic, sauvage wines of the past.

The wines were universally well received by a fine wine market that was open to new ideas. After all, in 1976, California wines had bested several First Growth Bordeaux in the famous Paris blind tasting, and changed the world by showing that newcomers could succeed in the hidebound world of wine. So the La Las changed Côte-Rôtie—as any extreme can do, they raised the ceiling of the region and shifted the center. They won new fame and respect for Côte-Rôtie and fueled an ongoing expansion. Today, the total vineyard area runs close to 300 hectares (735 acres) and prices for top wines stand with the best of the Rhône. The La Las also ushered in an era of changing style (though it probably would have changed anyway). Côte-Rôtie's characteristic finesse and brightness are still there, but more faint than they used to be. And, for those who crave the old style, the savory, gamy wines of the remaining arch traditionalists (Jamet, Barge, Stéphan, Bénetière) have never been more in fashion.

Côte-Rôtie effortlessly inspires awe. When it comes into view on the highway south from Lyon, the "roasted slope" commands attention. So massive and sweeping is the spectacle, focusing on the curving road requires steely discipline. And from this distance, the thousands of microscopic vineyard rows etching the great hill's surface look like mystical, primordial script on an ancient stone tablet. And, indeed, the hill offers much to decipher.

PARTICULARS OF PLACE

Most wine drinkers see Côte-Rôtie as a monolithic terroir—one wine. Of course it's more than that. Those with a little more experience may know about its two famous macro terroirs, Côte Brune and Côte Blonde. Separated by a stream, Côte Brune and Côte Blonde are vineyards, but they also give their names to the two unofficial lobes of the appellation. Occupying the northern two thirds, Côte Brune's soils of iron-rich mica-schist and clay are darker in color, hence the name (*brune* = "brown"). The wines too share these characteristics and are heavier, more tannic, muscular, and longer-lived. Côte Blonde lies to the south. Its basis in granite and gneiss provides a sandier surface, leading to a lighter-colored soil and a more finesse-driven, aromatic wine.

But beyond those divisions, Côte-Rôtie's jagged face contains countless climates known by name and character only to those who work its slopes. Stéphane would like to give these vineyards a larger voice, see them better known, and has an idea of how to accomplish this: through a Burgundy-style classification of vineyards. For his own vineyards, he's already adopted the rhetoric, referring to certain parcels as Grand Cru or Premier Cru, even though no such official designations exist. He even makes a "village" level Côte-Rôtie blend.

Stéphane's greatest terroirs are kept as single vineyards, which he already bottles separately: lacy, elegant Lancement on the Côte Blonde and ponderous, muscular La Belle Hélène in the Côte Brune half of Côte-Rôtie. But he's also bottling, in tiny quantities, vineyards he thinks have significant expression. There's the excellent La Viallière, in the far north on pure rocky mica schist, which makes an intensely mineral, but finessed and precise, Côte Brune. There's Champon, "one of my favorite parcels," Ogier says. "Parts are very steep, but we can still work them by horse. The vines see the sun all day, yet it's the last vineyard we pick. The wine is so rich, but always fresh with great acid."

It's a bold vision for a place he would like to see wine connoisseurs come to know as they know Burgundy. Beyond Côte Blonde and Côte Brune, a few great vineyards already have a reputations—Guigal's La Las (Mouline, Turque, and Landonne), for instance. But, more and more, others are bottling in a parcellaire fashion, in addition to making their larger blends. Clusel-Roch is famous for its Les Grandes Places. Jean-Michel Stéphane bottles wine from two vineyards, Tupin and Bassenon. When Ogier starts making larger commitments to his specific crus, will the world accept them? That remains to be seen, but history at least tells us that it's good for business.

How do you tell the Côte Blonde from the Côte Brune?

Wines from these two ends are great examples of the impact of soil on wine. The Côte Brune, with its deep brown mica-schists, produces dark, smoldering wine. Rarely accessible in its early years, it's tannic, brooding, and dense. Conversely, the Côte Blonde's lighter, sandier decomposed granites make a brighter wine with more verve and finesse. Its aromatics are floral with a mix of red and black fruit and a spray of white pepper. For comparison, pit the smoldering Côte Brune from Domaine Barge against the bright, perfumed Côte Blonde of René Rostaing.

RAJAT'S TOP PRODUCERS

◇ **OGIER** Ogier has a bold ambition in Côte-Rôtie, symbolized by his impressive new winery in Ampuis. He's expanded his vineyard holdings a lot over the years and is obsessed with expressing the facets of Côte-Rôtie's best individual vineyards. However, his blends are excellent too, and he loves the classic Côte-Rôtie style of acidity and finesse. Look for the basic Côte-Rôtie Le Village and the show-stopping single-vineyard Lancement.

◇ **BÉNETIÈRE** A very small, dedicated producer: Pierre Bénetière farms his tiny plots organically (although not certified) and makes wines traditionally. There's a wonderful purity to his wines, which are cleanly made and highly expressive. Cordeloux is the easiest Bénetière to find, but Dolium, not produced every year, is worth seeking out.

◇ **JEAN-MICHEL STÉPHAN** Another small, hardworking producer who is beyond organic in farming, Stéphan also works sulfite-free, putting him squarely into the "natural" category that so many people look for. But his wines are full of character and resonance, always paying attention to the notion of elegance and vibrance. He makes three wines: a basic Côte-Rôtie, which is great, and two single-site wines called Bassenon and Tupin.

◇ **CLUSEL-ROCH** Producing some of the most elegant, classic wines of the hill, this beloved domaine is focused on the Côte Brune, especially with anchor vineyards Les Grandes Places. The great La Viallière vineyard came in 2011. Clusel has farmed biodynamically since 2002. The basic Côte-Rôtie is very good, but the single-vineyard Les Grandes Places is legendary.

STÉPHANE OGIER
Côte-Rôtie

Hermitage

Before it ever even had vines, Hermitage would have been an impressive sight. Towering above the Rhône river and everything else for miles around, it rises from the water like Egypt's pyramids ascend from the sand. Photographs do it no justice; its form is so massive and bulky that it defies conventional framing. It looks like it was placed there by an alien intelligence—a massive solar panel tuned south to absorb maximum energy.

Today, of course, the place is teeming with vines. But it suffers from a lack of vignerons. As signaled by the commercial signs of the négociants who have claimed its faces, Hermitage belongs mostly to the Rhône's largest négociant houses. Nothing is wrong with négociants, of course. Many produce good wine. But the fact is that typically négociants just cannot express the potential of their vineyards in the way a small producer can. Simply and inevitably, this is a reflection of anything done on a large scale. Efficiency, economy, and consistency take precedence over nuance, personality, and risk-taking. When volume is the driver of a business, that which is improved by a more granular, hands-on approach will suffer—individual fermentations, individual plots of vines, individual vines themselves. Négociant wines tend to suffer from a lack of point of view, choosing instead an all-inclusive approach directed toward the assumed tastes of the greatest number of people. Of course there are still a few independent voices helping us make sense of Hermitage. They remind us of its fascinating localities and its unusual mosaic of soils. Let us listen to them and enjoy their wines, while they're still around!

PARTICULARS OF PLACE

Thanks to an inexplicable turn toward the east in the north–south running Rhône, Hermitage enjoys an uninterrupted gaze into the southern horizon. This is what makes it not only a grand terroir, but also a force of nature.

Conventional wisdom has it that Hermitage is a giant chunk of granite. This is hardly the whole truth. Granite is an important component, but Hermitage is a mosaic of different soils, and its terrain can change suddenly over just a period of yards. This complexity leads vigneron Jean-Louis Chave to say, "The big question is always: What is Hermitage?"

What indeed? We know it's a massive hill subject to the Nothern Rhône's continental climate—cold winters and hot summers with frequent interruptions from the frigidly dry, powerful mistral wind. For Jean-Louis, it is a blend of different soils and aspects, always a blend. Some producers bottle unique wines from Hermitage's single climats (the word they use for single vineyards located within the greater hill of Hermitage), but it's hard to argue with Chave's blended approach. Nevertheless, we ourselves are

THE RARE HERMITAGE BLANC

"They make the white [to] sell the red." That's Thomas Jefferson in a 1787 travel journal on Hermitage Blanc. He adds, "There is so little white made in proportion to the red, that it is difficult to buy it separate." In 1791, Jefferson followed up by calling Hermitage Blanc "the first wine in the world without a single exception" and ordered five hundred bottles for the White House wine cellar.

Jefferson was not alone in his love. In the eighteenth and nineteenth centuries, Hermitage Blanc was revered but hard to get, and Hermitage Rouge was on the rise. Red Hermitage was often shipped out of the port at Bordeaux, where the English had found a good use for it in adding depth and weight to Bordeaux reds. As the red also gained popularity in the powerful Russian market, white Hermitage began its decline. That decline has not just been in surface area devoted to the Roussanne and Marsanne vines that blend together for Hermitage Blanc. It's also meant a dearth of available plant material. Whereas there are many clones and selections of Syrah—especially the beguiling proto-Syrah, called Serine in Côte-Rôtie and Petite Syrah (no relation) in Hermitage—Roussanne and Marsanne variations are almost nonexistent.

Nevertheless, an older Hermitage Blanc is a beautiful and mysterious thing. "It's a wine that's not easy to understand," Raj says as we taste 1998 and 1985 with Jean-Louis Chave in his cellar. "It requires a very long time. It's amazing how it evolves backwards compared to most wines. It starts like a fat, unformed baby. And then gains muscle, shape, and minerality as it get older." And its subtle, almost faint flavors in youth gather strength too, becoming an irresistible mélange of honey, spring flowers, and nuts.

As a wine that needs many years to become its exotic, beguiling self and is not cheap to begin with, Hermitage Blanc will remain uncommon in a market that likes its wines young and cheap. But the beauty of a mature Hermitage Blanc is a rare pleasure in wine, so keep your eyes peeled, as back vintages can be found for between $100 and $200.

blends of many things, and to get to know someone is to hear about their parents, their upbringing, their school years. So it is with wine. And to get to know a great blend like Chave's Hermitage more intimately, it's instructive to spend some time with its constituent parts. These we experience as we taste through his barrel room with him one afternoon. And we learn several crucial details about Hermitage's nature. For instance, two famous sites determine the character of almost every producer's Hermitage, he says: a vineyard called Les Bessards and a vineyard called Le Méal. The amount of a domaine's holdings in these two plots drives the style of their wine. "In wine, we are who we are because of what we own," says Jean-Louis.

The natural place to start is with Les Bessards, the largest climat of Hermitage and its most definitive. Located right on the river's turn, it has full southern exposure and wraps around the end of the mountain. Bessards is the famous granite of Hermitage.

This granite was originally of a piece with the rock of St-Joseph, just across the river. What caused the Rhône river to divide this hard stone mound instead of taking a softer course around Hermitage is unknown. Bessards's granite produces a very complete, structured wine with finely integrated tannins and sense of core minerality. For many producers of Hermitages, Bessards is the wine's spine and the key to its longevity. "For us, we are so lucky to have the core of the Bessards. Yes, it's about blending, but many people feel if you don't have Bessards, it's not Hermitage."

Jean-Louis walks that statement back a little when discussing the other great Hermitage climat, Méal. "Well, for the red, it could be different with Méal. That, for instance, is La Chapelle," he says, referring to the famous wine of Jaboulet, which draws heavily on Méal. A contrast to Bessards, which lies just to its west, Méal's soil is glacial—pebbles and limestone bulldozed up the hill by an unstoppable mountain of ice. It's a warmer site and the light color of the soil reflects the sun, providing Méal wine with a richer, fleshier body than Bessards's wiry muscle. "You can imagine a Hermitage based on Méal," says Jean-Louis. "In Hermitage, either you follow the path of Méal or Bessards."

Above them both is a third climat, L'Hermite, which is sort of a meeting ground for all of Hermitage's soils. In various parts it features granite, loess, and clay, producing a wine a little lighter in weight, but with breadth and dimension. It gives freshness and spice, and many producers love it for white wines.

Below Méal is Greffieux, where there is some granite as well as glacier-driven limestone alluvia. The fantastic Hermitage vigneron Bernard Faurie tells us that for him, Greffieux mimics Bessards in its granite outlay, while the limestone portion adds lift and perfume. Sadly, Greffieux's base was put into shadow thanks to the ridiculous decision in the seventies by the town to build a multi-story building at the base of Hermitage. Not only is it an eyesore, but it also decreases the quality and value of the lower vines of Greffieux.

Other important climats to know are Beaume and Péléat, which lie to the east, across a small gully, from the vineyards described above. Beaume is made from limestone, clay, and sand that's been compressed to form a hard, brittle sort of agglomerate. It provides spine and backbone, says Jean-Louis. Péléat, just east of Beaume, is pure sand, "like a beach." It lacks the saltiness of limestone and produces a broad, lateral wine with a finer, silkier tannin. It makes a good complement to Bessards. "You don't have the same depth; it's more like baby fat. This softens the wines."

THE REYNARD VINEYARD
at Domaine A. Clape, Cornas

JEAN-LOUIS CHAVE
Domaine Jean Louis Chave, St. Joseph

FARMING IN THE RHÔNE

One of the most enduring images from our visits to the Rhône was the sight of the postage stamp–size vineyard that produces Pierre Bénetière's Dolium Côte-Rôtie. This vineyard sits literally in the middle of a famous vineyard, which surrounds it on all sides. Viewed from an opposite hillside in winter, it was obvious which vines were Bénetière's. He farms organically, and his plot was green with grass and other life growing between the rows of vines. Around it, the soils were as barren as the moon. But finding organic farming isn't easy on the slopes of the Northern Rhône.

This is sad but understandable. Thirty years of wars decimated the population of France, and rural regions like the Rhône were especially hard hit, as much of the labor force was wiped off the earth. Locals admit that it was chemicals like herbicides that allowed viticulture to continue. "If we had no weed killers on the hills, all the old vines would have disappeared," says Jean-Louis Chave. Steep hillsides, impoverished domaines, and a lack of workers make organic farming almost impossible. "Because when you have hillsides this steep, being organic is plowing by hand or working with a winch or a horse. In St-Joseph, few people can afford to be organic," Chave adds.

That said, many regions have recovered since the war and are now thriving. Farming organically seems an obligation to one's customers, if not to oneself. As Jean Gonon put it, "Do you want people to drink poison? We used to use herbicides. Now everyone knows the images of herbicides and what they can do to health. Wine is luxury; treat it like a luxury."

Olivier Clape, who since 2011 has been farming Domaine Clape organically, says,

"My grandfather and father used herbicides, and the wines were known to be good. So I knew it was possible. But in my mind and heart, I knew it was the right thing to do. And I'm the one working in those vineyards."

Chave reports that more and more producers in Hermitage are farming organically. Clape echoes this in Cornas. It's Côte-Rôtie that continues to be a disaster, as only five producers are known to be organic there (Clusel-Roch, Chapoutier, Jean-Michel Stéphan, Pierre Bénetière, and Stéphane Otheguy). It's also the region that has seen the greatest growth, which is not a coincidence. In a short amount of time, producers have doubled and tripled their holdings. Paying for organic farming when you've grown so fast is very difficult. This is one reason we have to commend the large négociant firm of Michel Chapoutier, which has dedicated itself to organic and biodynamic farming and is in fact France's largest biodynamic winegrower.

It's also a question of a wine's expression. And for that, organic farming is just the beginning of the story. The requirements to be certified organic are not all that strict and still allow hundreds of inputs. For Chave, truly being organic means going above and beyond what's required by certification, including greater attention to sustainability, soil health, and even the wellbeing of the workforce. It's a philosophy and a dedication: "The relation between the wine and the soil—the only way to understand it is through the taste. Even from the technical, scientific point of view, you have no correlation. So what we know is the soil needs to be alive. For sure, you have to be organic. But it's ultimately much more than that. Organic is even not enough."

What are the differences between a Chave Hermitage, based on Bessards, and something like Jaboulet La Chapelle, based more on Méal?

Bessards provides darker, more brooding fruit and a firm, long structure. It's a wine of heavy mineral ore that will take years, if not decades, to unspool. Méal wines lean toward brighter, gentler fruit, more perfume, and more ease. Their texture is more delicate and fine. These wines can also age well, but are usually more accessible when younger than wines from the Bessards tract.

◇ **CHAVE** For Hermitage, nothing else comes close. Chave is the gold standard for structure, density, longevity, and purity. Always a blend, Chave Hermitage is constructed to give a total image of the hill and all its soil types, yet the backbone is always Bessards. Keep an eye out for the rare Cuvée Cathelin. Made only in vintages where its production won't affect the main blend, it is simply a reconfiguration of the main Chave blend—not a reserve, and not more powerful or age-worthy, just another perspective. With Jean-Louis, we tasted the 1995 Cathelin, and it was wonderfully graceful. We also tried the 1949 Hermitage, a stunning wine of incredible youthfulness. (We tasted it blind and thought it from the seventies.)

◇ **BERNARD FAURIE** A true treasure whose wines will soon be gone, as he is retiring, Faurie is a small vigneron making wines out of a tiny garage cellar attached to his house. A consummate farmer and a fastidious winemaker, Faurie's wines are models of a graceful style. Like Chave, he's a Bessards guy, and believes granite is the true bedrock of any blend. Hilariously, he bottles two and sometimes three different reds to represent three soil types. One blend focuses on granite soils from Greffieux/Bessards. Then there's a Greffieux with some Méal, showing the graceful, comparatively airy aspect of the lighter soils. And occasionally, he'll bottle a true Méal. The challenge is that he doesn't explain this on the label. You must know that the Greffieux is bottled with a gold capsule, the Bessards/Greffieux is in cream, and the ultra-rare Méal wine is in a gold capsule with an M. From his little tasting area underneath his house, Faurie also occasionally sells beautiful cherry and apricot preserves.

St-Joseph

The Chave family is famous for Hermitage, but Jean-Louis Chave can't get over his obsession with St-Joseph, a much more obscure appellation across the Rhône river from the great Hill. After all, St-Joseph was where his family started in the wine business in 1481, when a landholding nobleman gave land to Chave's ancestors. Yet, despite the family's successful transition to the vineyards of Hermitage after phylloxera, Chave has dedicated a considerable amount of his energy and capital—not to mention twenty years of his life and counting—to restoring some places in St-Joseph that stopped making wine a long time ago.

While Chave's is considered the greatest Hermitage and one of the iconic red wines of the world, this fixation with restoring St-Joseph is tied intimately to his own family's history, to the ravages of bureaucracy, and the nobility of farmers. At the heart of the story, though, is wine. And the best wine from the heart of St-Joseph is a largely unknown, almost missing expression of Northern Rhône Syrah. It's a legitimate terroir unto itself—not as huge as Hermitage, less opulent than Cornas, and sculpted more precisely than Crozes-Hermitage (another region of the Northern Rhone, considered the least in quality and which we don't explore here). Great St-Joseph fills a gap in terms of flavor, structure, and price. The problem is, as Jean-Louis puts it, "St-Joseph means nothing, and that's a problem."

Let's go back to the beginning. What we now call St-Joseph started as an appellation in 1956. (In referring to times prior to 1956, we will continue to use the name St-Joseph for convenience, even though it was not in use.) It included six villages, but centered around a core of three: Mauves, St-Jean-de-Muzols, and Tournon, which is the village directly across the Rhône from Tain l'Hermitage. Good wine has been made at these places since at least the Middle Ages, but surely much longer.

The ability to ripen Syrah in the northern Rhône depends on south-facing slopes. As we discussed, Hermitage exists because the south-flowing Rhône takes an improbably west-to-east jog at Tain-l'Hermitage, opening the hill's slopes to a glorious, full-south exposure. The western side of the river benefits from no such turns; any southern exposures are dependent on the valleys cut by small rivers running perpendicularly into the Rhône. These streams open up five valleys, Jean-Louis tells us, each with a distinct terroir, though unified in their exhibitions of Massif Central granite: Chalais, Les Oliviers, St-Joseph, Ste-Épine, and Bachasson. "These valleys were the Grand Crus of St-Joseph, each with its own character," says Jean-Louis. "And the question is not what St-Joseph is about, but what Ste-Épine is about, what Bachasson is about, because these are different valleys, different places."

These valleys may have made great wine, but always in the shadow of Hermitage, which belonged to the nobility. St-Joseph belonged to the peasant farmers, who continued to grow fruits and vegetables as well as wine. After phylloxera, the region fell into a steep trough from which it's never recovered. Jean-Louis notes that replanting Hermitage after phylloxera's devastation was only just starting in 1910, and was quickly hampered by World War I, in which tens of millions of Frenchmen were killed. If Hermitage was barely being replanted, St-Joseph's fallow vineyards were completely ignored. On the St-Joseph side of the river, vineyards on the steep rocky hillsides were abandoned, as the vastly diminished community of farmers did all they could to survive. Any replanting of wine grapes occurred on the vastly inferior, but more accessible, river flats. World War II only further decimated the French population, and afterward, jobs moved to factories and cities, leaving France's farmland largely deserted.

Nevertheless, some hardy souls still worked the remaining vineyards of the St-Joseph slopes, explains retired winegrowing legend Raymond Trollat when we visit him in his small house, just opposite his vineyard. Jolly on this afternoon, he shares with us a bottle of his 1999 St-Joseph Blanc and remembers that, in the postwar years, there was still an understanding of what the real wines of St-Joseph were. While none of the wines were bottled—just sold in bulk to other regions or at local stores and bars—discerning palates would dismiss the wines from the flats and actively request the *"vins de bigot." Bigot* was the name for the special hoelike tool used by vignerons to work the high, rocky slopes. Indeed, even after more than fifty years of neglect, the St-Joseph wines still had enough reputation to warrant their own appellation, earning a consultation with the famous Baron Le Roy, who co-founded the appellation system in France in the 1930s. In 1956 he came to meet with the vignerons of St-Joseph.

Various stories about the origin of the name St-Joseph persist—most involving medieval monks—since there is no actual town of that name. But Trollat puts them all to rest with a tale far less romantic, and it occurred the evening Baron Le Roy was visiting. He was helping the local vignerons complete the paperwork, Trollat recalls, and he asked a question no one had considered: What do you want to call this proposed appellation? No one said a word. They hadn't considered it before. After some hesitation, one local farmer ventured, "I have a rather good-sized plot known as St-Joseph. . . ." Without hesitation, Baron Le Roy said, *"Bon! Ças'appelera St-Joseph!"* and filled in the application. That was that.

In 1969, due to political and social pressure, the region was expanded from six villages to twenty-five. (INAO, the governing body of the AOC system, told local growers it would never create another appellation for the Rhône. Therefore, if these vignerons not included in the original St-Joseph AOC wanted an appellation, the only solution was expansion of the current one. While the winegrowers of the original St-Joseph didn't favor expansion, they conceded to the desire of their fellow vignerons, who were colleagues, friends, and relations.) So, instead of 6 miles around Tournon, the vineyards stretched over 40 miles of the Rhône's western bank all the way up to the border with Côte-Rôtie and down past Cornas, including many soils and microclimates that had nothing to do with the renowned, original valleys. Before expansion, you knew what you were getting in a St-Joseph wine. To be part of the original villages meant being a holder of a specific terroir that had earned a reputation over centuries. Suddenly, thousands of new hectares were given a name, many of them unsuitable and up for grabs to even fledgling vignerons. An effort to somewhat dial back the expansion was made in 1992, but it was too late—the damage had been done. This is why Jean-Louis insists, "St-Joseph means nothing."

Sadly, this is true. But to dedicated vignerons like Jean and Pierre Gonon (Domaine Pierre Gonon) and Jean-Louis Chave, St-Joseph means everything. This is why the Gonons work so hard to make a wine worthy of the name. It's why Chave is twenty years into a project to restore and redeem some notion of St-Joseph, systematically purchasing old parcels of the original terrain, some of which had been completely reclaimed by nature. He's had to build roads just to get to some parcels. He's hired a team of stonemasons to rebuild vineyard walls long since crumbled. In search of original plant material, he's taken cuttings from old vines found growing wild in the woods to try to re-domesticate them; he's crossed oceans to track down descendants of pre-phylloxera vines that were shipped to Australia in the mid-nineteenth century. Even current vineyards that he purchased have proven reclamation projects, like the pristine Clos Florentin (never put under chemicals), whose plant material he found unsatisfactory and is therefore replanting. Those vines won't reach even early maturity for another decade or two. "It takes a whole life, and one life is not enough," says Jean-Louis.

Why do all this for wines that will never fetch half of what his Hermitage costs? For Jean-Louis, that is exactly the reason. "St-Joseph is so important to me because I believe the average person deserves some very special wines," he says. "And the problem with the *grand Hermitage*, unfortunately, it's for a different world. And why not? So we need to feed the new sommeliers, the new wine lovers, some really good stuff." But he also repeatedly emphasizes another point: "Without Hermitage, none of this could happen. What am I doing? I'm going back. That's my story, and I'm going back. And it's only possible because of Hermitage. For that, I am extremely lucky."

PARTICULARS OF PLACE

Jean Gonon of Domaine Pierre Gonon, one of the top producers of St-Joseph (and, for that matter, the Rhône in general), takes us on a tour of some of the original St-Joseph valleys. To get to them, you start along D86, heading south from Tournon. We're on the Rhône's right (western) bank, and it's a flatland, though still covered with vineyards. (Gonon's juicy, quaffable Les Iles Feray is down here, on lands so called because in older times they could be flooded by the Rhône and become islands. It's eligible for St-Joseph status, but out of respect for the appellation, Gonon labels it as *Vin de Pays de l'Ardèche*.)

From the flats, we take winding roads into the hills to discover the original sites. At Trollat's, we stand opposite the awesome Sainte Épine, a majestic, towering hillside stacked with stone terraces and 130-year-old vines. Gonon bought some land from Trollat on this hillside, but unfortunately most of it went to Trollat's nephew, who doesn't look after it as he should. Most of the grapes he sells become a very average wine from the Desestret family. There are a few treasures, though: for example, natural winemaker Hervé Souhaut of Domaine Romaneaux-Destezet makes a phenomenal Sainte Épine. At Trollat's one day, Gonon treats us to bottles of 1978 and 1979 Trollat

St-Joseph from this very site, true gems of a bygone era. Both held up beautifully and displayed a juicy vibrancy that is missing in much of the St-Joseph today.

We visit the rocky hillsides of Les Oliviers, between Mauves and Tournon. Here the soil is more clay and rounded stones with some loess on top, providing a richer medium for generous reds and fleshy whites. Indeed, Gonon's white is called Les Oliviers, a serious wine that mixes soft and fleshy textures with crisp and mineral tastes. It ages remarkably. Just to the north of Les Oliviers, we find the original St-Joseph climat, clearly visible from the road. Its soils are granite and clay, less starkly barren than the terraces above Tournon.

Finally, we clamber on those sheer terraces of the Vignes de l'Hospice, which climb like a steep staircase behind the town of Tournon. These famous vines belong to the big négociant Guigal, which won the privilege to buy the vines of the Hospice due to its dutiful restoration of the walls while just a renter. Here, we can gaze across the river at the looming goliath of Hermitage. Before the Rhône sliced it in two, this would have been a continuation of Hermitage's core vineyard Bessards. It's not Hermitage, though. The height of the hills blocks the sun here in the afternoon, while Hermitage continues to bask. The granite has evolved differently, too. Jean Gonon explains: "Granite de Tournon, blue granite, may be more complex than other granites. It's bluish-gray with jagged pieces of granite, but also more clay."

QUESTION OF TASTE

How does St-Joseph wine compare to Hermitage and Cornas?

We're just going to answer for core St-Joseph—that is, the wines we know are from the original five valleys before the expansions. While the wines all differ somewhat depending on their particular situation, they lack the size and structure of Hermitage. And they lack the breadth and richness of Cornas. But the best of them have a more precise and delicate structure than either Hermitage or Cornas, yet within that structure they can be intense and compact. Flavors are classic Rhône Syrah, but often more on the savory side—think olives, pepper, and thyme—and less brashly fruity than Cornas or as stony as Hermitage.

We agree with wine writer John Livingstone-Learmonth (who confesses "a soft spot for St-Joseph") that it's structure that defines St-Joseph's place in the Rhône firmament. He writes beautifully about this in *The Wines of the Northern Rhône*: "The tannic structure brought out by the granite is one of order and definition. It places a frame around the wines that keeps them tidy, subtle, and ready for an evolution that turns fulsome youth into complex middle age. The tannins give these wines a slightly pesky side, the fruit is grainy, a little taut at times, but always the aroma is vibrant and layered, never monotone." Great examples of classic St-Joseph are Chave's Offerus, Gonon's St-Joseph, and Hervé Souhaut's St-Joseph.

PIERRE AND JEAN GONON
Domaine Pierre Gonon, Tournon

◆ **GONON** By the sheer quality of their wines, brothers Jean and Pierre Gonon are doing more than anyone to elevate the profile of St-Joseph into a higher echelon. Their wines are painstakingly and organically farmed and impeccably treated in the cellar. In addition, the Gonons are incredibly humble, gracious, generous people whom we want to see succeed. Year in, year out, the St-Joseph is benchmark, while the Vieilles Vignes St-Joseph, made only in select vintages from seventy-year-old vines, is one of the rarest and most exquisite wines of the Rhône.

◆ **CHAVE** What else is there to say? The only reason Jean-Louis doesn't get more press for his St-Joseph wines (village and Offerus) is because everyone talks about Hermitage. In twenty years, when his full St-Joseph program is operational, get ready. But today, his stellar Offerus, a blend of sites, is a great deal (around $25), while his straight-up St-Joseph blend offers more structure, intensity, and density for about twice the price.

◆ **SOUHAUT** Hervé Souhaut's St-Josephs are terrific. The low- or zero-sulfur winemaking allows the wines to blossom fully with incredible floral notes, bacon, and dark, brambly fruits. Look for his basic Syrah, St-Joseph village, and the single-vineyard St-Josephs Les Cessieux, and St-Épine. All are terrific, showing progressive levels of intensity and complexity as you move up the line.

◆ **DOMAINE MONIER** Jean-Pierre Monier operates a tiny domaine with his son Samuel, sometimes working with a partner, Philippe Pérreol. The partnership is sensible given that each man's holdings of vines are so small; it's easier to combine their fruit and sell it together. No matter—the wines are exquisite, made with a remarkable grace and finesse given the ruggedness of the St-Joseph terrain. Look for the Domaine Monier-Pérreol St-Joseph Tradition and the Domaine Monier Terre Blanche and Laliefine.

Cornas

At just over 110 hectares (270 acres) in size, Cornas is one of the Rhône's smallest appellations. However, it makes a big impression. It's mouth-filling, with powerful blasts of dark fruit, and hearkens, more than any other Rhône wine, to Syrah's uninhibited wildness.

Cornas's small size has imbued it with a certain purity and modesty. The wines are big, but the producers are provincial and humble, none more so than Auguste Clape, one of the village's greatest wine heroes. Cornas really had no "golden age." Despite gaining its appellation in 1938 (almost twenty years earlier than St-Joseph), the area under vine declined to just 50 hectares (123 acres) in the 1940s and 1950s due to growing economic transition to industrialism and recovery from the wars, so there was hardly a chance for a real local wine economy to develop. Even through the 1960s, very few wines were put into bottle. One exception was Clape, who bottled his first wine under his name in 1955, one of the first in Cornas to do this. We visit Clape at his home. Ninety-two but still energetic, he tells us that in the fifties, he had only a slight indication that his wine was anything special. A local négociant would buy his wine in bulk and sell it to local restaurants and buyers; he said Clape's wine was up to par with some of the better producers in Hermitage. Another positive response came from the town priest, who, when sampling various local wines for use in the church, always preferred Clape's and a few other local low-yield vignerons.

Clape's wines helped Cornas develop its reputation. He still sold wine to négociants in the 1960s, but as the town made it through the tough economy of the 1970s and into the 1980s, its wines began to develop more of a name for themselves, thanks to vintners like Verset and Voge in addition to Clape. In the 1980s, Thierry Allemand got started, and in the last fifteen years, his remarkably energetic, powerful, and overwhelming wines have pushed Cornas into celebrity status. With the diminutive size of the appellation limiting production, the wines have always been scarce and expensive. But they deliver a great deal of character and substance for the price.

PARTICULARS OF PLACE

Cornas feels like its own little world. A tiny village just fifteen minutes down the road from Tournons, it has a quiet, almost empty atmosphere. The Rhône river squeezes the village between a steep slope of vineyards rising just behind. Those vineyards are not the best of Cornas, however. You must drive up past and through to get behind them, where their hill becomes one edge of a neat amphitheater of vineyards. Here is the secret to Cornas.

That bowl of vines—a crucible, really—traps heat and concentrates sunlight to bring Cornas the ripeness for which it's famous. The slopes rise steeply all around, with the great climat called Reynard located on a steep rise that faces south and is well sheltered. The soils here are resolutely granite. There's a northern section with a little clay and limestone, but the rest is just varying forms of granite; some are deeper and more decomposed, while in others, topsoils are thinner and rockier. This is why, Clape says, we don't see a big parcellaire trend in Cornas. "The soils are mostly the same. You can make a better wine by just blending." Indeed, back in the cellar, he demonstrates this with the tasting of two wines from 1997. One is the classic Cornas blend, the other an experimental single-parcel bottling of Reynard. The Reynard was not bad, but we all agree that the blend was more complete and had kept its balance with age.

Domaine Clape is now in its third generation under the stewardship of Auguste's grandson Olivier. Olivier has steered the vineyards in an organic direction, following the lead of Allemand, whom, Olivier says, was "for years the only guy out here plowing his vineyards. I have a lot of respect for him for that." Olivier reports that Cornas's hillsides are now bustling with a whole new generation of young winegrowers who are plowing more and using far fewer herbicides. The danger, he reports, is Cornas's newfound fashionability. "We're very nervous about how fast it grows, since people aren't really thinking about good and bad places to plant. They plant vineyards anywhere, just to have Cornas on the label."

QUESTION OF TASTE

What are the distinguishing characteristics of Cornas wines?

We put this question to Auguste Clape. "With a meal, first you have the Crozes-Hermitage, then the St-Joseph. Then you have the Cornas and finally the Hermitage." No Côte-Rôtie? Too far away (one hour)! "They sell that in Vienne and Lyon."

Both Hermitage and Cornas will be fuller-bodied wines than Côte-Rôtie. Hermitage may be a deeper, more structured wine, but Cornas is just as big and maybe even more mouth-filling. The wine is dark black, but can have some ripe, red cherry tones that Hermitage often does not. The tannins can be profound, but are dense and thick, and not usually as structured as Hermitage's.

RAJAT'S TOP PRODUCERS

◊ **CLAPE** One of the greatest producers of Syrah, and all the more impressive given the continuity and consistency over so many decades. The dedication to quality is a hallmark here, starting with Auguste and now with Olivier, who's farming organically. The wines are always savory and focused, with amazing complexity. Start with the entry-level Renaissance and work your way up to Clape's only other bottling: straight Cornas.

◊ **THIERRY ALLEMAND** Allemand is Raj's favorite producer in the world. He farmed organically in Cornas when no one else was. Allemand is as passionate, opinionated, physical, and determined as human beings get. A self-made man in every regard, he designed his own tools for working the soils—he plows with harnesses built for him, not for a horse. His own physical aversion to sulfur has taken him down the path of natural winemaking, and his wines—there are only two, Les Chaillots (younger vines) and Reynard (older vines)—are some of the most vibrant, lively expressions of Syrah ever made. They are savory and dark and full, but also gifted with a tremendous burst of joyful, vivacious fruit.

Châteauneuf-du-Pape

One of the coolest things about going to the Southern Rhône from the North is the feeling of passing between them on the A7. Some regional borders are not even noticeable. This one is a visceral experience. The Northern Rhône is a fairly tight valley rising steeply from the river with towering vineyards climbing the slopes. At the end of the north, you squeeze between the two walls of the Donzère gorge before being popped out into the vast, sunny, open expanse of the Southern Rhône. It's exhilarating and then relaxing. And that's how it should be, because you're now in the south of France.

Everything feels easy in the south of France. The sun is soothingly warm, and the wine is less mentally demanding. It's less exacting, less complicated, less wild. Of course, it can be equally delicious, but in a different way. Whereas in the north it's all about one red grape and what it's possible to express through that singular lens, here it's a blend of grapes. For all these factors, most wines from the Southern Rhone are the undistinguished blend known as Côtes du Rhône. However, in some places, like the world-famous village of Châteauneuf-du-Pape, they can become much more.

In 1936, Châteauneuf-du-Pape became the first of France's appellations d'origine contrôlée. This new program of geographical delineation was a legislative answer to the rampant problem of fraud plaguing the wine industry, which had been hobbled by phylloxera, allowing a glut of ordinary wine from Algeria and the Languedoc to flood the market, masquerading as fine wine. The rules for Châteauneuf were stringent. They specified that the land used for vineyards must be so dry and rugged that even thyme and lavender would grow there (they require a very dry landscape). They stipulated a minimum alcohol of 12.5 percent, still today the highest in France. And they detailed which grapes could be used.

"Since it was the first appellation, its crafters were especially methodical . . . as they knew they had to get it right," Marc Perrin says, as we walk with him through the deep, dark barrel cellars of his family's estate, Château de Beaucastel. "And I think they were very smart. They looked at geology to make the boundaries. They looked at the history of winemaking here for generations to decide which varieties would be allowed, and decided on thirteen of them. They knew that the climate here can change dramatically from year to year. The varieties balance the climate, and the magic is in the blend."

THIERRY ALLEMAND
Domaine Thierry Allemand, Cornas

Given only these lasting prescriptions, the region's wines have evolved in unusual ways, leading to the transitional period Châteauneuf-du-Pape finds itself in now. The boundaries have remained the same, although, thanks to advances in mechanical equipment's ability to break rock, plantings have occurred in places that were impossible in the 1930s. Attaining the minimum alcohol level has not been a concern. In fact, the opposite is true; alcohols, especially in warm years, can be some of the highest in the world.

And when it came to selection of grape varieties, the wide range of choices presented by thirteen varieties has not proven to be a problem. "At some point, everyone took the easy path," Perrin says about the dominance of Grenache. "It's easier to grow one grape rather than thirteen." He believes too many Châteauneuf-du-Papes rely too heavily on Grenache, a dependence that, in the context of climate change, is becoming a problem. "Harvest here is two weeks earlier than it was twenty years ago," says Perrin. "With Grenache, the sugars are coming in well before phenolic maturity. It's a warm climate problem." Indeed, a hotter climate sends the maturity clocks for sugars and phenolics out of sync. If producers want ripe wines, they must wait longer for the phenolic ripening. But that sends sugars—and therefore alcohols—out of control. The result can be hollow but corpulent wines that sting like a shot of vodka.

Raj remembers when Châteauneuf-du-Pape started to go off the rails. "In 2000," he recalls, "I used to buy a lot of Châteauneuf-du-Pape for myself, for the restaurant, and it was always balanced. But after that, I saw the numbers shoot up. The low end was 14.5 percent alcohol and it was getting up to 16 percent. That's when I stopped buying it." A certain sector of wine drinkers happens to love that bigger style, though. Indeed, the dark, extracted form of Châteauneuf-du-Pape helped skyrocket it to new heights of popularity in the eighties and nineties. Châteauneuf-du-Pape was France's answer to the "big red" Napa and Australia obsession that had gripped a new generation of wine drinkers.

The duality of these two reactions presents problems for winegrowers here. As Jean-Paul Daumen, proprietor of the small, excellent Domaine de la Vieille Julienne, tells us, "It's a difficult situation. A young producer today, if he wants to get a good score, has to produce a wine of 15 to 16 percent alcohol. If he doesn't, he won't get a good score. At the opposite, if you put 15 degrees on the label, sommeliers don't want the wine."

Grenache may be king in Châteauneuf-du-Pape, but its skyrocketing sugars in advance of true ripeness may be pushing it out of the game, remaking the appelation's vineyards. "Everybody is planting Mourvèdre now," Perrin tells us. "It ripens two to three weeks later, almost four where we are located. And you never go higher than 13.2 percent. But the problem is you need old vines." How old, exactly? Well, Daniel Brunier says that his family's winery, Vieux Télégraphe, won't use their Mourvèdre in the main blend because their vines are too young—at thirty-two years. But, no matter how many decades it takes for Mourvèdre to be ready, the eventual change supports Marc Perrin's earlier point that the framers of the AOC provided the tools for Châteauneuf-du-Pape to deal with its climate. To find the best, most balanced Châteauneufs today, the surest path is the one those framers used: look back, rather than forward. The best wines come from classic producers with estates that were carved out from the beginning to best take advantage of Châteauneuf-du-Pape's diversity of grapes and soils.

PARTICULARS OF PLACE

We're down in the sunny south of Châteauneuf-du-Pape, and the wind is blowing. Really blowing—as in, this is no joke, "hope it doesn't sweep our little compact rental off the road" kind of blowing. Despite that it's blasting our hats off and making it hard to hear someone standing just a few feet from us, the famous mistral is a good thing to experience. They say it blows 120 to 150 days a year here, and you can't really imagine it until you're in it.

"It's a small mistral. A good mistral," says Vieux Télégraphe's Daniel Brunier, comfortingly. Brunier runs Vieux Télégraphe, which has been an icon in Châteauneuf-du-Pape since his ancestor founded it in the 1890s. "We like to feel the wind in the wine. The idea is to feel the wind. It's the purity; it's mineral, it's brisk. That's the target here: to feel the wind in the wine."

The wind is one of two features of the terroir here about which the textbook entries on Châteauneuf-du-Pape terroir are often misleading. They mention the mistral, but do not do justice to its impact. A powerful wind blowing so much of the time impacts the grapes enormously, especially in a place where the humidity often hovers only between 20 and 40 percent. It dehydrates them, concentrates them. And it keeps them dry and safe from threats that thrive in moisture. It's such an oxidative force, says Brunier, that it pushes good vignerons to be meticulous with Grenache, a variety prone to oxidation. Poorly handled Grenache often results in jammy, exhausted, caramel-flavored Châteauneuf-du-Pape.

The other distortion put forth by conventional wisdom has to do with the famous *galets roulés*—those iconic heavy, polished stones that mesmerizingly blanket certain sections of vineyard here. The rocks are impressive, to say the least. But their function in the wine is inevitably described as absorbing the sun's heat and radiating back onto the vines at night. That may be true, but there's no lack of heat here to ripen the grapes. The stones' greater function is to protect the soil underneath and to mediate the vine roots' ability to gorge themselves on the clay beneath the stones.

Making Châteauneuf-du-Pape agreeable for viticulture is the presence of clay over the vast limestone basement underlying the vineyards. The clay here is damp for much of the year. Since Châteauneuf-du-Pape lies right next to the river, water is constantly filtering down through its soils to the Rhône from higher lands to the east.

Simply pull up some of the galets roulés, put your hand in the earth, and you'll feel the dampness. The rocks protect these clays through the summer, allowing them to be a water source for the vines despite the punishingly hot, arid climate.

Speaking of soils, those red clays are rich in minerals: iron and magnesium. But they're only part of the equation in Châteauneuf-du-Pape, which boasts a multitude of soils. The terrain can change shockingly over a distance of a few feet. One minute you'll be risking ankle sprains while trundling over galets roulés, and suddenly you'll be padding around in sand, trudging through clay, or blinded by limestone.

The most classic—and easy-to-recognize—wines are singular to one general terroir or to an estate. For example, Rayas is singularly recognizable for its red clay-sand. There are no big stones. The vines are very old. It's a cool, northerly place made even cooler by the bordering forest. Hence an instantly recognizable wine, light in color, but powerful and ripe in the mouth. Vieux Télégraphe is also known for a singular wine from a stony terrace called La Crau, where the rocks run very deep and the wine shows amazing depth and richness but never lacks energy. Château de Beaucastel occupies a unique spot at the farthest northern tip of the appellation, where it points into the mistral like the prow of a ship. It's the windiest, coolest spot in Châteauneuf, and it shows in the balanced, savory, precisely-drawn wines.

What are the different tastes of Châteauneuf-du-Pape on sand, limestone, and clay?

Of course, the tastes are always determined by the varietal blend and altitude and orientation. But if you take Rayas as the quintessential sand of Châteauneuf-du-Pape, but a unique style in its lightness and finesse, you can look at Domaine Charvin as another exponent of sand, also from the northern side of the appellation. The textures of both wines are smooth and elegant, with a fine structure and floral notes, though the Charvin is a more robust, richer style. Clays make the wines quite fleshy and deep, but some clays are found mixed with sand and limestone under the galets roulés, as exemplified in the wines of the northerly Beaucastel and the eastern Vieux Télégraphe. Both have power and flesh, but also great energy and vitality. Finally, the limestone, as found in Vieille Julienne's Les Hauts-Lieux, has that distinct linear edge and spark of limestone as well as angular tannins that tighten into a penetrating finish.

RAJAT'S TOP PRODUCERS

◇ **DOMAINE VIEUX TÉLÉGRAPHE** One of the all-time greats of Châteauneuf-du-Pape and of France—meticulous winemaking and winegrowing from the classic plateau of La Crau. The wines are always powerful, crunchy in youth, but provide a vision back to the ripe yet earthy, savory minerality of classic Châteauneuf-du-Pape. A blend of sites, Télégramme is the entry-level wine, easy to drink in its youth. The single-vineyard La Crau needs some time, but can age for generations.

◇ **CHÂTEAU DE BEAUCASTEL** Another classic, unimpeachable, family-run winery, maybe Châteauneuf-du-Pape's most famous. The northern location defines the wine, which even in hot vintages has incredible acidity and verve. Famous for using all thirteen varieties, what really signifies Beaucastel is the high proportion of Mourvèdre, which gives it its dark, savory, gamy cast. Every wine here is great, from both the Châteauneuf-du-Pape white and red to the rare and resplendent Hommage à Jacques Perrin, produced only in the best years.

◇ **CHÂTEAU RAYAS** At once the heart of Châteauneuf-du-Pape and an outlier, Rayas is a bit of a mystery. Its light-colored and somewhat elegant wines sometimes seem more Burgundian than Southern Rhône, and have caused people to wonder if they're really made of Grenache. They are—they're just evidence of a singular terroir. At their best, the wines are a mesmerizing blend of flavors and aromas, mixing flowers, earth, game, and wild, brambly fruit. If you can't find (or afford) Rayas Châteauneuf-du-Pape, look for its second wine, Pignan, which is also delicious. And, lastly, they produce Côtes du Rhône wines from just outside the Châteauneuf-du-Pape borders, which are well worth seeking out: Pialade and Fonsalette.

ALSACE

The most curious wine region in France is also one of its most beautiful. The beauty is obvious in the mountain-lined valley with its perfect medieval cobblestone villages, vineyard-lined hills, and half-timber homes. The curiousness is apparent upon meeting the people. Ask producers in the region if they feel more French or more Germanic, and almost all will say French. But it's a peculiar sort of French, as most have a Germanic accent and bearing—stiff, precise, tucked in, intellectual.

Alsace has shifted back and forth between France and Germany multiple times in Europe's long history. It was even a front line in World War I, with some of its greatest terroirs seeded with land mines. Alsace is defined by the Rhine, which originates in Switzerland and flows through Germany as one of the world's great wine rivers. And of course, its greatest wine comes from Riesling, a grape of German origin. "We are at the farthest eastern point of France," André Ostertag of Domaine Ostertag notes, "but we are the most western region for Riesling." Perhaps because of this, over the years Alsace (and its customer base) has dealt with its own confusions; as a result, Alsatian wine has somewhat fallen off the map for the latest generation of wine drinkers and sommeliers.

We choose to focus on Riesling here, as it's the greatest grape, but Alsace also notably produces single-variety wines: Gewürztraminer, Pinot Grigio, Pinot Blanc, Muscat, Sylvaner, Auxxerois, and Pinot Noir. With so many varieties, tastings at wineries can quickly get out of hand, making it hard to remember any of the wines. Alsace has also sowed confusion over sweetness through the years. Without a convenient method describing the wines' sweetness levels—Riesling as well as the others—ordering Alsatian wines could be seen as a crapshoot. When a region is capable of making some of the world's driest Riesling (like Trimbach's Clos St-Hune), it can be disappointing, to say the least, to buy a bottle only to find it cloyingly off-dry.

Alsace's wine classification system is also difficult to understand. An evolving Grand Cru system has been in place since 1975, but for years many producers spurned using Grand Crus on the labels. This was because delineating regions is always tough work, and the results—now fifty-one Grand Crus with sizes ranging from 80 hectares (Schlossberg) to 3.2 (Kanzlerberg)—were disputed over factors both political and terroir-related. Consequently, many producers' names, especially those who are brand names for specific wines (Clos St-Hune, for example), were stronger than the names of the vineyards from which they came (Rosacker).

Fortunately, the region seems to be working its way through these problems. More and more domaines are accepting the Grand Cru system and labeling as such, allowing us drinkers to get down to the business of tasting and recognizing the wines. Sweetness levels have been somewhat addressed by some soft EU guidelines, not to mention that most producers have agreed that dry (or dry-tasting) is the way forward, especially for Riesling. As for the confusion between a French or German identity? That one won't get solved any time soon, but nor should it. While this dual identity sometimes may bewilder us, it provides a tension, which, at its best, defines Alsace's wines.

PARTICULARS OF PLACE

As with everything else concerning Alsace, understanding the elements of its terroir is both simple and complicated. Simple is the fact that it's a very narrow strip of vines following the Rhine river on a 75-mile north–south stretch from near Strasbourg to around Mulhouse. Bordering the wine region on the east side is the broad Rhine valley, the river itself that defines the border with Germany, and then Germany's Black Forest mountains. Of more importance is the western border, the Vosges mountains. It's a small range, but significant in that it delineates Alsace's climate. It's the Vosges that leave Alsace in a rain shadow, thanks to the fact that Atlantic weather coming from the west drops its water on the western side of the mountains, unable to pass over the peaks. Amazingly, Colmar, Alsace's wine center, has been France's driest town over the last ten years. This leaves the region with a continental climate, featuring hot summers, cold winters, and large diurnal swings—perfect for Riesling. The wine areas occupy a thin ribbon spreading from the foothills of the Vosges to the edge of the broad valley floor.

Things get much more complex when you talk about soil types, about thirteen in number, which run an impossibly wide gamut that gives Alsace the world's greatest diversity of soil. The Vosges provide the oldest soils, about four or five types—granites (with and without mica), sandstone, slate, schist, and various volcanic products. Besides these igneous and metamorphic rocks, Alsace boasts a number of sedimentary soils, with limestones, marls, and accompanying clays. Over time, the older soils have shed more of their marls and clays, leaving pure rock. Finally, to complete the mix there is a healthy dose of loess and gravel.

It's not only the number of soils that boggles the mind; it's also their arrangement. Olivier Humbrecht of Domaine Zind-Humbrecht spells it out for us one day during an epic conversation at his winery. Like Burgundy, he says, Alsace experienced faulting along the north–south axis. This just means that some buried soil types have been brought up and others lowered, creating vertical stripes of soils. "But in Alsace, the difference from Burgundy," says Olivier, "is that you also have fault lines that run east to west." So now imagine these vertical stripes being shifted in horizontal stripes. Suddenly your neat stripes have become a chessboard in which all the soils are intermixed in three dimensions.

ZIND-HUMBRECHT VINEYARD
Grand Cru Rangen de Thann, Clos St-Urbain

"You don't need to know about all the geology to appreciate the wines," says Olivier, "but traditionally growers would have chosen specific varieties [of soils] to favor a specific situation." If the soils are so muddled that there's no hope of ever being able to generalize about their locations, it would make sense that exposition becomes more important. And, indeed, elevation and aspect play important roles. For instance, it's not hard to distinguish most of Alsace's Grand Cru vineyards from non–Grand Crus. Most look the part, towering over their areas with perfect south- and southeast-facing exposures.

But soils do explain a lot about what grows where, Olivier explains, because almost all the soil types are interesting for wine and only a few are dull. "On the valley floor, the gravelly soil is good, but never will be brilliant; it's just average. You can find bad soils sometimes on the hills. There's loess, not very interesting. The other characteristic that can be bad is the richness of the soil, mostly on the valley floor."

In looking at the good soils, the general dynamic is one between the warmer soils based on granite (and sandstone, schist, and slate) and the cooler limestone marls. Soil can either increase the effects of heat and drought, or decrease them. For example, marl and granite are radically different. "A granite soil will by nature offer much better drainage and be drier and lighter," says Olivier, "thus the temperature travels through the ground much faster and you will see a big divergence of temperature between day and night."

Marl soils are different because they're denser and hold water. Because of this, "the temperature travels much more slowly," Olivier continues "It takes longer for the soil to warm up in spring. Also, every morning, it takes much more heat and sunlight to warm it up from the night before. It also decreases more slowly, in the evenings."

Hence: The granite emphasizes climatic variations and marl soil tempers them. For vines planted in limestone marl, growth of the vine is more directly correlated to the temperature at root level than at leaf level. Therefore, if you plant a vine in a soil that stays colder longer, it's as though you planted it in a much more northerly place that's cooler. Conversely, if you plant it in a very dry soil that warms quickly and drains the water easily, it's like increasing the temperature of the climate. So granite, a dry soil, will allow a vine to grow more quickly, but it will also make the vine burn more acid. Marl limestone is the opposite. Vines grow more slowly but more evenly because the water supply is consistent. Because the soil is colder, the vine will burn less acidity.

Growers must consider all this when choosing their grapes and planting locations. Riesling always has too much acidity and struggles to produce enough sugar during ripening. Gewürztraminer, on the other hand, is always lacking in acidity and produces a surfeit of sugar. To produce dry Gewürztraminer with verve and not too much alcohol, growers plant it in cool limestone marls. To balance the searing acidity of Riesling and encourage it to produce body and flavor, the "hot stones" of granite, sandstone, slate, and volcanic rocks are a good growing medium.

Let's consider a few Grand Cru vineyards. Schlossberg, the first Grand Cru, is a granitic site famous for Riesling. Towering over the town of Kaysersberg like a terraced colossus, Schlossberg's Riesling is inevitably graceful, carved by stone, and poignantly dry. Rangen, a crazy steep face of volcanic rock, produces many things, but its Riesling is one of the world's greatest and most idiosyncratic—with smoky, iron, and exotic fruit flavors like tangerine and pineapple. Hengst, on the other hand, is calcareous marl and known as a stellar Gewürztraminer terroir.

To keep things interesting (or confusing), Alsace doesn't always follow the simple pattern of grape selection that Olivier pointed out. For instance, that famous Clos Ste- Riesling of Trimbach grows in Rosacker, a cool limestone, marl, and clay terroir. The coolness and slowness of the soil is evident in the wine, which, especially in youth, is one of the most famously austere Rieslings on the planet. With screaming acidity and a chiseled, merciless mineral character, it usually takes years of bottle age to reveal much flavor and improves not for decades, but for generations.

Of course, soil is not all. The profound, spiritual biodynamic farmer André Ostertag took us to his prime Grand Cru, Muenchberg, which has red sandstone and volcanic rocks. More of a big, broad hill, Muenchberg is visually less impressive than Schlossberg or Rangen. But Ostertag is sensitive to more than just soil and aspect. He looks for a deeper harmony and sensibility of site.

"Beauty is for me the most important thing when you get a feeling of a place—the beauty and the energy you get," he tells us, standing below the rise of the vineyard as the sun goes down. "If you feel beauty and energy and are full of peace, it's a sign that's a good place for vines. The wine is the result of the place. So if the place has no vibration, if you don't feel it, how can the wine have vibration? Even in a great place, if you don't have the right attitude, you can break the connection."

Whatever the connection is, it's clear that many vignerons—not only Ostertag—feel a spiritual link between themselves and their vines. And who are we to say differently? After all, it is they who spend most of their lives tending row after row of individual plants, head under the sky, feet on the earth. No doubt a life spent doing this work can give rise to spiritual and philosophical bonds to place and plant. If in the past, this connection has been muddled or broken in Alsace, it's clearly being repaired.

OLIVIER HUMBRECHT
Domaine Zind-Humbrecht, Turckheim

How to differentiate dry Alsatian Riesling from dry German and Austrian Riesling?

Compared to the finely etched, medium body of German Mosel dry Riesling, Austrian and Alsatian will be more broad in body, slightly lower in acidity, and have riper, richer flavors. Between Austrian and Alsatian, the difference can be harder to discern, especially if the Austrian is from the Wachau. Both are temperate to cool regions containing warmer, rocky soils. But Alsace is drier and warmer than the Wachau overall, and the wines are likely to be bigger in alcohol and body, with riper flavors of orange, apple, and tropical fruit compared to the herbal, citrus-inflected Austrian wines.

RAJAT'S TOP PRODUCERS

◇ **ZIND-HUMBRECHT** Long a leader in Alsace, Olivier Humbrecht's biodynamically farmed wines reflect the traits of the man. In general, they are large and powerful, but also deep and complex, representing a great deal of thought, nuance, and hard work. Any Zind-Humbrecht Riesling is worth seeking out (as are the non-Riesling wines like Gewürztraminer and Pinot Blanc), from the basic blend to the epic single vineyards from Grand Cru sites like Brand and Rangen.

◇ **ALBERT MANN** Brothers Maurice and Jacky Barthelmé have raised this domaine to be one of the leading producers in Alsace. Over the years, the Rieslings have slowly found their style, which is restrained, poised, mineral, and dry. The entry-level Cuvée Albert Riesling is peppy and bright, while the Grand Crus Steingrubler and Furstentum bring more depth and structure. Don't miss the Pinot Noir—it is Alsace's best.

◇ **ANDRÉ OSTERTAG** Ostertag makes some of the most lyrical, elegant, and tasteful Rieslings in all of Alsace. Also a biodynamic farmer, he never imposes a style, but lets the vineyard dictate it, meaning that his very dry wines are always rich in diversity. His most beautiful Rieslings are from the single vineyards Fronholz, Heissenberg, and Muenchberg.

THANN (LEFT) AND HUNAWIHR (ABOVE)
Alsace

THREE
ITALY

If France is the world's greatest wine country, Italy is the world's most exciting. This is not to say that Italy doesn't also produce great wines. It does—many that easily go toe-to-toe with the best of France. It's only to say that it's fascinating to examine the two wine cultures and the perception of both in the United States. France's grand terroirs are known and well explored, infinitely dissected and discussed. For centuries, France has been secure in its eminence. Italy, on the other hand, is a moving target. It still has mysteries, capacities to surprise and delight, in a way France does not. Italy's wine culture may date back further than France's, but in many ways it's also much newer, just getting restarted in modern times.

The sense of wild creativity and discovery one gets when exploring Italian wine can be credited to history. After all, the Risorgimento, the Italian unification process that brought together all the diverse states of the boot-shaped peninsula, was only ratified in 1871, almost a century after the French revolution. France has its unique regional cultures, but some sense of shared French identity has existed much longer. How might this stable French identity impact the ways terroir is constructed and wine is shaped? The process of identity creation is happening fitfully to this day in Italy, a country whose wine culture, post-Risorgimento, still had to deal with phylloxera and two world wars before even beginning to examine some larger concept of what it means to be Italian.

So, what *does* it mean to be an Italian wine? Nothing . . . and yet a lot. A lot, because a lot of wine is made in Italy. While there are significant swaths of France that don't grow vines, practically the entirety of Italy seems to sport vines in one form or another, ever supplying novel flavors and textures. But "Italian wine" also means nothing because of the impossibility of imposing order on the country's delightful cacophony of disparate regions, languages, grapes (over five hundred different varieties at last count), and stories. In many regions, efforts are well underway to bring some order and organization—always a messy process, but especially so in Italy.

Yet, after all this, somehow almost magically, it often happens that one of us holds a glass of unidentified wine to our noses and sniffs, before declaring with confidence, "Smells Italian!"

How is this even possible, given the crazy clamor of that country? How can it be that a country that can agree on no singular identity for itself finds one in wine? Chalk it up to wine's eternal ability to confound. We bow respectfully to that aspect of wine, and to Italy's unsurpassed ability to channel it. In this chapter, we look at just a few of the regions that we consider classic—meaning, they've achieved enough presence and identity in the global marketplace to command international attention and study—in a country so full of great wine that no book can do it justice.

BAROLO

Tasting—even just smelling—Nebbiolo, the great red grape of Italy's Piedmont, never gets old. It is truly *sui generis*. What other variety can seem so stern, with strict, crunchy tannins and jaw-clenching acidity, yet also seduce with the most alluringly sweet perfume, smelling like something between a cherry and a warm river rock, and, finally, fill the mouth with a liquid at once graceful, juicy, and dry? Very seldom do you find a wine so utterly emblematic of its place and people—ravishing and dramatic like Piedmont's landscape; closed at first, but ultimately supremely friendly; and an amazing match with everything eaten in the place, from agnolotti to truffles. We're fortunate to be living through the greatest period in the existence of Nebbiolo. Never have the wines been better, thanks to a warming climate, stable politics, better economies, and winemaker education. We're on an unprecedented fifteen-year string of good to great vintages (with a couple of slight hiccups). And the wines of yesteryear, the ones that were criticized for needing thirty years to come around? Well, it's been thirty years! And they're drinking wonderfully.

And, to think: Barolo, despite an all-time high in popularity, is still somehow undervalued. How could this be? One answer might be simply because it's Italian. No matter how much we may prefer Italian cuisine and love Italian wine, they are cursed to always appear less polished and sophisticated than things French. This is simply reflective of a bias we have against the simplicity and casualness. Italy is more Mediterranean: warmer, brighter, more easygoing. Classic French food is more complicated, baroque. French wine regions spawned complex classifications. Italy's sheen of simplicity—for which it is beloved—is, ironically, what keeps it second fiddle to French wine. Of course, this is ridiculous. Italian wine is equally complex, and no region more dizzyingly than Barolo.

The other quality that slightly holds back the reputation of Barolo is recency. It's a relatively new wine. Of course it feels old ("King of wines, wine of kings" and all that nonsense), but the fact is that dry red Nebbiolo didn't even exist until the 1830s and 1840s. The wine industry only became close to what we see today starting in the 1970s and 1980s. Just as in France, phylloxera and two world wars set the region back immensely, as did the post-WWII abandonment of rural areas for industrial jobs in the cities. Some rural parts of the Piedmont didn't even have a consistent clean water supply until the 1980s. Furthermore, until this time, few growers bottled their own wines. In the 1950s, only a handful of bottlers existed in Piedmont, and they were mostly négociants (and a few small grower-producers like Bartolo Mascarello). They bought grapes and bottled regional blends. The single-vineyard approach didn't begin until the early 1960s (led by Beppe Colla, then of Prunotto) and didn't become widespread until the 1980s. For people just coming to wine today, the name of Barolo may carry a sense of tradition-soaked profundity, but in many ways the modern industry is the same age as Napa Valley. But, of course, the culture of winemaking goes back much further.

Barolo's fifty-year sprint to modernity was not without its convulsions. Consider that for a century, little progressed in this place, while the world around had moved on. In the seventies, young winemakers in the region found themselves limited by a struggling economy and what they saw as primitive winemaking. The value of tradition in Barolo therefore came under attack in the mid-1980s, leading to an internal conflict commonly referred to nowadays as "The Barolo Wars." For its combatants, at stake in this war was nothing less than the identity of Barolo.

The conflict between the so-called Modernists and Traditionalists isn't so rare a tale. It just played out over ten to fifteen years more stridently and emotionally (and publicly) in Barolo than in many other places. The battleground was the style of wine. Historically, when traditional Barolo was good, it was great—ethereal and perfumed, pale in color yet intense in flavor, mixing elegance and power in a way only matched by Burgundy. But it didn't always get to this place. When it did, it was only after thirty years of bottle age. When it didn't, the wines were thin, acidic, and often bloodcurdlingly tannic. Sometimes you'd wait thirty years to open a bottle, and when you finally did, it was still a cudgel of acid and tannin. In addition, cellars were rustic and dirty, equipment and casks were antiquated, and vineyard management techniques were likewise outmoded.

The young Modernists had been to France and seen a different, more current approach to wine, where instead of blending all the grapes together, vignerons took pride in every single parcel, treating each as precious. The young Barolo winemakers were also aware of the rapidly changing global wine culture, thanks to an uptick in tourism and the burgeoning wine media. So they adopted techniques popular around the world to make darker, more accessible wines that

MARIA TERESA MASCARELLO
Cantina Bartolo Mascarello, Barolo

could be approached earlier. To the dismay of their elders, they concentrated their crops in the vineyard with green harvests, they used rotary fermenters to speed fermentations and extract softer tannins, and they employed the great emblem of the "international style": the small new oak barrel, instead of the traditional giant wooden cask. As was intended, the wines tasted very little like their antecedents. They were dark, extracted, fruity, and oaky. And the media, entranced by such qualities, showered them with praise.

A decade-long standoff ensued until, at long last, tensions began to ease. What allowed the détente? Many things, including the greatest salve: time. But also, the market matured. After more than a decade of sampling internationally styled wines from all over, more and more wine drinkers and sommeliers (who, at that time, were on the rise and generally gravitated toward traditionally styled wines) wanted to taste the purity and identity of Nebbiolo, not only juicy fruit and oak. The Modernists tempered their approach. At the same time, the Traditionalists benefited from new investment made possible by an expanding Italian economy and growing interest in Barolo (no small part of which was due to the press this feud generated). They could replace old and dirty equipment, invest in better cellar hygiene, and afford to drop some fruit. Eventually, the Traditionalists ended up modernizing a bit, and the Modernists took a step back. Today the extremes are no longer so extreme. Instead of radically opposed poles of style, a wide spectrum of techniques coexists, and the wine has never been better. Finally, as Raj likes to point out, when it comes to the only thing that matters—the wine in the bottle—both styles ended up in the same place, anyway. After enough time in bottle it's hard to tell the difference.

PARTICULARS OF PLACE

There's no better guide to the vineyards of Barolo than Luca Currado of Vietti. Not only is Currado an engaging host, with delightfully singsongy Italian-inflected English, but also the winery his family founded in the nineteenth century has perhaps the most extensive and wide-ranging holdings of top vineyards across the region. Vietti produces at least eight different bottlings of Barolo and Barbaresco, but owns land in many, many more vineyards that don't see their name on the label. An eager student of the region his whole life, Currado knows Barolo inside and out. When he was younger, he plied his elders for wisdom. Now that he's (slightly) older, he dispenses it.

It's Thanksgiving, and later Currado and his wife Elena will treat us Americans to a large dinner featuring a golden, roasted *tacchino* (turkey) and, better yet, white truffles, just coming into season. But first, on a cold, foggy, rainy, classically Barolo day, we start with a little geology seminar. Currado explains that, like Burgundy, the Langhe, a hilly area in the Piedmont zone of Italy bounded by the river Tanaro, was a sedimentary basin uplifted by the collision of tectonic plates. Like any ocean floor, over eons sediments were deposited in layers of clay, limestone, and sand. Eventually, as the water receded and the land rose, the hills of Barolo were formed.

When you're there—thanks to the endless twisting roads snaking up and down the slopes—Barolo can feel impossibly tangled and circuitous. However, it actually makes sense. The easiest way to understand it is to envision three parallel ridges running roughly north to south. These extended "tongues" of land (*langhe* is local dialect for "tongue") are divided by two narrow valleys. Vineyards lie on both sides of the valleys with east and west exposures. Furthermore, smaller sub-ridges extend perpendicularly off the tongues, creating southern and northern exposures. So the Langhe is really a kaleidoscope of vineyard exposures, but those facing west and south are warmer sites than the eastern-facing ones. (North-facing sites are rare for Nebbiolo and usually feature Dolcetto.)

The first ridge, on the western side, begins in the north with the village of Verduno. It then runs south to the village of La Morra and concludes with Novello. In between La Morra and Novello, but seated slightly lower in the valley, is the namesake town of Barolo. The entire Barolo zone is bounded on the north and west by the Alps. The western side of this first ridge is directly exposed to the cold winds from the mountains, as are parts of Verduno on the top and Novello on the bottom. So, you can surmise that these villages are cooler sites (especially Verduno) and that their most famous vineyards lie on their eastern slopes, protected from the mountain winds.

The second (middle) ridge is shorter and features Castiglione Falletto on its northern end and Monforte d'Alba to the south. Shorter still, the third and easterly ridge contains the village of Serralunga. The two interior valleys are the most protected areas. Like anywhere, altitude plays an important role. La Morra's vineyards reach the greatest heights (up to 1,800 feet), followed closely by Monforte d'Alba.

Now let's talk briefly about soil. In general, Piedmont being a former ocean floor and sedimentary basin, the soils are mostly variants of clay, limestone-rich marls, and sandstones. There are two things to remember: First, limestone is everywhere, providing structure, acidity, and that magical limestone lift. Second, the force governing the wine's structure involves the dynamic of clay and sand. As we've found in so many places, clay produces more dense, powerful, tannic wines. And sand produces lighter, fruitier wines.

Standing in his little tasting room as the rain pours outside, Currado tells us that Barolo's principal soils formed mainly over two epochs (the older Serravallian and the younger Tortonian). The older epoch's soils define the southeastern, Serralunga side of the region. "This is the first part that elevated from the sea," he says. "And it's why in Serralunga, Castiglione Falletto, and Monforte d'Alba there are very few sandy places. You find much more clay, blue clay, and marl. The sand is very hard and compacted. This is also the reason why we say that in

Serralunga and Castiglione Falletto the Barolos are more powerful, more tannic, more aggressive."

The ridge of La Morra, defining Barolo's western edge, elevated later. Its younger soils explain why, Currado says, the soil is a bit sandier and "the Barolo from La Morra is more elegant, more fruity, and the tannins are more approachable." Yet another small area of different soil exists on the western side of the La Morra ridge, going up to Verduno. It's sandy, he says, "but there's lot of chalk in the soil. In the past there was a quarry there. And the wines are even lighter and more elegant. This same chalky soil appears again in Barbaresco."

In general, the lighter wines are found in Barolo's north, and the heavier toward the south. This is evident, Currado notes, in comparing wines from the extremes: a Barolo from Verduno is notably lighter and more elegant than one from Monforte d'Alba. But he also assures us that he's only painted the big, broad picture. Once you move from the extremes toward the center, differences are a lot less obvious: "In the ground, things are much more complicated and soils a lot more jumbled," he says. "Generalizations always fall down." Soils change dramatically within one vineyard. Elevation and exposure also play huge roles in Piedmont, giving each vineyard a remarkable specificity.

Indeed, Barolo makes the recognized champion of complicated wine regions, Burgundy, seem simple. Burgundy may have more vineyards to memorize, but the logical consistency of its singular slope and climate is easy to grasp. Comparatively, Barolo is a grab bag of soils and exposures. It's very hard to make sense of, and the only comfort is that we are not the only ones who suffer under the strain. The producers of the region do too, even more maddeningly. Spend any time in Barolo, and this becomes apparent, as pretty much every conversation about wine becomes a discussion about the delineation of vineyards. In most regions producers have passionate arguments about classification (which vineyards are better than others). But Barolo isn't even there yet (and run for cover when it does get there). No, right now, basic delineation (the boundaries and names of vineyards) is still an issue in certain villages. Mapping and classifying the vineyards has been done several times over the years—by a producer and civic leader in the 1970s, by Slow Food, by a cartographer, and most recently by wine critic Antonio Galloni—and the results always leave unresolved issues and continuing discussions.

The only way to learn Barolo is just to dive in—preferably during truffle season.

CARLOTTA RINALDI
Cantina Giussepe Rinaldi, Barolo

Barolo

It can be confusing: the name Barolo originates with a village, but also gives its name to the surrounding wine-producing zone and the Nebbiolo wines that come from it. The centerpiece village of Barolo is at the heart of the region, boasting tasting rooms, restaurants, and a stately castle. It's the setting of Cannubi, which some think is Barolo's most iconic vineyard, and also Brunate and Cerequio, other top-drawer vineyards. In general, Barolo wines, especially Cannubi, are said to embody and blend the different traits of the Barolo region's extremes, represented by the famous layering of soils in the vineyards: clay marl over sand. With balance, wines from the commune of Barolo marry the tannic conviction of Serralunga with the perfume and verve of La Morra. And finally, Barolo is home to two of the greatest traditional producers in the whole region: Giuseppe Rinaldi and Bartolo Mascarello. Indeed, it's not a stretch to call them two of the greatest domaines in Italy. So, naturally, we must visit both.

It's stopped raining for long enough that young Carlotta Rinaldi, taking over from her father, the legendary Beppe Rinaldi, agrees to take us out to the Brunate vineyard. This was a mistake, as we soon find our shoes sinking into deep mud. Brunate is a large vineyard and spans both Barolo and La Morra, with the greater extent of it lying in the latter. Brunate wines also offer a helpful lens through which to examine the character of the two villages. Brunate is considered a fairly silky, elegant wine with a slightly lighter color when compared to the generic idea of wines from the commune of Barolo. But those in La Morra see Brunate as a harder, more powerful and dense wine. Carlotta explains that her family has three separate plots in Brunate, and each contributes something different to create a wine her father calls emblematic of the classic, austere style of Barolo, with great structure and much tannin and acidity. But after much aging, its softer, lilting side comes out. And after much washing, the mud comes off our shoes, and we escape to have lunch with Carlotta from a much better vantage point—a restaurant facing the vineyard slope.

We are lucky to get an appointment at the tiny, venerable domaine of Bartolo Mascarello, whose wines are ever too low in production and too high in demand. This most traditional of domaines has been run since 2005 by Bartolo's daughter, Maria Teresa, though she had essentially been the winemaker for years before that. True to her father's famously traditional vision, she's not changed a thing, and her Barolo remains one of the great wines of the world. She makes only one wine, a blend of different (in her case, elite) vineyards, as was the practice before modern times and the obsession with parcellaire wines in the Burgundy style. It's a blend of three vineyards in the Barolo commune—Cannubi, San Lorenzo, and Rué—and one, Rocche, in the commune of La Morra. Each site, she says, is crucial to the blend; she has no interest in making single-vineyard wines. "In a dry year, the sand of Cannubi does not always produce the best Nebbiolo. The best wine, the truest wine of Barolo, comes from the vineyards together." From harvest, her wine is a true blend, an *assemblaggio*, as referred to in Barolo—the grapes from each vineyard are mixed together, added to the fermentation when they are picked. "My father said that the pieces must begin to come together from the first day," Maria Teresa adds. We taste the 2012 and 2013 Barolos—very different years. The former was a classic year, but very dry; the latter much cooler and wet. The differences are stark, but also highlight the inescapable power of clay.

Mascarello's Rué—one of the vineyard components of the blend—contains a big streak of clay, making it often "the most tannic, backward, and late-harvesting vineyard," explains Alan Manley, Maria Teresa's right-hand man. In 2012, Rué got hit by hail, and a large portion of the crop was lost and therefore wasn't in the blend. Thus the 2012 Barolo, lacking a significant clay component, was incredibly delicate and ethereal with a perfume-bottle spray of fragrant raspberry and cherry fruit. In 2013, Rué was back, and, with a cool, wet vintage, made a dark-fruited and much more deeply structured wine. The 2012 is drinking beautifully, but Manley reminds us this is not typical, as Bartolo Mascarello wines are usually not accessible so young.

Castiglione Falletto

Another twisty road takes you to Castiglione Falletto, a village so small it's easy to miss. Perched over one edge of the hillside is Vietti's winery and cellar, from which Luca Currado explains to us the complexity of the soils. "You can find almost every kind of soil of the Barolo region in Castiglione Falletto," he says. "Marl, sand, and sandstone." As such, the wines can have a variety of expressions, but in many ways bring home the diverse talents of the region—somehow weaving grace, heavenly aromatics, and structural depth into one wine. The village of Castiglione Falletto, Vietti's stronghold, is well represented with two of Currado's single-vineyard wines, Villero and Rocche di Castiglione. Rocche is historically important to Vietti because in 1961 it was among the first crop of single-vineyard wines to emerge. "It's incredibly steep," he says, "and the soils are very white." Rocche makes an ideal Barolo—known for its delicacy, finesse, and approachable-in-youth floral aromatics. And, as if by magic, it's also capable of aging for decades, allowing the tannins to soften, the wine to stretch out, and the flavors of bright, fresh cherries to turn to mellow, dried cherries surrounded by hints of earth and leaves.

Vietti produces Villero as a *riserva*, meaning it's only made in years in which Currado finds that the character of the vineyard is expressed clearly. This requires two extra years of aging in barrel, for a total of five years before release. When Villero emerges, however, it's an amazing wine. Currado loves to describe the nose as "balsamic," and indeed a great Villero mixes the sweet, spicy tones of an aged balsamic with floral and licorice notes and dark fruit flavors. All of this is captured in a firm, austere structure that needs upwards of ten or fifteen years to loosen up. But when it does, an inner elegance emerges.

The other universally great site of Castiglione Falletto is Monprivato. While not technically a monopole, it is almost synonymous with the domaine of Giuseppe

Mascarello. With its great southwest exposure and white marly soils, Monprivato makes one of the most balanced, precise, and finely knit of all Barolos. There's power and intensity, but it's not upfront. Just as a Ferrari's massive engine is hidden inside a body of tremendous grace, so do the elegant curves and mineral-tinged red fruits of Monprivato make it easy to overlook its concentration.

La Morra

La Morra is the highest town in the region, and from the winery of Elio Altare this is clear—we have a commanding view over the valley. When we arrive, we are greeted by energetic, frizzy-haired Sylvia, who tells us, proudly, that she officially bought the winery from her father, Elio, a few months before. "So now I am officially the owner, and my dad is the employee!"

Sylvia has bought into a good legacy; her father Elio was a principal and contentious figure in the transitional years that brought Barolo into the contemporary era. In the 1980s and 1990s, he was one of the lead Modernists, though his modernizations were hardly just stylistic. It was also about making cleaner wine. We discuss this as we venture deep into Altare's hillside cellar and look at the library of wines, going back decades. "We don't have any wines from before my grandfather," Altare says, "and just a few from him. When you find a good bottle, it's only thanks to a rare and lucky combination of good cork, a strong vintage, and proper storage. His wine was made in an *interesting* way, let's leave it at that."

We're impressed by the number of bottles saved from her father's era. "My dad took over in 1974, and he was smart. When he started doing these experiments with a different style of winemaking, everyone said, 'Your wines will be dead in five years.' Now, we know it's not true." Indeed, we taste through some vintages of Arborina, one of Altare's signature La Morra vineyards, and the wines have held up magnificently.

Arborina, with its perfume, verve, and bright fruitiness, is emblematic of the way most producers see La Morra. Of all the villages, it has the most area under vine and thus a diversity of exposures and soils, but finesse and perfume are the key takeaways. La Morra's altitude is the highest, at over 1,640 feet, but it also has vineyards at 650 feet, giving it a great disparity in vineyard height. Additionally, it has vines on two sides of the ridge with different soils. The lesser-known vineyards to the west are exposed to cooling of the Alps and are on the light, chalky sand of Verduno. The eastern-facing slopes feature the famous blue marl as well as some of Barolo's most iconic vineyards: Brunate, Cerequio, and Rocche dell'Annunziata. These vineyards produce wines with tannin—"This is Nebbiolo, after all, there will always be tannin!" Sylvia says, noting the grape's inherent quality—but are regarded for their grace as well as strength. The classic tannic structure associated with La Morra is even lighter, and the wines can be approached younger.

SILVIA ALTARE
Elio Altare, La Morra

Monforte d'Alba

Almost equal in size and with a similarly wide range of altitudes, Monforte is La Morra's southern counterpart. Monforte's soils (like Castiglione Falletto, which lies just to the north on the same ridgeline) are a mixture of various types. There is hard sandstone and clay, which produces firm wines with muscular tannins; there's some blue marl with sand, producing wines of some perfume and elegance—and everything in between.

As we found out, Monforte is still much talked about in the entire region, but not in the way most villages would want to be mentioned. Discussions of Monforte are colored by ridicule and dejection over how its producers treated the commune's vineyards in the last governmental delineation in 2010. For this official process, producers in each village were asked to come together to decide on their own vineyard lines. Every commune took the traditional cru divisions and upheld them, unless they made them even more precise. For instance, the producers of Serralunga decided to become more granular and specific, upping the number of specific crus to thirty-nine from the thirty-two listed in a 2000 atlas published by Slow Food. Monforte, however, took the opposite tack, reducing the number of specific vineyards and vastly enlarging the ones they kept. So now, Monforte lists just eleven vineyards, all of giant size, down from twenty-four in the 2000 delineation.

Bussia, Monforte's most important vineyard, is now so big that a common joke about it goes, "It begins in Milan and ends at the seaside." Luca Currado tells us, incredulously, "You cannot tell me that Bussia is the same size as the village of Castiglione Falletto, that an entire appellation is as big as one cru!"

The problem is that the vineyards used to be more specific. Famous and important climats like Dardi and Pianpolvere officially do not exist anymore, swallowed up into the giant mass of Bussia. But also swallowed up was lots of vineyard not before included. Now someone with an inferior vineyard at the bottom of the hill can sell his wine as Bussia, just the same as some with vines in the heart of what was Bussia Soprana, one of the greatest locales. "Bussia, unfortunately, is losing a little bit of its appeal," Currado tells us. This is undeniably true. Everywhere the topic comes up, the mood turns to one of mourning. "Who wins in Bussia?" Currado asks. "Nobody wins. Everybody lost."

Serralunga

The high ridge that defines the commune of Serralunga is one of the most impressive in the Barolo region. You sense it as you pass the stately, traditionally striped buildings of Fontanafredda and take the snaking road up to the top of the hill. The road heads south through the little community of Baudana, with vineyards cascading to the right and left, until you reach the village of Serralunga and its soaring castle.

The wines from this area are as impressive as the scenery. The clay-limestone soils and compact, unyielding sandstones make for wines of phenomenal tannic structure, built for depth, power, and aging. The vineyards that produce some of Barolo's most epic wines extend from the west-facing side of the ridge, where they have southern exposures and are protected from cooling winds by the sheltered valley. Temperatures can be extreme here, leading to Barolos of great strength, with alcohols of 15 percent. However, the temperature is somewhat mitigated by altitude: many of the best vineyards enjoy privileged heights, which moderate to some degree the heat that comes from the south and southwest exposures.

Most famous, of course, is Francia, which becomes Monfortino Riserva and Cascina Francia, two wines from Barolo's most cultish producer, Roberto Conterno (of Giacomo Conterno. Don't be confused by the labels that say Monforte d'Alba; that's where Conterno's winery is). There's so much power in the plots that become Monfortino that the wines get to age seven years in cask before release, by which time they can still age for decades. They are supreme examples of a marriage of power and finesse.

The other great vineyard of Serralunga's southern end is Falletto, which, at its best, shows similar attributes to Francia. The amphitheater-shaped vineyard produces wines of great depth and substance, but also impressive perfume of spice, roses, and warm rocks. The late, Barbaresco-based great Bruno Giacosa (he died in January 2018; the winery had been run by his daughter Bruna for years, though) makes two wines from this vineyard, the white label Falletto, which is approachable at a younger age. Le Rocche del Falletto, a part of Falletto, comprises a few southwest-facing parcels with older vines higher on the slope. This wine, which is sometimes bottled with a white label and sometimes with a red (denoting a reserve-level wine) needs decades to mature, but produces staggeringly complex and seductive wines.

Just north of these two spots is the other most famous Serralunga cru, considered by some to be the greatest vineyard of the region: Vigna Rionda. It was Giacosa's Vigna Rionda, made from purchased fruit, that won the vineyard much acclaim and was in the 1980s and early 1990s one of the most famous Barolos made. Sadly, he lost the contract on the parcel, and Giacosa's last wine was 1993. We visit with Pietro Oddero, a La Morra producer, who is lucky to own a piece of this Serralunga gem. Pietro tells us the vineyard's soil is loaded with minerals like manganese and potassium and has a relatively high content of active limestone, resulting in wines of good structure that can last for decades but still have that characteristic limestone lift. Back at the winery, Pietro treats us to a tasting of Vigna Riondas—1996, 2006, 2007, and the unreleased 2015. Even with its due-south alignment, in a hot year like 2007, Vigna Rionda maintained incredible freshness, along with bright red cherry and pomegranate flavors. "We have learned to handle the hot vintages," Pietro says, "but having soils as you find in Vigna Rionda helps nourish the vines through a tough season."

DOMENICO CLERICO
Monforte d'Alba

NO BE ONE, CANNUBI!

If the wrangling over Bussia in the 2010 delineation has caused ongoing commotion in Barolo over the last many years, a similar cloud has hovered over another—arguably *the most*—celebrated vineyard of the region: Cannubi. And, yes, it all comes down to boundaries. It's a long and complicated story, but we'll try to sketch it out. Cannubi is one 15-hectare (37 acres) sweet spot on a long mostly south-facing hill outside of the town of Barolo. To give an idea of the almost biblical primacy of this place, consider this: the oldest surviving bottle of Langhe wine is labeled not Barolo, not Nebbiolo, but Cannubi 1752. No one disagrees that the center of this hill is Cannubi. At issue is the size. Is there just one Cannubi? Or are a bunch of neighbors also entitled to the name?

Cannubi is surrounded on the same hillside by a bunch of neighboring vineyards with their own identities: Valletta, Muscatel, San Lorenzo, and Boschis. For years, producers making wines from those plots have attached the name Cannubi to them (much as, say, the Montrachet satellites originally did in Puligny): for instance, Sandrone's famous Cannubi Boschis bottling from Sandrone, or Ceretto's Cannubi San Lorenzo. In 2010, at a council meeting, a winery operative of Marchesi di Barolo somehow got passed the right to simply use the name Cannubi for any of these satellites. Barolo's most important vineyard had just swelled to 34 hectares (84 acres) from 15. There was instant opposition from landholders in the original Cannubi (now often ruefully referred to as "Cannubi-Cannubi"), including Maria Teresa Mascarello and Beppe Rinaldi. They won their first appeal in 2012, but that was reversed in 2013. Another appeal to Italy's highest court failed in 2016.

So, Cannubi can be much larger than it originally was. However, that doesn't mean every producer will use the new rules to simply label their wines Cannubi. Sandrone was a member of the group fighting the expansion, and Cannubi Boschis is already an established brand and won't change its name. Maria Teresa Mascarello owns Cannubi-Cannubi (though won't use that term), yet doesn't bottle it on its own, but includes it in her magnificent blend. The point is that the soil underneath the vines hasn't changed. Producers say the terrain is composed of alternating layers of sandy soils and blue marl, where the two dominant soil types of Barolo come together to produce its most emblematic wine. Hopefully, in the future, the owners of Cannubi can do the same.

LUCA CURRADO
Vietti, Castiglione Falleto

Verduno

"When I was a young boy," Fabio Alessandria of G.B. Burlotto recalls, "and I saw the dark clouds of a storm pass by, many times I heard my mother say, 'San Tanaro! Grazie, San Tanaro!'" The Tanaro is the major river of the region, marking the line that separates the Barolo zone from the less-heralded Roero, and it runs straight past the vineyards of Verduno. His mother praised the saintly river because of its influence on the village; it is key to Verduno's microclimate. Its air currents tend to divert hailstorms and other dangerous weather from Verduno's hillside and off toward the (unfortunate) Roero.

The village of Verduno is the least known of all Barolo's villages, but that's changing rapidly, as a new generation of wine drinkers discover its wines, which are the most distinctive of Barolo. Perhaps the village went unnoticed by previous generations because the style produced here is a far cry from the dense, powerful Barolos of Serralunga and Monforte d'Alba. The wines in Verduno are even lighter and lacier than those of La Morra, defined by true grace and finesse as well as a cheerful dash of red fruit—a style that appeals to many sommeliers and younger wine drinkers alike. Flying under the radar is also easy when you produce very little wine. To this day, only three producers of consequence are based in this small town—Burlotto, Castello di Verduno, and Fratelli Alessandria—and all come from different branches of the same family. Of course, light and elegant, hard-to-get red wines are all the rage these days, which explains Verduno's newfound celebrity.

Verduno's greatest vineyard is Monvigliero, which Fabio says is distinctive because of its northern orientation toward the saintly Tanaro river, which we can see flowing by below. The soil in Monvigliero, he says, is a version of the same blue marl of great vineyards far away like Cerequio and Brunate. But it's the river that brings cooling air at night that helps Monvigliero's wines remain nervy, even in hot vintages. When it all comes together, as it does for the three producers listed above, Monvigliero is one of Barolo's most exciting wines, combining racy acidity, incredible perfume of cherries and spice, and a delicate structure that nevertheless keeps the wine upright for decades.

The rest of Verduno is known for lighter, sandier soils that produce more delicate wines, especially the rare Pelaverga, a grape that only flourishes in Verduno. A wine popular with hipsters everywhere, Pelaverga is the quintessential light red. Heavier than a rosé, but more quaffable than any structured red, it's supremely easy and juicy—and affordable, at around $20 a bottle—and it has only added to Verduno's newfound popularity.

Novello

It's very easy to miss this small town just south of Barolo; turn your head to marvel at one of the sweeping views, and you've missed the turnoff. Novello may be small in its number of crus (seven) and its number of producers (not many), but it is home to celebrated vineyard Ravera. Ravera has good altitude and a southern exposure onto the valley of Cuneo that exposes it to the influence of the perpetually snow-covered Alps. The mountain effect is profound; at night, drafts of cold air billow across the expanse. And the first recipient of these winds is Novello.

Known for Vietti's fantastic single-vineyard bottling of it, Ravera is even more closely associated with the late, beloved figure of Elvio Cogno, a chef from Novello who operated a successful restaurant in La Morra. Besides being a talent behind the stove, Cogno also had a great touch in the vineyard and left his partnership in wine (at a brand called Marcarini) at age sixty to start his own thing, teaming up with his young winemaker and future son-in-law, Valter Fissore. Together they purchased Ravera and started the Elvio Cogno wines entirely based on this vineyard site. Since Cogno's death in 2016, Valter and Cogno's daughter Nadia carry the brand forward.

Before Cogno, Ravera was known to winemakers in Barolo, but not beyond. There were no separate bottlings of it; rather, its fruit was used to add energy and acidity to many blends. One reason Ravera flew under the radar was that it could be difficult to ripen fruit there. But, with much riding on its success, Cogno showed that with a deft touch in the vineyard, great wine could be made. Even Luca Currado, after buying his part of Ravera in 1994, didn't make wine there for ten years because he "didn't understand the tannins." Despite its underdog status, Ravera is making a steady climb. As Valter Fissore tells us, "I'm sure this is a very important cru, and

I always show my wines beside other famous crus without fear, because I'm sure of the quality of my wines." Today, Ravera is known for wines of great freshness, crystalline fruit, and electric acidity. In the future, it's poised to ascend even higher to become one of Barolo's truly profound crus.

What are the major differences between Barolo villages?

Barolo soils and exposures create a wide dichotomy, from the lighter, more racy wine of Verduno in the north to the heavier, more tannic and powerful wines of Serralunga in the south. As you get closer to the center of the region, the commune of Barolo, those two styles come ever closer together. At least, this is the simplest version. The more complicated version is . . . there is no answer.

Despite its standing as one of the world's great wines, Barbaresco will ever be saddled with the role of Barolo's little brother. It's much smaller than Barolo, less than half the size. Its production is likewise smaller. And the wines are often a little lighter and, truth be told, more elegant.

RAJAT'S TOP PRODUCERS (BAROLO)

◇ **BARTOLO MASCARELLO (BAROLO)** One of the few estates to uphold the region's tradition of blending great vineyards to produce one wine, Bartolo Mascarello's classic, poignant Barolos never disappoint. Today, the small estate is run exquisitely by the firm but elegant hand of Maria Teresa Mascarello. Nebbiolo offerings are limited to Langhe Nebbiolo and Barolo.

◇ **GIUSEPPE RINALDI (BAROLO)** Like nearby Bartolo Mascarello, Rinaldi makes wines in the traditional blended fashion, and with the same purity and precision. The estate is now in the capable hands of the next generation, Beppe's daughter Carlotta Rinaldi. All the Barolos are fantastic and come in a few signature wines: Brunate, Tre Tine, and Barolo. There's also a Langhe Nebbiolo that's a good indication of Rinaldi's graceful, elegant style.

◇ **VIETTI (CASTIGLIONE FALLETTO)** Under Luca Currado, Vietti continues to be one of the most important of all Barolo domaines. Besides beautifully producing a panoply of the region's most important sites, Vietti remains accessible and outgoing and is a beacon to all those discovering Barolo and Barbaresco. Vietti makes a number of wines, but Currado's regional blend called Perbacco is always ready to drink and a steal at around $25. Of his single crus, he's most known for Castiglione, Rocche di Castiglione, Lazzarito, and Ravera.

◇ **ACCOMASSO (LA MORRA)** An obscure but brilliant traditionalist, Accomasso makes wines that are rare birds indeed, but worth buying if you run across a bottle. The delicacy and detail are always inspiring. In particular, keep your eyes out for the Rocche.

◇ **GIACOMO CONTERNO (MONFORTE D'ALBA)** It's impossible to overstate the importance of this estate and its current owner, Robert Conterno, whose grandfather, in the 1920s, was one of the first to craft Barolo for bottling. His winemaking innovations forever changed the region, and, two generations later, the domaine continues to produce some of the greatest wines in the world. Besides farming expertly, Roberto has only sustained and refined the techniques, continuing to set the standard for the entire region. His greatest wine is Monfortino Riserva (only produced in some vintages), but for half the price or less you can find his wine from the same vineyard, Cascina Francia. And don't sleep on his Barbera—a lesser grape, but delicious nonetheless.

◇ **CAPPELLANO (SERRALUNGA)** Under the great traditionalist Teobaldo Cappellano, this house developed a reputation for purity and grace. Today, under the direction of Teodoro's son Augusto, Cappellano goes on producing the perfumed, heady Barolos from Serralunga it has for decades. Like other traditionalists on this list, the wines speak to a blend of grace and power. Don't miss the delicious Barolo Chinato.

◇ **BURLOTTO (VERDUNO)** The shining star of Verduno, Burlotto is headed by the brilliant Fabio Alessandria, who every year makes some of the most lyrical Barolos of the entire region. His wine from Monvigliero is a benchmark not just for Verduno, but for the whole Barolo zone. And don't miss the Pelaverga.

BARBARESCO

Barbaresco is simply the growing region to the northeast of the city of Alba, while Barolo lies to its southwest. In both regions, the grape is Nebbiolo and the winemaking is generally the same. The salient differences between the two is that Barbaresco is lower in average altitude and lies closer to the river Tanaro, which provides a warming influence. Thus, the harvest in Barbaresco usually starts about a week earlier. Its soils, in many parts, are very white, representing a high degree of chalky marls and sandstone. The greater preponderance of sand may be responsible for the lighter weight of the wines.

"Barbaresco is smaller, like a country town," says Andrea Sottimano, one of Barbaresco's finest producers. "Here you find more small producers than in Barolo, which has many more of the big estates."

BURLOTTO
Verduno

Barbaresco's hills ripple around three towns. Closest to the Tanaro is the namesake town of Barbaresco, which produces a third of the appellation's wines and has in its orbit an embarrassing wealth of the most important vineyards: Asili, Montestefano, Rabajà, Roncaglie, and Rio Sordo. All of these vineyards face south or southwest and have some of the chalkiest marls and silt. The combination of the limestone and the warming of the river give the wines the structure to age for decades, while remaining elegant, such as in Produtorri del Barbaresco's Asili. It's no surprise that this is where Barbaresco winemaking legend Gaja made his name. And this is where we are tasting with Andrea, just three minutes from the heart of Barbaresco town, though his address is in Neive.

"Neive is by far the warmest commune," Andrea says, "it's very low, almost flat in parts." The western side of Neive is known for its blue marls, very hard and dense, resulting in wines that express the clay with a firm structure and great density. Here is the Santo Stefano vineyard (located within the less-famous Albesani cru) made world-famous by the legendary, Neive-based Bruno Giacosa. On the eastern side of the village, the soils are sandy and make lighter, easier-drinking wines.

The third town is Treiso. "Treiso is the coolest," Andrea goes on, "because it's the highest. It's much windier here, too." These factors, as well as a higher content of sand, make Treiso wines the most elegant and fragrant of all Barbaresco. The most famous vineyard of Treiso is without a doubt Pajoré, which, in Andrea's plot at 1,315 feet in altitude, holds sixty-year-old vines that produce a most silky wine, bursting with spice, dried herbs, and dark cherry fruit. Indeed, it's classic Barbaresco.

QUESTION OF TASTE

How can you tell Barbaresco from Barolo?

As discussed, both wines are made from Nebbiolo and from neighboring regions. The differences can be subtle (indeed, some producers claim there are no basic differences), and it can be almost impossible to discern the two if the Barbaresco is made in a heavily extracted style and aged in new oak barrels, as was the fashion for a time. But classically, Barbaresco has a finer structure and more gentle tannins, while Barolo will be the denser, more voluminous wine. As a comparison, try a couple of wines from the same vintage and similar prices, say 2013 Vietti Castiglione (around $40) and Produtorri del Barbaresco's Barbaresco (around $30). You'll find a heavier structure in the Barolo and richer, chewier tannins.

- ◇ **SERAFINO RIVELLA (BARBARESCO)** A tiny but brilliant producer working powerfully calcareous soils in Montestefano to yield buoyantly graceful wines that are nonetheless very firmly structured for long aging. Barbaresco Montestefano is the one to seek.

- ◇ **GAJA (BARBARESCO)** As a brilliant winemaker and tireless emissary, Angelo Gaja is not only important to Barbaresco, but to the Langhe and to all of Italy. His wines and his actions have helped define the region for over forty years. His basic Barbaresco is often approachable and can age, while his cru wines like Sorì Tildin and Sorì San Lorenzo are legendary (and legendarily expensive—several hundred dollars a bottle).

- ◇ **ROAGNA (BARBARBESCO)** Run by the young, fiery Luca Roagna, the domaine's style has remained consistent over generations, prizing purity, structure, and complexity over trendiness. Perhaps his most famous wines are the ethereal Pajè and the stalwart Asili.

- ◇ **PRODUTTORI DEL BARBARESCO (BARBARESCO)** Not a producer, but the cooperative of local grape growers, who bring their wines together and see them guided into wine by the expertise of the great Aldo Vacca. This producer holds up as one of the highest quality co-ops in the world and is always a great value, as even their esteemed crus like Asili, Montestefano, and Rabajà can be found for under $100.

- ◇ **CASCINA ROCCALINI (BARBARESCO)** Paolo Veglio's family grew grapes for generations and sold them to local winemakers before the young man decided to hold onto the fruit and make a go of it himself. We're grateful he did, as he makes beautiful, graceful, aromatic Nebbiolo. Production is small, so look out for either the basic Barbaresco and Riserva or for the Langhe Nebbiolo.

- ◇ **SOTTIMANO (NEIVE)** Andrea Sottimano brilliantly crafts the personas of many important Barbaresco crus to create a nuanced and beautiful image of the region, making some of the most graceful, elegant, soulful wines in the Langhe. He trained in Burgundy and remains inspired by it, making Barbaresco with some Burgundian methods, using some new oak—so it's good to give the wines a few years to absorb the wood. Among his wonderful crus, look for Cottà, Currà, and Pajoré.

TUSCANY

Tuscany, that beautiful land on Italy's western flank, brings together ocean and mountains in a way that's perfect for wine, as well as tourists, artists, chefs, and everyone else who wants to be ravaged by beautiful light, a warm, fresh climate, and bucolic scenery. Tuscany's muse in wine is Sangiovese, one of Italy's great red grapes and one that, perplexingly, has posed problems for many modern sommeliers.

The existence of the SSP (Sommelier Sangiovese Problem) cannot be denied. Sangiovese is the most widely planted grape in Italy, but how often do sommeliers talk about it? How many Sangiovese wines do most sommeliers gush about? Montevertine. Perhaps Soldera. Maybe a great Chianti Classico or two. When it comes to Italian wine, in general we hear more from sommeliers about obscurities like Pelaverga than we do Sangiovese.

At first look, it seems easy to blame the SSP on sommelier snobbery, but that doesn't seem right. The only grape sommeliers are really snobby about is Zinfandel. Maybe we can pin SSP on Tuscany fatigue. After all, by the end of the *Under the Tuscan Sun* era, everyone was burned out on the golden light, olive groves, and picture-perfect hillsides. Or perhaps responsibility for SSP lies at the feet of Italy itself. So long were American's Italian wine habits dominated by Chianti and Barolo that, when the awe-inspiring diversity of Italy—from Aglianico to Zibibbo—was "discovered" in the early 2000s, we turned our backs on the old grapes and embraced the new. That argument seems sound but for the fact that we never turned our backs on Nebbiolo; in fact, we continue to clutch it ever more tightly to our hearts.

No, the answer to the SSP must lie in Sangiovese itself—or, more accurately, with the Italian treatment of it. Many a sommelier has claimed dislike of the grape, but for a rare couple of expressions (Montevertine and Soldera, usually). But if sommeliers love those wines, they can't hate the grape, as both are 100 percent Sangiovese (or close). So what causes SSP? Perhaps it's testament to the possibility that Sangiovese is perhaps one of the world's most finicky grape varieties.

How could so ubiquitous a grape ever be considered finicky? Well, consider how rarely it's successful. Sangiovese wines are often compared to other famously fussy varieties like Pinot Noir and Nebbiolo. Yet that comparison might not be fair to Pinot Noir and Nebbiolo. After all, consider how many diverse places produce good Pinot. And, despite being much more obscure, even California's Nebbiolo has been more successful than its Sangiovese (as seen in Jim Clendenen's Nebbiolos from California's Central Coast). Now think of how many places outside Tuscany are known for world-class Sangiovese. Now, think of how few places even in Tuscany are known for world-class Sangiovese!

In his inspired *Native Wine Grapes of Italy* (2014), Ian d'Agata takes pages to detail the extreme demands of Sangiovese. "There have been, and still are, countless obstacles in the variety's path to stardom," d'Agata writes. "Poorly chosen vineyard sites were the main problem; at other times, selection of less than stellar clones. As Sangiovese does not grow well just anywhere, poor sites have long contributed to limiting the expression of Sangiovese. . . . This led to, among other things, the conviction that it was neither a noble cultivar nor a possible source of world-class wines unless 'helped out' with international varieties such as Merlot and Cabernet Sauvignon."

Why plant Sangiovese in poor sites? Because it's difficult to find great ones. The grape prefers south- and southwest-facing slopes, mainly between 820 and 1,640 feet of elevation, d'Agata notes. The climate can't be too hot or too cold, but large diurnal shifts are preferable, as well as warm summers and falls. A touch of limestone is necessary, and a little clay, but not too much.

Unlike many grapes whose origins can be found in their genomes, Sangiovese's remain elusive. Genetic researchers can't figure out exactly where it comes from—not for lack of trying—and it's been postulated that Sangiovese isn't even a single variety, but a "variety-population." It has the highest number of clones listed in the National Registry of commercially accepted wine grapes, with, as d'Agata notes, "a whopping" 108. And that doesn't even include the other myriad biotypes growing in the wild.

All this is to say, it's understandable sommeliers don't know what to make of Sangiovese, because many producers barely do either. A great many of them simply haven't been focused on producing Sangiovese of the highest quality and expression. This likely has to do with the fact that Tuscany is one of the world's most beautiful places and attracts settlers from all over. Since the 1980s, much like the Napa Valley, it's been flooded with wealthy people—from abroad, or Florence or Rome—who buy land and want to make wine. Their site selections rarely hinged on discovering the greatest Sangiovese terroirs.

"They would make huge initial investments, buying land or vineyards at often astronomical prices, creating hype and spending lots of money on marketing and public relations. The winery would then have to produce results in a hurry and so barely two or three years after its purchase we would see the release of 'marketing oriented' wines. Very dark, concentrated and fleshy, and bearing little relationship with the land where they were theoretically born." That's journalist Carlo Macchi in his 2016 book *Giulio Gambelli: The Man Who Could Listen to Wine* (Slow Food Editore).

The late Gambelli was known as the "maestro of Sangiovese." As a consultant, taster, and wine guru for sixty years, he lent his expertise to such estates as Soldera and Montevertine, helping develop the wines that most spectacularly embodied Sangiovese's greatness. Gambelli knew that when grown in the right place, vinified with care, and matured for long enough in cask, Sangiovese can be one of the world's most distinguished wines.

And he was right: when it all comes together, Sangiovese is undeniably world class. At its most beguiling, it speaks to red fruit. Bright, tart cherry, sometimes black cherry with native notes of high-toned spice—cinnamon, nutmeg—and suggestions of licorice, rocks, and graphite. Like Nebbiolo and Pinot Noir, it doesn't need deep color or extraction to get its point across, evincing great power and concentration while remaining a luminous, translucent red. And it can age so beautifully in the bottle, as well as any Burgundy or Barolo, transforming from bright cherry to intense dark cherry garlanded in notes of underbrush and even more spice. Its acidity remains vibrant, even as the tannins melt away.

The keys to ethereal Sangiovese are intent, effort, and time—and, of course, a great location. When all these factors are present, wines of great purity are possible. This doesn't happen everywhere in Tuscany. Brunello di Montalcino is the only mandated 100 percent Sangiovese wine. The two other famous appellations of Tuscany, Vino Nobile de Montepulciano (see box, page 272) and Chianti Classico, only require 70 and 80 percent, respectively. But even in those region's blends, the most ambitious and beguiling wines will always be the ones with the highest proportion of Sangiovese.

PARTICULARS OF PLACE

While Tuscany's coast has beautiful beaches, sandy soils, and a temperate, Mediterranean-influenced climate that is more famous for growing Bordeaux varieties than Italian ones these days, it's the hilly, bucolic interior of the region where Sangiovese truly makes its home. The painterly skies and luminous glow here conjure daydreams of vacations punctuated by long al fresco lunches and aperitifs at sundown. But that tranquility belies the fact that this is indeed rugged country. The dense forests grow on craggy, rocky soils. The hills and valleys are often steep and relentless—flat ground is hard to find. The climate is more extreme than on the coast, with roasting summers and frigid winters. This is the world Sangiovese lives in—not a gentle, easy one but a hardscrabble existence where enough water and soil nutrients can be hard to come by. The grape has somehow learned to thrive in these conditions and makes good, often great, wines.

In trying to account for Sangiovese wines, in trying to understand the keys to making the great ones, we pay attention to several things. We look for that uniquely Tuscan marl called galestro, which so many claim to be a hallmark of great Tuscan reds. We pay attention to altitude, as the most elegant and aromatic wines seem to come from the cooler high spots. And we inquire into winemaking—are big barrels required to make the purest wines?

In the end, Tuscany often leaves us with more questions than answers. It's a dazzlingly complex landscape with millions of exposures and contours, endless expressions of this hard-to-define grape, all making it difficult to come up with generalizations about the wines. Perhaps a dreamy vacation is the best answer after all.

Montalcino

The stately, hilltop town of Montalcino—or rather, the vineyards that adorn its slopes—is a place where it comes together for Sangiovese in every way d'Agata describes above. It has the well-draining, crumbly soil with a streak of limestone and a dash of clay. It has many microclimates with altitude, warm days and cool nights, warm summers and autumns. There is a reason why Brunello di Montalcino is the only appellation requiring its wine be 100 percent Sangiovese: with great viticulture and classic vinification, Sangiovese here can make one of the most compelling wines on earth.

Following the example of the Biondi Santi family, who reputedly created the first Brunello in the late nineteenth century, producers found a place around the mountaintop village of Montalcino that could produce wines like this. But, as with the rest of Tuscany, Montalcino started to get popular. According to *Brunello di Montalcino: Understanding and Appreciating One of Italy's Greatest Wines* by Kerin O'Keefe, production in the zone increased tenfold from the late sixties to the late seventies, as drinkers discovered the wines. Then in the early eighties the big international companies came in, leveled hillsides, and planted vineyards on land that had only previously grown grain. By the late nineties, there were over 120 producers, up from 13 thirty years prior. Then, in 1997, Brunello producers successfully lobbied the appellation to expand its boundaries even further. You get the idea.

Of course, all this expansion led to a familiar pattern. First comes the crisis, next the medication. By the early 2000s, most Brunello di Montalcino, trying to appeal to some idea of an international taste in wine, looked nothing like the style created by Biondi Santi. In 2008, "Brunellogate" erupted when it was reported that some Brunello producers were under investigation for illegally adding other grape varieties to a wine that, by law, must contain only Sangiovese. We'd love to say the wine world was scandalized by the news, but in fact, observers had been suspecting adulteration for years: so many Brunellos had taken on dark purplish hues, softer and rounder bodies, and lower acidity. The "international style" had been dominant in Italy for some time, but still many wines were pushing credulity of what even new oak and heavy extraction could do to Sangiovese. A few people pled guilty, some vines were torn out, and several hundred thousand gallons of wine were destroyed. But, since then, it's been business as usual.

We know what truly great Sangiovese tastes like. And we know the zone of Montalcino is one of the rare spots that can produce it—but only in certain places, and there's the rub. For all but those willing to do some research (like reading a book on wine), consumers don't exactly know which spots produce good Brunello di Montalcino and which are crap. This very obvious product flaw has led many critics to call for a delineation of zones. As O'Keefe writes, "Brunello remains totally unregulated in terms of where vines can be planted . . . unfathomable given the stature of the wine and the indisputable complexity of both the growing zone and Sangiovese."

We think of Montalcino as a hill, and it is. But in reality it's much more than that: a vast circle of land with around 3,500 hectares (8,575 acres) under vine (up from 80 [200 acres] in 1968). However, the hill is where it all started, and if you're looking for classic expressions of Brunello di Montalcino, that's where you start. Therefore, one morning our little car can be found climbing the curvy road to the top, where we're meeting with producer Riccardo Campinoti of Le Ragnaie (perhaps one of the more difficult Italian names to say: *Lay Ron-YIE-yay*). A young and affable guy, Riccardo operates a little *agriturismo* on the top of a hillside just down from the town of Montalcino. The bucolic property is surrounded by woods and vineyards and has a commanding view of the rest of Tuscany (it's is well worth staying there if you are in the region). Riccardo ushers us out of his old stone headquarters and winery into one of his several vineyards.

As opposed to dark-fruited, oaky, massively extracted, and high-alcohol Brunello, Riccardo makes a classic lovely, gently colored wine that tends toward red fruit and spice, with good acidity and sometimes notable tannins. One of the reasons for his more graceful wines, he explains quite simply, as we stand in his vineyard, is elevation. Reaching up to 2,038 feet, his vineyards are in fact that highest in the zone. While the danger of being so high is not getting ripe, the benefits far outweigh the risks. "The soils are poorer—mostly sandstone with a clay base—and the wind influence is strong. We have a southwest exposure, but it always cools down at night." Riccardo also has a vineyard far down below in Castelnuovo dell'Abate. Just a fifteen-minute drive away, the harvest there is often an incredible six weeks earlier than up here at Le Ragnaie.

We noticed that a number of traditional Brunellos are made here in Montalcino on the upper and middle sections of the hill, classics like Biondi Santi, Salvioni, and Il Marroneto. Some are on the north-facing side and others are on the south, but either way, all seem to be able to pull off this classic style. Classic in no way means "delicate." In a warm year, alcohols will be 15 percent and colors will be a crimson red. But it's all within the framework Sangiovese seems to want to allow, which is never too voluminous and round, and always with a skeleton of fine-boned acidity.

Winemaking naturally plays a role, too. "Here we try to work gently to tame the fruit a little," Riccardo adds. "We try not to get too much power, too much concentration." To that end, his winemaking is quite traditional. He vinifies with native yeasts in concrete tanks and ages in large Slavonian oak casks for three years. This is the pattern we see at Il Maronetto and Salvioni as well—as traditional as can be. Something about the long, slow maturation in a giant wood cask seems important. Smaller barrels encourage more exchange between wine, wood, and oxygen; they speed things along. Sangiovese—at least this classic expression of it—seems to enjoy a slower, plodding development, which keeps its edges tucked in and concentrates its flavors.

Down in the vineyards, we're looking for galestro, the famous soil type of Montalcino (and elsewhere in Tuscany) that's said to be Sangiovese's best friend. Everyone claims they have it, but all offer differing accounts as to what it is. Galestro, along with sandstone (both an iron-rich red and yellow) and alberese, a very hard, compact limestone marl, are the main soil types in Montalcino. The recent Brunello extensions feature clay (out to the northeast) and some parts feature deeper sand. Riccardo says that he and various like-minded producers are eager for geologists and cartographers to come do a thorough soil mapping of Montalcino. But, he adds that it hasn't happened yet, because of resistance from the larger bodies that dominate the *consorzio*. Who wouldn't want accurate soil mapping to help illuminate Montalcino's terroir? Those who already know their soils are poor, of course.

Finally, we appear to find galestro when we visit Jan Hendrik Erbach of Pian dell'Orino. He confidently rips a chunk off the side of a building on his property, proclaiming galestro definitively. It's a crumbly schistous marl, gray in color. Beneath the ground, he says, it's extremely hard, but when exposed to oxygen it becomes friable, able to be cracked without difficulty. Galestro certainly seems to be an ingredient in the most supple form of Brunello; its looser knit allows more oxygen to the roots than clay or dense sandstone do. The ever-present limestone also provides its magical combination of weightless structure. On the contrary, alberese soils are hard and often make hard wines. Likewise, the wines from clay are dense, closed, and unyielding.

Pian dell'Orino, which Jan owns with his wife, Caroline Pobitzer, is a reflection of its owners' fastidiousness. Their viticulture is certified organic but they also use biodynamic principles, and they tailor their approach to fit the soil profile and exposure of each of their four vineyards. Great care is taken, for instance, with specific cover crops—they seek out the precise mix of grasses and flowers each year that will treat the various maladies that may afflict the vineyard. The winery is treated like a holy space. Tanks are arranged in a large circle, light is kept low, and we speak in hushed tones while proceeding around the circle as Jan draws a sample of Brunello from each tank. They handle the fruit and wines gently, and the wines, shimmering like rubies in the half light, reflect that. They are lovely examples of finesse, with complexities and delicacies easily apparent on the expressive bouquets. However, they also hide impressive muscle, with a powerful intensity and significant tannin.

Finally, we descend the Montalcino hill, pass through the village, and head down the southern side to the region of Castelnuovo dell'Abate, which, should zoning ever occur, is considered a likely candidate for its own sub-appellation. Ranging from 650 to 1,475 feet, the altitude in this area is considered ideal by Brunello standards for ripening. The summer heat, which would normally be intense down in this valley due to punishingly hot winds off the Mediterranean, is moderated by the nearby Orcia river and a neighboring ridge. Here we visit another unusual producer, Stella di Campalto, whose wines impressed us at a recent dinner.

Stella's mere existence in Brunello de Montalcino provides an instructive view of wine style here. Having lived in Rome and Milan, she arrived in the 1990s with her two daughters to convert an old, unused family farm into a vineyard and winery. (When she arrived, Stella didn't even drink wine, and still today she drinks only rarely.) The land had not been used since the early 1940s, so it had never seen chemicals and had returned to a state of startling purity, inspiring Stella to continue farming in harmony with nature. The estate, called Podere San Giuseppe, climbs between 985 and 1,310 feet and is now farmed biodynamically.

Originally, she experimented with making a fashionable style of wine, but eventually realized that wasn't the right path. So she explored the range of wines being made in Montalcino at a dinner with friends. "I gathered some of the highest scoring wines from *Wine Spectator* and then some wines from my few friends at the time," she remembers one afternoon at her winery. "Everybody admired the *Wine Spectator* wine. They said: 'Look at the color! Feel the smell! This wine is excellent! And the mouth is incredible!' But at the end of the dinner, that bottle was still full. A wine that everybody loved, they didn't drink. The wines they drank were the less impressive wines. I realized I needed a wine easy to drink and digest. Not a big wine—easygoing, compact, and simple." Her Brunello di Montalcino has achieved this, and is one of the most elegant and mineral versions in the district. Indeed, it's dangerously easy to drink, despite having a great deal of concentration.

As she suggested, in her Brunello and Rosso di Montalcino is that wonderful quality the French call *digestibilité*, which writer and critic Eric Asimov described beautifully in the *New York Times* as "beginning with deliciousness, but it also indicates wines that are easy to drink without weighing heavily in the gut. It's an immediate, unmediated pleasure that nonetheless may be complex and contemplative." Indeed, that quality describes the best wines from Montalcino, made from soils and altitudes that prevent the wines from being too heavy.

Chianti Classico

The heartland of Chianti was first zoned in 1716, making it the oldest wine appellation in Europe. In the fight against counterfeiting in the 1930s, the appellation was to be officially demarcated, but instead, in a move foreshadowing future bureaucratic incompetence, the committee surprisingly and dramatically expanded the appellation of Chianti and created six new subzones. The word "Classico" would have to be officially appended to Chianti to define the true heartland of the wine, around the villages of Radda, Gaiole, Castellina, and Greve.

The identity of Chianti Classico remains in flux. Pre-nineteenth century, wines from this area were likely based on Canaiolo, with Sangiovese in the blend. In 1872, Baron Bettino Ricasoli famously created the modern recipe, basing the wine on the more aromatic Sangiovese, with a number of other blending grapes, including white ones. Almost unbelievably, until 1996, Chianti Classico still required whites to be part of the blend, and 100 percent Sangiovese wines were illegal. (It was in defiance of these rules that the so-called Super Tuscan movement began.) All that changed in 1996, when Chianti Classico was given its own DOCG appellation (no longer a subzone of Chianti), imposing stricter standards of quality. While many producers make 100 percent Sangiovese today, the law requires only 80 percent, with the remaining fifth allowed to come from any combination of an absurd forty-nine other red grapes.

Lacking in Chianti Classico is any delineation based on subzone or terroir. The area already has nine communes, but subzone labeling, though heavily discussed, is not allowed. When asked about it, most local producers wave their hands and claim delineation by terroir is next to impossible. "We are not there yet," says Roberto Stucchi of Badia a Coltibuono, noting the familiar argument that the soils—mainly galestro, alberese (hard limestone), and various forms of sandstone and clay—are so mixed that regional zoning based on soils can't be done. Altitude, says Piero Lanza of Poggerino, is the most salient factor, allowing recognition of zones in blind tastings. The wines of Radda, Gaiole, and (little known) Lamole tend to display

VINO NOBILE DE MONTEPULCIANO

In the minds of Tuscans (and some others), a third appellation rates mention in the same breath with Chianti Classico and Montalcino: the wines from the gorgeous hilltop town of Montepulciano. However, this "noble" wine often gets lost in the shuffle, as a good deal of mass production through the 1970s and 1980s left it lagging behind its neighbors, and the area is still trying to make up the ground. Furthermore, blending rules here are even more lax than in Chianti Classico, requiring only 70 percent of Sangiovese. With vineyards planted on a ridge of high hills in between the Val d'Orcia and the Val di Chiana, which straddles the border between Tuscany and Umbria, soils can run from sandy to rather heavy calcareous clay loaded with marine fossils, allowing a style that theoretically occupies the middle ground between lighter Chianti Classico and more structured Brunello. Density and tannin from clay soils suggest many of the wines need a few years in bottle to soften up. As everywhere in Tuscany, the styles are somewhat split between those who blend and those who concentrate on pure Sangiovese aged in large oak casks. When taking the latter approach, many estates here can reach the same heights of expression as Tuscany's other greats, often at even better prices. For excellent examples of this style, Avignonesi (Montepulciano's most iconic estate), Il Macchione, and Le Casalte are great places to start.

the most elegance and acidity, and all come from higher elevations. Recognition by blind tasting becomes even more difficult based on the blended nature of Chianti Classico. Distinction of terroir would be helpful if the region had a classification for the increasingly popular category of 100 percent Sangiovese.

Alas, an opportunity to create such a category seemed to present itself in 2014 when the consorzio introduced the top-level category of Gran Selezione. How smart would it be to have a 100 percent Sangiovese to showcase Chianti Classico terroir against Montalcino terroir on the same playing field? But instead of creating such a wine, the bureaucrats made another confusing category. A wine designated Gran Selezione is still made from the same 80/20 blend, though it can be 100 percent Sangiovese. It must spend at least six more months in barrel than Chianti Classico Riserva (thirty months versus twenty-four), be from estate-grown fruit, and pass a taste test by committee. The scuttle in Chianti Classico is that the new category was simply created to help wineries move back vintages of unsold Cabernet Sauvignon, Merlot, and other international varieties that are suddenly not fashionable. They can blend them into a prestige wine with extra age and sell it off as something special.

The only hopeful thing about the situation is that the possibility exists, when these international wines are finally depleted, to change the rule to mandate 100 percent Sangiovese wines. The trend here is encouraging. Pure Sangiovese wines continue to proliferate. And more and more producers are speaking of grafting Cabernet Sauvignon and Merlot vineyards to Sangiovese or its traditional blending partners.

The words "elegance" and "perfume" are coming up more and more, as people likewise speak of turning away from small barrels and new oak back to the traditional vessels of mid-size and large wooden casks. Despite the mucking of bureaucrats, the future of Sangiovese seems bright. Giulio Gambelli would be proud.

QUESTIONS OF TASTE

How to distinguish wines from different sectors of Montalcino?

It's not always clear-cut, but wines made from the north-facing slopes and the highest altitudes facing south are more likely to show elevated acidity, high-toned fragrance, and lightness of body. Wines from the slightly lower south-facing slopes of Castelnuovo dell'Abate are softer, with more gentle tannins and a pronounced minerality.

Can you taste regionality or village signature in Chianti Classico?

This is the big debate in the region right now, as it looks to create subzones that may both generate new and more focused interest in the wines and help better define a sprawling area. But are there natural, consistent differences in the way wines from various places taste? Some tasters from older generations insist this used to be the case, but homogenized winemaking styles and clones of Sangiovese make it much more difficult. For us, the only obviously distinctive place was Lamole, sometimes referred to as the "rooftop of of Chianti," thanks to its high altitude. The wines here were uniformly lighter and leaner in body, finer in tannins than most others. Though, of course, there are individual wines from places like Radda and Greve that are also from quite high altitudes.

RAJAT'S TOP PRODUCERS (MONTALCINO)

◇ **LE RAGNAIE** Riccardo Campinoti's wines are elegant and red fruit–driven. Vineyards are spread out across different altitudes, including the highest site in the appellation as well as a few lower sites, to create a multifaceted wine with great complexity. The single-vineyard Fornace (Furnace) is the biggest of his Montalcino offerings, while his basic Brunello always shows lovely grace and balance. And his Rosso di Montalcino is a fantastic drink and can usually be found for under $35.

◇ **PIAN DELL'ORINO** Jan Hendrik Erbach and Caroline Pobitzer focus obsessively on their soil and vine material to achieve a maximum of site expression. Their Brunello is a wonderful example of a new, gentler side of Brunello de Montalcino (which hearkens back to classic, elegant, less ripe styles).

◇ **STELLA DI CAMPALTA** A great example of the marriage of elegance and strength possible from the area of Castelnuovo dell'Abate, which is southern and warmer.

The grapes are grown biodynamically, on basically virgin land, at moderate altitude. Light extractions and gentle winemaking produce lovely, graceful wines in a spot where wine is typically much more opulent and forward.

◇ **SALVIONI** Operating from a tight little building right in the middle of Montalcino, the grapes are farmed from vineyards of galestro soils and southeast exposures at about 1,310 feet of altitude. The winemaking is staunchly traditional, with aging in large Slavonian oak casks. These are wines of incredible perfume—very pure and smooth.

◇ **IL PARADISO DI MANFREDI** This tiny domaine was started in the 1950s by Manfredi Martini, a former employee of Biondi Santi, and continues under the next generation to produce Brunello of great character and purity.

RAJAT'S TOP PRODUCERS (CHIANTI CLASSICO)

◇ **BADIA A COLTIBUONO** Roberto Stucchi is one of the great winegrowers in Italy. The key here is his longtime cultivation of his own plant material, which, coupled with the clay-limestone soils, brings rich and on-point wine. Aged in large casks, the Chianti Classico and Riserva are blends of Sangiovese and native varieties, while the Sangioveto is 100 percent Sangiovese, aged in barrique.

◇ **MONTEVERTINE** Sergio Manetti acquired and planted vineyards on his majestic dome of a hill south of Radda in 1967. Even the first vintage of 1971 showed great promise. With the winemaking guidance of Giulio Gambelli, Manetti devoted Montevertine to the expression of Sangiovese with just minor plantings of Colorino and Canaiolo. In small quantities, these grapes go into the wines labeled Montevertine and Pian del Ciampolo. The colorfully labeled Le Pergole Torte is 100 percent Sangiovese, and one of the world's great wines.

◇ **POGGERINO** Just across the road from Montevertine, Piero Lanza is as much a true vigneron as you'll find in Tuscany, preferring to spend his time in the vineyards and cellar instead of the boardroom. His excellent 100 percent Sangiovese wines fly under the radar, but are some of the purest expressions of the grape in Italy.

◇ **ISOLE E OLENA** The De Marchi family bought and combined these two estates into one in the 1950s. Since his arrival in 1976, Paolo di Marchi has been improving the vineyards and wines, turning this estate near Castellina into one of Chianti Classico's standout properties. The iconic 100 percent Sangiovese bottling is called Cepparello and is aged in barrique.

◇ **CASTELL'IN VILLA** Founded in the late 1960s, this top Chianti Classico estate is still run by the Principessa Coralia Pignatelli della Leonessa. She has never strayed from ultra-traditional winemaking, and her Chianti Classico and Riserva are both 100 percent Sangiovese, as is the single-vineyard Poggio delle Rose.

ETNA

Etna—the mountain and the wine appellation surrounding it—provides a jaw-dropping landscape, one every wine lover should see. Millions of gnarled old vines grow out of avalanches of dark, crumbling lava soils with a massive, commanding peak looming in the background. The theme of Mount Etna is ever destruction and renewal, fueled by a boundless energy residing deep within the earth. The active volcano is always erupting—sometimes spectacularly, with fireworks and rivers of molten rock, and other times with just a distant plume of smoke.

The current cycle of creation and destruction, though, isn't emanating from beneath the surface of the earth but on top of it. With smoke billowing from its top, Etna seems a giant factory, and long ago it was. In the late nineteenth century, it was one of the most vital and productive wine zones in the world, with 50,000 hectares (122,500 acres) of vines planted. Then the standard ravages of modernity hit—phylloxera, war, economic crisis, de-population due to industrialization—and the mountain fell into a deep hole. And there it remained for practically a century until a revival began in the 1990s. This revival is exciting in that it's introducing the world to a beguiling wine from an exotic place, but it's also putting new pressures on this quiet town that had until recently been long slumbering.

No one is more important to Etna wine than Salvo Foti, and no one is more conflicted about this current renewal. A winemaker with deep local roots, Foti has been at the center of the new Etna. He was the oenologist hired in 1988 by a local man, Giuseppe Benanti, when Benanti ambitiously decided he would try to produce quality wine from a place that was only producing dreck. His gambit worked, as Benanti's wine, made by Foti, put Etna on the map. Soon outsiders came calling, and Foti was often the man they would ask for when seeking vineyards, winemaking, or advice. But it wasn't Benanti or Foti who would make Etna into a global wine sensation. It was outsiders—the plutocrat Andrea Franchetti of Tenuta di Trinoro in Tuscany, the famous American wine importer Marco di Grazia, the Belgian Frank Cornelissen and his idiosyncratic but highly sought wines—that brought the press and the attention of the wine world.

Foti has seen things change dramatically in just thirty years. In 1988, only three Etna wine labels existed. Now there are more than 130. Money has flooded in and prices have shot up. "We have two different Etnas," Foti says, as we drive around the perimeter of Mount Etna one evening after looking at some vineyards. "We have the Etna people, the Etna place, the Etna grapes. And then we have all the other people who have come." He laments Etna's culture being swallowed in the tide of outsider interests. Locals can no longer afford to buy land and share in this expanding economy. Traditional—and in his mind, superior—viticultural methods and grape varieties are threatened by imports. But Foti can't turn his back on and recede

SPARKLING ETNA

Nerello Mascalese is often compared to Pinot Noir. Both produce wines of low color, moderate tannin, and good acidity. Both age well. And both have extraordinary site sensitivity. However, Nerello Mascalese also shares another Pinot Noir trait that few people know of: bubbles. The rainy, foggy, cool eastern side of Mount Etna is not only good for white wine, but it's also excellent for sparkling Nerello. The innovator of this style was the enviably named Baron Emanuele Scammacca del Murgo, who discovered it in the 1980s. The grapes are picked just before they'd be considered ripe for red, and then made using the Champagne method. The wines have all the vivacity and structure of great Blanc de Noirs, with hints of red berries and memorable creaminess. Best of all, they deliver outstanding quality at a low price. Murgo's is the best (look for the rosé, too) and can usually be bought at felicitously low price.

from the modern Etna, lest he become another casualty. So, he has to engage the newcomers, has to hope he can preserve things by acting from the inside. At the same time, he has advocated in word and deed—usually alone—for the traditional people and culture of Etna. Foti split from Benanti in 2011, but still consults for many other producers and has recently begun a partnership with wealthy venture capitalist Kevin Harvey of California's Rhys Vineyards.

But it's not all bad news. Indeed, Foti has had some success in getting his message across, as many producers today listen to what he has to say. For instance, he grieved when new big interests steamrolled in like arrogant conquistadors. They leveled hills and destroyed ancient terraces to plant Pinot Noir and Chardonnay instead of native Nerello Mascalese and Nerello Cappuccio. They trained their vineyards on wire trellises instead of in the head-trained, wireless *albarello* style used for centuries. They made flashy, oaky wines. But, it seems, some also have learned. More and more are turning to Nerello, which is perfectly suited to express the volcanic terrain. Many are returning to albarello as the perfect system to allow the grapes to ripen without getting burned by the sun.

And while there's been an explosion of winemaking that's edged out locals, there may soon be a contraction, too, says Antonio Benanti, co-proprietor of Benanti, one of Etna's best wineries. The problem has been a lack of investment in the region: people look at Etna as a cash machine rather than setting down roots there. "There are probably 150 different brands from Etna these days, but on Etna we have not more than fifty or fifty-five cellars," he says. "So, on average, each cellar is making wine for three brands, which are produced by people who don't live here or own land. At some stage either people will properly invest, which would make them more credible or, they will have nowhere to make their wine."

Though the recent wave of carpetbaggers may be fostering resentment on the mountain, the early wave of outsiders like Franchetti, de Grazia, and Alberto Graci must also be seen as being beneficial. After all, they were the ones who prized the old vines. Their critical mass created a true market for Etna wines when before there was none. "They were very good at highlighting and leveraging, marketing-wise, those unique features we always took for granted," Benanti admits. "I'm saying that in the positive way."

Transitions are always tough. Despite the grumbling over who is doing what and how much money they're paying, it's important to remember that there's plenty of room left to grow. After all, remember that a couple of hundred years ago, 50,000 hectares (122,500 acres) of vines completely encircled the massive mountain. Today, only about 1,000 hectares (2,450 acres) are planted, and only in certain places on the north, east, and south faces. Etna's production today is only a small fraction of what it once was. There's still much to do.

PARTICULARS OF PLACE

After a heavy rain one afternoon, we go out into a dark, volcanic vineyard of a producer called Murgo on Etna's eastern flank. The sky is still clouded and misty, and the air is cool. The fear is that our shoes are going to get stuck in the mud, much as they did in Barolo. And we hesitate before taking that first step into the glistening, black vineyard trail. But, our feet don't sink at all, for it isn't even mud. This deep, black volcanic terrain is crystalline ash and is practically dry—the rain just disappeared right through.

This is just one of the mysterious and delightful surprises of a land Jancis Robinson called "the strangest wine country in the world." Everywhere you look, there are mesmerizing lava flows: dark, screaming rocks twisted and contorted into painful postures. Some are black voids, where nothing grows. Yet on others are crowded vineyards full of robust vines, over a century old. Some trails are full of razor-edged black rocks. Other trails are softer, and you can pad along on what feels like a gentle, bouncy bed of moss. And the terraces climb the slopes like staircases until the height becomes too great to fully ripen grapes.

As the terrain here makes a strong visual impression, so it is with taste. This strong-willed volcanic ground speaks through the Nerello. The wines seem to have a smoky, rocky mineral note underneath a vibrant dose of ripe cherries and strawberries. We try a Pinot Noir from the same soils as a Nerello, and it tastes similar to the Nerello; the soil simply overwhelms the variety. Nevertheless, the Nerello pair that create Etna Rosso are the best for the job. Nerello Mascalese, which typically provides at least 90 percent of an Etna Rosso, provides tannin but lacks color. Nerello Cappuccio has color, but almost very little tannin. The light color of so many Etna Rosso wines is due to the prevalence of Mascalese. Cappuccio is planted much more sparsely. It also thrives on the southern face of the volcano, whereas most Etna Rosso comes from the cooler norther face.

Every so often the mountain erupts, issuing rivers of lava. These flows may destroy in moments what it took generations to cultivate. But they also present new opportunities as future soils, though no one ever knows what the magma will bring. Because of an inhospitable mix of minerals and rock, on some flows nothing will grow; it may take eons of weathering and degradation before the first blooms of *ginestra* (broom), the first plant to root and break down the volcanic rock, serving as a bellwether of future soil. However, other lava flows become ready much sooner and can support vineyards after just a few hundred years. Consequently, different lava flows imbue different characteristics to the wine made from them, which explains much of the fascination behind Etna today.

More and more, single-vineyard wines are labeled by the name of their *contrade*. Contrade are simply former names of places, a way of organizing what were sometimes large farms, properties, or communities. Contrade are not delineated by terroir. They often coincide with a certain lava flow, but not always. For instance, Antonio Benanti says in Benanti's wine from the Contrada Rovitello, "The upper part is a 1911 lava flow, but below that is one from 1646." In the context of wine, however, the contrade function like Burgundy's crus. For instance, Andrea Franchetti's Passopisciaro makes five different single-contrada wines: Chiappemacine, Porcaria, Guardiola, Sciaranuova, and Rampante. As in Burgundy, different producers often produce wines for the same contrada. For instance, both Passopisciaro and Terre Nere produce wines from Contrada Guardiola. And, both wines have a high-toned nose of stony red fruit and a tight, austere tannic structure.

Producers are just starting to understand more about the various vineyard soils. For example, with Marco de Grazia we taste 2015 wines from two of his best "Grand Cru" sites (de Grazia uses Burgundian classifications to indicate quality levels in his sites; this is not official as Etna has no classification): Calderara Sottana and San Lorenzo. Both are astonishingly good, yet they have different profiles. Calderara is dark and spicy with floral notes, at once heavy and rich, yet not at all ponderous. On the other hand, San Lorenzo is silkily smooth, effortlessly light on its feet, and bursting with bright red fruit. It was only fairly recently that de Grazia learned that both contrade are composed of a very rare instance of the same sixty-thousand-year-old soil from the collapse of an earlier version of Etna called Ellittico. Only four or five contrade display Ellittico soils at all, and in all but these two it's been mixed with other material. "These are the only two soils on this side of the Etna that are purely from the same geological area, and both are consistently the finest wine we have. So there must be something that links them." There are differences too, he adds. San Lorenzo is a much cooler site. (Girolamo Russo also makes a San Lorenzo, and it has much in common with Terre Nere's, including an almost inexplicable poise and balance.)

As with any terroir, soil is only part of the equation. On Etna, altitude and exposure also play huge roles. The altitude limit of the Etna Rosso appellation is 3,280 feet. Above that, conditions are too cool to ripen Nerello in most years. The aforementioned Guardiola, for instance, runs between 2,625 and 3,280 feet, leaving no doubt as to why its wines are so tightly strung. Another important terroir consideration: the south gets hit with the *sirocco* winds, which originate in the Sahara and bring cold, wet weather in winter and heat in summer. Nerello Cappuccio loves the heat, says Antonio Benanti, which is why it finds a home in the south. The north face is relatively cooler and drier, making viticulture easier. Light abounds. The east side of Etna is only about 5 miles from (and directly facing) the sea. The exposure to the sea means a lot of rain and fog here, which is why this zone is good for white wine and lighter reds, like those you'll find at the producer Murgo, who also makes sparkling wines here (see box, page 276).

The eastern flank of Etna is home to arguably Italy's greatest white wine, Pietra Marina, a lyrical, structured, complex white evocative of the sea and the flowers and fruits that grow on Etna. The grape used is Carricante, which Ian d'Agata calls "potentially one of Italy's greatest cultivars, white or red." When it's produced well, he writes, "It yields wines of great longevity and very intense mineral character." That minerality is often of a memorably salty character, as if the grapes were licked by the sea. Pietra Marina is a name trademarked by Benanti, but the wine was created by Salvo Foti from a vineyard in the town of Milo, and Foti remains obsessed with the grape. Though it's now planted on other parts of the mountain, Carricante originated in Milo, Foti says, and still finds its greatest expression there. "Here there's no Sicily, no Etna, only Milo," he says. "It's cold, foggy, the weather is always bad.

ALBERTO GRACI
Graci, Etna

But when you drink 100 percent Carricante from Milo, it's different. They can age twenty years and still be fresh and young." Felicitously, government regulations agree even with Foti's assessment. For a wine to be labeled Etna Bianco, it must contain 60 percent Carricante grown anywhere in the Etna zone. But Etna Bianco Superiore requires at least 80 percent Carricante and can only come from Milo.

RAJAT'S TOP PRODUCERS

◇ **BENANTI** The producer who sparked the Etna renaissance remains one of its best. The Etna Rosso wines are balanced and pure, with a red-fruit lushness upheld by stiff acidity and polished tannins. The salty, mineral-laden Pietramarina is simply one of Italy's greatest white wines.

◇ **I VIGNIERI** This is the label for Salvo Foti's wines and represents his core convictions about tradition, culture, and Etna identity. A true naturalist, Foti farms with no vineyard additions but copper and sulfur, and winemaking is done by native yeast fermentation without temperature control. The vines that produce his Etna Rosso are mostly very old, some at extremely high altitudes, worked by hand and mule.

◇ **TERRE NERE** Marco di Grazia's stake on the north face of Etna just gets better and better. To its great credit, the basic Etna Rosso is one of the most reliable affordable reds and easily found. The single-contrada wines—especially San Lorenzo and Calderara Sottana—are often extraordinary, with complex, delicious red fruits sharing the stage with earthy and mineral notes. These are great wines of texture.

◇ **GRACI** Alberto Graci is from another part of Sicily, but came to Etna in 2004 to take over family land. He makes lusty Etna Rosso from high on the slopes of the north side, with a big and rich expression of Nerello that is impressive without being overwhelming. His rosé is also delicious. In 2017, he announced a new joint venture on Etna with Barbaresco legend Angelo Gaja.

◇ **PASSOPISCIARO** Famous Tuscan producer Andrea Franchetti was an early believer in Etna and his wines continue to be among the most eloquent voices of the terroirs here, especially his suite of single-contrada bottlings such as Guardiola, Rampante, and Porcaria. But his basic Etna Rosso, called Passorosso, is terrific and not hard to come by.

FOUR

AUSTRIA AND GERMANY

It's always amusing to catalog the differences between Austrians and Germans. In 2010, a book was published in German on this subject called *Streitbare Brüder* (*Quarrelsome Brothers*). Asked about the divisions by talkshow host Conan O'Brien, Academy Award–winning Austrian actor Christoph Waltz compared them to "the difference between a battleship and a waltz," suggesting Germans are brusque, hardheaded, and graceless. O'Brien, in disbelief, said, "There's really not a lot of similarities is what you're saying. I know the Germans . . . there's the cliché that they have no sense of humor. . . ." Waltz: "That's not a cliché."

Indeed, Germany and Austria are neighbors and share many things, including a great deal of history and a language. They also share a grape, a wonderful, magical wine grape—Riesling—whose expressions vary as widely between the two countries as their mentalities.

In contrast to Waltz's characterization of the people, Austrian Riesling is the one that tends toward greater, raw power—famously dry, muscular, powerful wines. No less profound, German Riesling is awash in complexity. Germany vinifies a dizzying number of styles of Riesling, unwilling to let any expression of the grape fall by the wayside. In this way, the Austrian approach seems more simple and practical, while the German more searching and philosophical. Which Riesling is better? A silly question, to be sure, and with only one possible answer: whichever one is in your glass.

AUSTRIA

It's no exaggeration to say that today the chances of getting poorly made wine are lower in Austria than in any other place. This is slightly ironic only in that the nationwide display of winemaking excellence may be a result of one of the most notorious wine scandals of all time. In 1985, German officials discovered that a few Austrian producers had been adding the solvent diethylene glycol, a component of antifreeze, to wines imported to Germany to make them seem sweeter and rounder-bodied. The uproar that followed got Austrian wine banned from export into many countries. But it also stirred all of Austria's producers to reform and hold themselves to higher standards of quality than almost anywhere else.

Since the scandal, Austria has focused on what it does best: bone-dry whites of great structure and minerality. A great white from Austria is a thrilling experience, combining the sensual pleasure of a rich, voluptuous-in-body white wine with a firm spine of electric acidity. Fruits and herbs and flowers and grasses emerge from the glass, while a broad, persistent minerality is interwoven into the wine's very fabric. You can find these characteristics in both of Austria's two great white wines, Riesling and Grüner Veltliner.

Riesling reaches its greatest heights in Austria's most famous white wine regions: Wachau, Kremstal, and Kamptal. While Grüner Veltliner is more widely planted than Riesling in all these regions, it proves itself Riesling's foil in almost every way. Grüner grows in heavier, deeper soils lower on the slope; Riesling grows high on the slopes, basically in sheer rock. Grüner needs a good deal of water, while Riesling is more drought-resistant and hardy. Grüner needs a lot of warmth to ripen, while Riesling can ripen without it. Grüner may be domestically Austria's most popular wine, and it can be excellent, but sadly, it often falls flat these days. The warming climate and Austria's propensity for planting the grape in the warmest sites and least interesting soils has resulted in a preponderance of flabby, overripe, high-alcohol Grüners without structure or acidity. Simply put, Riesling is the superior grape, which is why we've chosen to focus on it in this chapter.

But even Riesling has found itself the subject of a stylistic debate in Austria in recent years. While the dynamic in Germany has involved dry versus fruity, in Austria, it's been the question of how ripe is too ripe. Any observer will have noticed that in the last twenty years, Riesling as well as Grüner Veltliner from many Austrian producers has often become overinflated, its noble traits contorted. We see its crisp, precise fruit turned cloying and overblown, its crystalline structure saggy. The place where this has become most pronounced is the Wachau, Austria's most iconic and influential region. However, in other places, a cleaner, racier style has emerged as a result.

Austria produces wine in about a third of the country, from its eastern borders with Hungary, Slovakia, and the Czech Republic, heading west until the rising Alps make it impossible. The area we focus on, where the best Riesling is grown, is right outside of Vienna. Simply take the A22 headed north and west from the capital city, following the Danube until the gentle rolling hills get bigger and bigger, eventually turning into massive hillsides and low mountains. The Danube remains the binding thread, snaking its way through the increasingly more rugged landscape all the while carving facets out of the rock. As it does so, it exposes some of the world's greatest locations for growing Riesling, high on the rocky terraces of the Wachau and climbing the sides of its various tributaries. The result is Austria's version of what Riesling always seems to offer— amazing wines and amazing landscapes.

The Wachau

One of Riesling's gifts to humanity is that, simply by becoming exponentially better in some places, it inspires people to plant it in the most steep and rugged locales, creating not only outstandingly mineral wines, but also breathtaking visual spectacles. One of these is the Wachau, a narrow, largely east–west strip of the Danube just an hour west of Vienna, stretching 25 miles between the villages of Melk and Krems. Very little flatland exists here on the banks of the river before the valley sides soar upward to form walls of vineyard terraces carved into the pure rock and upheld by thousands of hand-stacked stone walls.

Most of the vineyards are on the north side, facing south. At the base of the valley, the soils are composed of loess, a light, windblown soil, mixed with the weathered particles from other stones to form a fine topsoil. In the Wachau the loess is much shallower and less common than in the Kamptal and Kremstal. But soon the topsoil begins to disappear or is present in such small amounts that most vines on the slopes appear to grow straight out of the rock. And indeed they do: up high is Riesling country. The rocks here are igneous and metamorphic types like gneiss, amphibolite, and granite. The climate is continental with very cold winters and warm summers. Austria is known for the Alps, but here in the northern, lower part of the country, the weather comes more from the Pannonian plain of central Europe, which produces powerful, hot, dry summer winds. But those Pannonian winds directly affect the Kremstal and Kamptal more than the Wachau, which is sheltered by its tight valley.

There can be no question that the loess soils produce wines—usually Grüner Veltliner, but some Riesling—of less structure and depth. Loess wines may display a mineral grain, but it's not the firm, insistent kind that comes from rock. Producers tell us that the various rock/forms—gneiss and granite, mostly—don't produce individual flavors but promote acidity, firm structure, and minerally texture.

The reasons why ripeness has escalated here is a common topic of conversation. The warming climate no doubt plays a role, allowing ripeness levels previously unachievable. But of even greater significance has been the will of the producers. It all started in the mid-1980s with the creation of several wine categories for Wachau wines, based on potential alcohol. Initially, the Steinfeder category was introduced, a category for wines under 11.5 percent. Then Federspiel, for wines between 11.5 and 12.5 percent. And, finally, Smaragd, for wines 12.5 percent and over. These categories were to help consumers make quick choices based on wine style.

Emmerich Knoll, producer and head of the Wachau winegrowers association, acknowledges that these categories have had a complicated impact, but defends them. "Pretty often we get the comments that this is an old-fashioned system, that one should concentrate more on vineyards and origins. I don't entirely agree," he says. Of course, place of origin is crucial, he agrees, but "before the modern area and the wine scandal, origin didn't mean anything to people. The growing area is so small, with its 1,500 hectares (3,675 acres) and eight villages, that it's not so easy to communicate its speciality, as the output is small. My antecedents said we need a tool that focuses on the Wachau with its special working circumstances, with the terraces that take three to four times the labor. And we need a tool that has marketing power for every producer."

Steinfeder is for everyday drinking wines. One step up is Federspiel, itself a lighter, more refreshing, less powerful style than Smaragd, the most powerful wine, good for long aging. Any single vineyard, no matter how great, may produce any of the categories. "The problem is that consumers misunderstand them as quality," Knoll continues, "not just as weight class. Definition by sugar ripeness makes people think higher sugar is better." Indeed, further complicating things is that Smaragd wines tend to come from the best sites, as these are the vineyards capable of making stronger wines. And they fetch the highest prices and earn the highest scores from critics. So, the implication that Smaragd is the best quality, and not just a style category, is inescapable.

Confusion in the minds of consumers is understandable, but apparently producers have also fallen into the same trap. The bigger scores and prices of Smaragd wines led to an escalation of the wine style, which just got heavier and heavier. It became a Wachau trope to harvest later and later, using even botrytis-infected grapes and fermenting them dry, giving the wines a sweet, honeyed flavor and even higher alcohol levels, reaching 14 or 15 percent. The results may be impressively intense and even complex, but they come at the expense of freshness, energy, and balance.

When we visit the Wachau, the claim is that ripeness levels are being dialed back, but we didn't see that in many of the wines, which is why we were drawn to Peter Veyder-Malberg, whose Veyder-Malberg wines have developed quite a following over the past couple of years. Peter is not from an old family in the region, such as Hirtzberger or Knoll, and is thus somewhat an upstart in his willingness to challenge the status quo. He has opted out of the Smaragd system, as has his neighbor Martin Mutenthaler, and chooses to label his wines without any designation of category.

"My philosophy is different from the traditional producers who were born here," the measured, intellectual winemaker tells us one night over dinner at his modern house, high on a hillside. "What I tell you is just my thoughts from my nine years here. I came to Wachau because my idea was to make different wines, because I couldn't drink those heavy wines from the recent years that got such high scores. I thought it must be possible to produce a style that's original to the area. For some reason it worked. But it's not about high sugars, I think. It's more about ripeness, and ripeness is achieved much earlier than what the numbers of Smaragd, Federspiel, and Steinfeder tell you."

Ripeness comes less easily where Peter is based: the Spitzer Graben, a narrow, cool valley that branches off from the Danube, tracing an ascending path to the high, forested plateau above. "When I came to Wachau in 2008, producers said, 'Forget the Spitzer Graben because the fruit never gets ripe,'" Peter says. "But in my opinion sugar doesn't define ripeness. And because I like high acidity, I concentrated in this area." That was then. Peter now has vineyards all over the Wachau, and he's showing that his precise, lean, edgily mineral style can still be made anywhere—even in Grüner Veltliner.

Veyder-Malberg may have opted out, but many in the Wachau who use the categories still produce wonderfully energetic, balanced wines more middle-of-the-road in style, like Prager, Alzinger, and Knoll. And don't forget that Federspiel does not mean lower quality, but simply a lighter weight.

LEO ALZINGER
Weingut Alzinger, Wachau

Kremstal and Kamptal

The Kremstal and Kamptal used to be considered one region, so it seems fair to talk about them together. Indeed, no easily identifiable geographical border between them exists. Together they form a little pocket, bordered by high hills on the western and northern sides, the Danube to the south, and a broad, flat plain to the east. This flat expanse connects the region(s) to the vast Pannonian Steppe of eastern Europe, a broad terrain of rangeland, marshes, and dunes that covers parts of Slovakia, Serbia, Hungary, Romania, and Bulgaria as well. The winds emanating from the steppe bring strong doses of continental climate and can mean blasting heat in the summer and frigid gales in the winter.

In the last 100,000 years, squalls from the steppe have deposited a massive pile of fine, windblown sediment, sometimes 30 feet or higher, onto the Kremstal and Kamptal, often mixed with material weathered from the local rocks. This is loess, and it's a dominant soil in both regions. Loess is mainly the medium for Grüner Veltliner, but can produce tasty Riesling. Yet it's not a soil that provides any interest or imprint to the wines. Loess can yield tight, acidic, and somewhat mineral wines. But, especially in a warming climate (as loess is a warm soil), it also appears easy for growers to lose their grip on the vines' ripening curves, resulting in lots of wine from loess that simply loses its structure, falling apart into a mess of low acid and high alcohol, with overripe Riesling flavors.

This is why the Kremstal's best Riesling spots are more Wachau-like. These include the rocky outcrops just west of the town of Krems in the hamlet of Stein, and its two elite vineyards Pfaffenberg and Steiner Hund. Both technically reside in the Kremstal but are really a continuation of the Wachau gneiss and granite (the regional border is political, not geographical) and make Rieslings that have the classic Wachau spine. Knoll's zesty, stony Pfaffenberg is a great example of that vineyard, while the famous Steiner Hund vineyard is beautifully interpreted in the deep, savory Rieslings of Nikolaihof and Stagård.

Kremstal's other significant zone is in the steep, rocky valley that accompanies the Krems river's path into the Danube, cutting through the same primary rock that forms the Wachau. The great wines of this little valley start in the town of Senftenberg and end where it emerges at the town of Krems. Nigl is by far the most famous estate here. The sheer faces of gneiss that comprise Nigl's Höchacker, Pellingen, and Piri vineyards produce, in Martin Nigl's talented hands, some of the most mineral and precise Rieslings of Austria. Due to its narrow confines, this valley collects the cool air pouring from the forests above and avoids the heat brought by the Pannonian winds, making for cooler temperatures than in surrounding regions and thus incredibly racy, acid-driven wines.

The Kamptal is basically the northern continuation of the Kremstal terrain, taking its name from the river Kamp, which flows through the village of Langenlois, the center of Kamptal winemaking. On our visit, we learn the two features that most set the Kamptal apart from the Kremstal: the singular, epic vineyard of Heiligenstein, and the Kamptal's winemaking culture. No doubt, great wines are made in the Kremstal, but wines of the Kamptal have an edgier, more electric buzz, driven perhaps not so much by terroir, but by intent.

Asked whether this fiery style comes more from the soil or the people, young winemaker Alwin Jurtschitsch answers, "I think it comes more from the winemakers' attitude, because the times of the big, fat stuff is over. We have the chance here to really go razor sharp, crystal clear. And this is something which started some years ago, actually." Indeed, the original stars of Kamptal winemaking—Bründlmayer, Loimer, and Hirsch—are still going strong, having set the tone decades ago with intense, lean, piercing wines that take Austria's predilection for dryness seriously. But that mantle is now in the hands of a group of fiery young winemakers, including Jurtschitsch and Lorenz Haas of Weingut Allram, who confidently want to take Kamptal wines to even more thrillingly electric extremes.

How to distinguish the Wachau, Kamptal, and Kremstal Rieslings?

At their best, the Wachau wines still bring together a generous fleshiness with rock-hard acidity and structure. Structurally, this plays out on the tongue as layers of ripe fruit and green vegetables wrapped around a stony pillar. Most Kremstal wines, grown more on loess, typically lack the Wachau's muscle and breadth. There are exceptions (Nigl's and Stagard's wines, wines from areas of Pfaffenberg, and Steiner Hund), as the best of them can show an even grainier minerality than the Wachau's on a leaner body. Kamptal wines can be indistinguishable from the Kremstal, but the best of them have adopted a racy, very edgy style that is sleeker than anything from the Wachau, except for perhaps the sharpest wines of the Spitzer Graben. The heavier style of the Wachau is notable for its huge extract, muscle, and the somewhat honeyed and earthy flavors supplied by botrytis.

ALWIN AND STEFANIE JURTSCHITSCH
Kamptal

◇ **ALZINGER** Classy and smooth, Leo Alzinger's wines are also as zingy as the name suggests. They have incredible energy and force, but also great restraint. His Hollerin and Loibenberg, especially, layer citrus and herbal notes atop a stony core.

◇ **KNOLL** A leader and standout producer, Emmerich Knoll works masterfully in many styles depending on the needs of the vineyard, from rich and full-bodied to airy and mineral. But mostly, Knoll is known for command of the rich, powerful style, crafting majestically full wines out of sites like Schutt and Pfaffenberg, while still keeping them firm and structured.

◇ **VEYDER-MALBERG** The brilliant rebel Peter Veyder-Malberg is not afraid to follow his own taste, no matter what challenges that incurs, and the result is some of Austria's greatest wines. His style is more restrained and acid-driven than any other Wachau wine. The result is crystalline Rieslings like Bruck and Buschenberg that marry power with an ethereal lightness.

◇ **MARTIN MUTHENTHALER** Hard-driving and determined, Martin may be the Thierry Allemand of the Spitzer Graben. And his wines have the same powerful personality too: brusque, structured, and mouth-filling, but always delicious and satisfying.

RAJAT'S TOP PRODUCERS (KREMSTAL)

◇ **NIGL** Soft-spoken and reserved, Martin Nigl lets his wines do the talking. Eloquent, balanced, complex, and poised, these are always benchmark Rieslings that deftly meld citrus, floral, and herbal notes with a persistent stoniness. Dornleiten, Höchacker, and Goldberg are great wines to start with.

◇ **STAGÅRD** Stagård's brash, insistent, and intense wines are helping to remind other Kremstal producers what is possible in this region. The wines are full-bodied, but don't seem heavy, as the acids are beautifully woven into the larger structures.

◇ **SALOMON UNDHOF** So good for so long, it's easy to overlook Salomon Undhof, whose deeply mineral and transparent wines are some of the country's most profound. Elegant and refined are words that come to mind. These wines dazzle with their quiet, staid solidity.

ALOIS KRACHER

It's impossible to talk about Austrian wine without bringing up the name of the late winemaker Alois Kracher, one of the world's greatest makers of sweet wines. Today, the Kracher name is upheld by his son Gerhard, who runs the winery with the same panache and soul as his father. Like all sweet wines, Kracher's come from a unique climate.

More exposed to the extremes of the Pannonian climate than the Wachau is the region of the Burgenland, in far southeastern Austria at the border with Hungary. Here stretches the vast Lake Neusiedl, an incredibly long but absurdly shallow body of water (only about 5 feet deep), which moderates the region's temperature and often casts it in a dense fog—perfect for the growth of botrytis, aka noble rot.

Kracher turns the cultivation of botrytis into an art form, bringing its vineyards of obscure grapes like Welschriesling, Zweigelt, Muskat Ottonel, and Scheurebe to degrees of sweetness rarely achieved anywhere else. For each vintage, the sweet wines are numbered, starting at one and reaching as high in some years as twelve or fifteen. The numbers indicate only an ascending level of concentration, as the wines can be different blends of grapes. Always balanced by extreme acidity, the sweetness doesn't so much flavor the wine as embody it, with essences, depending on the individual cuvée, of candied fruit, citrus, apricot, and spice. Kracher's wines are hardly cloying, but are instead shockingly powerful in their delivery of sugar. But don't be deceived by their balance and drink too much—it could set off a sugar rush that's hard to come down from.

RAJAT'S TOP PRODUCERS (KAMPTAL)

◇ **HIRSCH** Perhaps the most consistently elite producer of the Kamptal, if not all of Austria, Johannes Hirsch makes wines of crystalline precision and complexity that nevertheless have the same charm and friendliness of the man himself. The wines' piercing edge may startle the tongue at first, but then it relaxes into the comfort of deep, rounded fruit and floral notes. Gaisberg and Heiligenstein are the most famous vineyards.

◇ **JURTSCHITSCH** Alwin Jurtschitsch is the best young producer in Austria. In a tasting, Jurtschitsch's wines blew us away. His Rieslings from Loiserberg and Heiligenstein are penetrating, lasting, and intense. Thrilling in their edge and precision, they vibrate on the tongue and sides of the mouth. The Heiligenstein Riesling is a showstopper, but we have to call out the brilliant Grüner Veltliners at this estate, too.

◇ **BRÜNDLMAYER** A Kamptal legend, Willi Bründlmayer's wines are better today than ever. They harness the power and energy of the Kamptal terroirs, yet manage to contain it in a beautifully restrained, elegant way. His Heiligenstein and Steinmassel are benchmarks.

JOHANNES HIRSCH
of Weingut Hirsch at the Heiligenstein

HEILIGENSTEIN

VINEYARD FOCUS

"Heiligenstein is probably the most unique soil for Riesling in Austria," says Andreas Wickhoff MW of Weingut Bründlmayer, an estate lucky enough to be the major owner of the great vineyard. The singularity is apparent in both soil and situation, as Heiligenstein towers over the Kamptal from its northern location, reaching up to 1,150 feet. From the top terraces, it's easy to gaze out over the entire Kamptal and Kremstal valleys to the Danube. It doesn't take much to imagine the hot Pannonian winds blasting in during the summer and the long rays of setting sun ripening the Riesling until the last moments of the day. Without any moderating effects of the Danube or any other mountain range, this place captures the Kamptal's exposure to all the features of its climate, and Heiligenstein is the most prominent recipient.

Heiligenstein's massive face of 37 hectares (91 acres) sits on steeply terraced slopes of primary rock. However, the primary rock here is a bit different than much of that in the Wachau. Its gneiss and granite are even more eroded, leaving a face of deeply metamorphosed sandstones, very hard and layered with bands of fossilized plants and volcanic rhyolite. Why this produces a distinctive wine with volumes of spice and brilliantly warm citrus notes is anyone's guess.

The major exposure of Heiligenstein is south-southwest, but it wraps around the edge of the hillside to face somewhat east at the commune of Kammern and to face west near the town of Zöbing. The western side is cooler, more sheltered from those hot summer winds, while the eastern side is more exposed to them, creating a warmer zone.

From its 10 hectares (25 acres) right in the heart of the hill, Bründlmayer produces three Heiligenstein Rieslings—a standard one, an old vine cuvée, and one called Lyra, which is from a set of vines in a unique Lyre trellising system. Splitting the vines' canopy into two V-shaped planes to increase sun exposure and airflow, the Lyre system was intended to make a wine showing more fruit and early approachability, and this is apparent in the tasting—it's a fuller, more intense version of the standard Heiligenstein bottling, with brighter citrus notes. The system is also very expensive to install and keep up. And while Lyra is slightly different, it's not necessarily better: the Alte Reben ("old vines") is itself stunning in its depth and purity, all from vines grown on standard trellis.

With the great Johannes Hirsch, we taste a selection of vintages of his excellent parcels in the Heiligenstein vineyard against the same vintages of the vineyard's almost-as-famous neighbor, Gaisberg. In each vintage, the Gaisberg was excellent, but is rounder and fleshier than Heiligenstein, which is more muscular, lean, and taut. What comes across most about Heiligenstein in these wines, as well as in excellent bottlings by Jurtschitsch and Birgit Eichinger, are the high tones of spice and a profound citrus brightness—not lemon or lime or orange, but all of them twisted together in a cable of citric intensity. Heiligenstein is Kamptal Riesling at its zenith.

GERMANY

The appreciation of Riesling's particular magic simply requires a comprehension of scale. Riesling's versatility and outrageous expressiveness expand over different orders of magnitude than other grape. It's like when a football field is used to show the brevity of human existence compared to the history of the earth. The entire 100-yard field represents earth's history, while the appearance of humans occurs a mere half inch from one end zone. Well, consider the ripening window of most grapes to be the brief blip of human existence; they must be picked at a certain time to make great wine. Riesling? It's the whole field. No other grape can be picked anywhere on that entire massive span while still making epic wine and expressing its terroir.

This great range, this talent for versatility, conveys awesome potential but also confusion. If good wine can be in any style—from sparkling to ice wine, and bone-dry to syrupy sweet—how to know which kind to make? This is something Germans and lovers of German wines have grappled with over the years—and, in particular, the question of sweet or dry. Actually, the word "sweet" confuses things, because of Germany's mastery of intentionally sweet after-dinner wines. Off-dry wines meant for the table (referred to by the familiar terms Kabinett, Spätlese, and Auslese) are referred to as "fruity," as in the question "Fruity style versus dry style: which is the truest form of German Riesling?"

This is a question that's plagued many of us for years: what is the original style of German Riesling? What did the earliest practitioners of Riesling intend for it before modernity and technology entered the picture and altered everything? It's a compelling question because the past informs the present. As silly as the word "fruity" might sound, it's not reflective of wine quality. The most profound, balanced, mineral German Rieslings of the twentieth century were in the so-called fruity style. Until a decade ago, no one used the term "fruity style" when talking about German Riesling; we just called it German Riesling. But today the style of German Riesling is on the move: after dwelling in the realm of the fruity for as long as anyone alive can remember, it's now on a determined march toward dryness. Given the change now occurring, it seems reasonable to inquire what is traditional. After all, we all need to know where we came from.

Fortunately, author John Winthrop Haeger deeply researched this very question in his 2016 book *Riesling Rediscovered* and came to some convincing conclusions. The answer to the question what is traditional, is, of course, not so simple. "By the end of the nineteenth century, and probably earlier," Haeger writes, "the dominant Riesling style—albeit one among several—was an occasionally dry but typically off-dry wine, fermented until the fermentation stopped naturally." This makes sense. Without the technological ability to stop a fermentation (temperature-controlled tanks, sterile filtration), a wine would either ferment until dry or leave a little residual sugar because yeasts stopped working thanks to a high alcohol content and a cold enough outside temperature. Haeger's conclusion is that German table wine (wine never intended to be sweet) was either dry or "dryish" (which we take to mean "mostly dry").

This changed in the twentieth century, when, Haeger says, table wine that "had been generally dryish until the beginning of the twentieth century, turned noticeably sweet after World War I and became sweeter still during the 1960s and 1970s . . . Judging from the lack of surviving evidence, the change happened rather quietly, and even at best it is poorly understood." Haeger offers a few theories to explain why. One is that the Western world developed a greater taste for sugar during the twentieth century as it became cheaper and more available. The collective sweet tooth was further stoked in wartime generations who experienced severe sugar rationing during both world wars. Thus, market demand for sweeter styles drove German producers to continue sweetening them. A common theme in several of the theories is simply that a global market wanted to drink sweet wines, and Germany now had the ability to easily make them. This led to a surge of cheap and popular sweet Riesling exports, most famously the insipidly sweet jug wine Blue Nun.

And it was precisely the overwhelming success of wines like Blue Nun and the reputation they gave to German wine (which still exists today) that spurred serious German producers in the 1970s to begin countering the sweetness trend with a series of measures to bring back dry wines. The *Trockenwelle*—"dry wave"—we are experiencing now is the direct result of their efforts. However, Haeger says, many producers always preferred the drier style and were guilty of selling sweet while drinking dry themselves.

The greatest vehicle in the move to dry wines has been the creation and promotion of *Grosses Gewächs* vineyards ("Great Growths"). Abbreviated simply as GG (specifying the vineyard, or the wine that's made from it), these are the equivalent of Burgundy's Grand Crus, the top wines from the top sites. But to earn GG status, the wine from a GG-rated vineyard must be technically dry (a numerical threshold calculated by the Germans from a wine's sugar and acid content) as opposed to just *tasting* dry. (Off-dry wines from GG sites are labeled *Grosse Lage*.) Over the last thirty years, the classification of German wine was rigorous, employing the historical record, geologic and climate analysis, and taste to designate certain vineyards GG or not. GGs can now be found all over the German wine country. Paragons of dryness, power, and minerality, GG Rieslings are now Germany's most celebrated and serious wines. And while other, off-dry styles of the twentieth century (Kabinett, Spätlese, etc.) are still made and can still be beautiful, GGs get most of the attention.

The path from sweet to very dry has not been without its stumbles. In their rush to return to dry wines, many producers forgot why sweetness was ever left in wines to begin with: to balance Riesling's incredible acidity. The first several years of widespread dryness brought wines that were often undrinkably austere and acidic.

Over time, German producers learned how to deal with that acidity. They've also learned that their regions and terroir have something to say. Dry wines are more natural fits in warmer places like the Rheingau, Baden, and Pfalz. In the cool Mosel, having a little more residual sugar to balance the elevated acidity makes sense.

But the Trockenwelle has more than anything been a celebration and showcase for the brilliance of German winegrowing today. As famed producer Johannes Leitz tells us, "To make a dry Riesling is much more difficult than a sweet one. Much more. I always call dry wine 'naked.' Sugar provides a very nice cover to mask flaws and deficiencies in a wine."

Leitz is only in middle age, but he's been at this a long time, taking over his family's small winery when he was only approaching his twentieth year. Since then, his progress has been remarkable, growing the small estate from 3 hectares (8 acres) to over 40 (100 acres) today and cementing it as one of the great domaines of Germany. He remembers a different climate, a change in which has also propelled the shift toward dryness. "When I was a child, the grapes would only start to ripen in the first week of October," Leitz recalls. "And the bad weather for sure was coming in November. So you had three weeks to pick all your grapes, meaning they were all of the same quality and mostly not very good. Look to decades of German wine—forties through eighties. You had two good vintages in ten years."

Today's climate tells a different story. "Now, grapes are ripe in the middle of September, and like with a tuner, you can decide what you want to do with them," Leitz says. "Pick them earlier for something lighter with high acidity, in the middle for something of mid-weight. And later for something full-bodied and rich."

We're in a new era for German wine. And, as recent years suggest, it is likely a golden era, much like in Italy's Piedmont. The sun is shining on German Riesling, and the winemakers are turning the beautifully ripe fruit it provides into ever more brilliant wines.

PARTICULARS OF PLACE

The German wine regions we cover here— Mosel, Saar, Ruwer, Rheingau, Nahe, and Rheinhessen—are all very near each other, an interconnecting tangle of rivers and valleys that begins just thirty minutes west of Frankfurt in far west Germany. The regions lie on the northernmost limit for ripening Riesling, and many of the vineyards are collected around river valleys that provide airflow, sun-catching hillsides, and moderate temperatures. Each river—be it a monumental waterway like the Rhine or a smaller tributary like the Ruwer—is a unique body with its own identity.

A note on slate, the predominant soil of German Riesling. Slate is derived from shale and neither are as defined by their composition as by their form. As geologist Alex Maltman writes in the publication *The World of Fine Wine*, shale "can be of any chemical/ mineral composition. The weathered rock that started it all could have been anything . . . clay minerals could be rich in potassium, say, or calcium, manganese, zinc . . . " though "most shales are dominated by aluminum-bearing clay minerals and consequently, without much carbonate around, yield soils that are quite acid." Slate is simply shale that pressure and heat have metamorphosed into a harder substance with a tendency to break into planar sheets. Furthermore, Maltman advises, "There is no defined boundary between shale and slate. This is why reports on a particular vineyard area might seem a bit confused if the slates have only reached an early stage of development." We take this to mean, don't get bogged down arguing about whether a vineyard is composed of highly developed shale or young slate.

German producers talk of various forms of slate in their vineyards—red and blue mostly—each imbuing wines with different qualities. Blue is often spoken of as making the most precise, savory, mineral-driven wines with citric flavors. Red slate also gives mineral impressions, but is said to offer warmer flavors of fruit and spice. The iconic soil of the Mosel is blue slate (though there are pockets of other slates and soils), and the Rheingau's is quartzite (a metamorphosed sandstone).

The different colors are due to very small amounts of trace substances (red usually indicates iron), which Maltman says are unlikely to influence flavor in the wines. Nevertheless, winemakers attest to variance among wines from different-colored

JOHANNES LEITZ
Weingut Leitz, Rudesheim

slates. Why might this be? Haeger cites research that suggests the red wavelengths of light reflected by red slate may be a key. "Reddish surface soils," he writes, "tend to correlate with faster sugar accumulation—helpful in cooler climates but not in warmer spots—and with increased content of anthocyanins in grape skins." Perhaps it's this impact of slate colors on ripening that produces the differences in taste that winemakers note; this isn't something that would have been tested by a geologist.

Mosel

Germany's most famous wine region is renowned for a reason. A great majority of the country's outstanding wineries and sites reside here, producing Riesling of remarkable precision, verve, and longevity. Mosel's exceedingly narrow river valley creates the iconic image of Riesling grown on steep, terraced slopes carved from the almost vertical face of the rock.

This geography reaches its pinnacle in the Lower Mosel (to the north, near its intersection with the Rhine), which is why producers there are pushing wine lovers to embrace the more evocative name Mosel Terrassen. We are more than happy to oblige. The producers here are heroic, as a drive up to the top of the Uhlen vineyard with young Matthias Knebel attests. Matthias, the owner and vigneron of Weingut Knebel, based in Winningen, takes us up in his Jeep, parking as casually as one would outside a grocery store. In this case, however, he's unflinchingly placing the front wheels just a few feet from a stone ledge overlooking a vertiginous free fall to the river over 650 feet below. Some parts of this vineyard reach a slope of 86 degrees, and to even approach the edge, with crumbly, slippery slate beneath your feet, feels like placing your life in immediate danger. We can't imagine what it must be like to prune vines here, let alone harvest grapes. The difficulty of this work is the region's greatest challenge.

"In the town of Winningen, we have about 80 hectares (200 acres) in total," Matthias says. "One hundred years ago, we had 120 hectares (300 acres). But that was the golden age of Mosel Riesling, and you can imagine especially in this area here the need for hired labor is big." It's big because the only way to work these slopes is by hand. "I don't even own a tractor," he says. "This is and will be a much bigger problem in the future because nobody is willing to spend the money that we would need to work all these vineyards."

So the next time you purchase a bottle of Knebel Riesling, be grateful it's not twice the price. Incidentally, Knebel's wines—and those of the Mosel Terrassen in general—have all the fineness associated with the general Mosel typicity, but even a more precise, etched structure and a greater verve thanks to the altitude and absence of topsoil, as the vines grow in pure rock. And while the immediate fortunes of the Mosel Terrassen may sound dire due to labor shortages, encouraging signs also exist. Matthias tells us he has a number of friends roughly his age—late twenties to mid-thirties—and all are attacking the problem (and their family vineyards) with gusto. We see this in action upriver in Bremm, where youngsters Kilian and Angelina Franzen are not only tending some of the world's steepest slopes in the famed Calmont vineyard, but they are also actively replanting it. There is hope yet for the survival of these steep terraces.

The vineyards of the Middle Mosel are also remarkable, if not quite as steep. If there is a Rodeo Drive of Riesling, this is it. As the river loops and traipses in a beautifully carefree path full of 320-degree "oxbow" turns, it exposes its mosaic of red and blue slate to a variety of expositions. The wine characteristics vary, but the fame of these villages is a constant.

The Middle Mosel starts in the area of the bustling industry town Traben-Trarbach, where we visit with Alexandra Künstler of the amazing new(ish) producer Weiser-Künstler. She and her husband, Konstantin Weiser, make wines in dry and off-dry styles that show a remarkable balance and integration of acidity and body. They are not quite as warmly ripe as wines from the towns farther up the river, but they have remarkable energy.

Next up is the famous town of Erden and its warm, red-slate wines from the Treppchen and Prälat vineyards on a shelf overlooking the river. Ürzig follows with its famous "spice garden" vineyard Würzgarten, all tropical fruit and aromatic spices. The villages of Zeltingen, Wehlen, and Graach face their shared slope, which holds vineyards Himmelreich, Sonnenuhr, and Domprobst. If you love Riesling, this is hallowed ground, as the producers that work these slopes are some of the biggest names in German wine: J.J. Prüm, Willi Schaefer, and Dr. Loosen. Bernkastel, Brauneberg, and Piesport all follow as we continue upstream.

The iconic wines of the Middle Mosel have different modulations based on producer and style. What is true about most of them, though, is that many still adhere, at least in most of their wines, to the "traditional" fruity style of the twentieth century. In general, this style is considered to be very natural for the Mosel, since it's colder than the Rheingau and needs to balance its elevated acidities with a bit more residual sugar. Altogether, though, these are wines noted for their balance and poise, but also generosity and verve. They are not austere, but rather robust, richly fruited wines that vibrate in the oscillations between electric acidity and the suggestion of sweetness.

The Mosel is considered the coolest of the major Riesling regions in Germany. But its coolest areas are the rivers no longer included in the label: the Saar and the Ruwer.

MATTHIAS KNEBEL
Weingut Knebel, Mosel

Saar and Ruwer

Tributaries of the Mosel (which itself, remember, is a tributary of the Rhine), the smaller rivers of the Saar and Ruwer are famous for being home to Germany's greatest non-Mosel producers. But they also have a good claim on their own style—or at least the Saar does. The Ruwer is almost too small to have a lot of personality, beyond its excellent winery Maximin Grünhaus.

Besides the wine, one of the greatest things about the thousand-year-old estate of Maximin Grünhaus is its proprietor Carl von Schubert, one of the true gentlemen of wine. Let's hope his son, who will soon be taking over, is as thoughtful, congenial, and generous. Those are enormous shoes to fill. When comparing the Ruwer to the Mosel, von Schubert says the difference is "a question of body. The Ruwer has a lighter body." The estate comprises two epic vineyards, Abtsberg and Herrenberg, consecutive hills of blue slate and red slate, respectively. These two vineyards, which every sommelier should know, are epic showcases for Riesling's abilities, as von Schubert wrings every conceivable style out of them—from very sweet and rich, to delicately balanced off-dry, to the bone-dry power of a GG. The differences are also the classic blue-slate/red-slate divide (no joke intended). "Abtsberg shows typical blue slate traits: fine structured, hard and focused minerality, which makes the wines need more time to open up. Herrenberg's mostly red slate soils make for a warmer, more accessible wine with hints of spice."

The Saar has a little more to say about terroir, as it is even cooler than the Mosel and the Ruwer. This is due to the fact that it's more of a wide-open valley, says Florian Lauer of Weingut Peter Lauer, one of the best producers of the region (and, indeed, all of Germany). "Soil is not the main influence here in the Saar," he says. While the soil is important, "our terroir is the microclimate. The Saar valley is much more open, with more cool winds that blow through the valley." The little river Saar, he notes, is important as a temperature regulator. It keeps things warmer in cold times, and more moderate in hot times. The vineyards closest to the river most often are good for dry wine because they get riper more consistently. Vineyards farther from the river make for better sweet wine, because they don't achieve such levels every year. Lauer also considers position on the hill very important, as soil erosion creates deeper, denser soils down below, giving a richer, more heavy texture to the wines. Lauer's range of wines studies these effects by fermenting separately grapes from all different exposures, altitudes, and soils. The attention to subtle details of terrain is impressive. Even more impressive is that all have the brilliant, racy, dry style that perfectly captures the windblown Saar.

Lauer would be the most well-known Saar producer if it weren't for Egon Müller. Perhaps Germany's most famous producer, Müller farms the Scharzhofberg vineyard, just a short walk from his house. As if proving Florian Lauer's point, the Scharzhofberg stands alone, far from the river, and thus gets blasted by cool air all year long. This is one reason why Müller's wines remain in the sweet style—getting the maturity levels that support total dryness is almost impossible here. But the off-dry and sweet wines from this house are some of the most powerful, poised, and expensive in Germany (fetching over $200 a bottle). Powerhouses that can age for generations, the wines deserve the fame they bring and can be considered truly emblematic of the Saar, the flip side to Lauer's brilliant dry evocations of this impressive valley.

Rheingau

After the Mosel, the Rheingau is Germany's other heavy-hitter. That's not because of size, as its vineyards cover less than half the geography of the Mosel, but because of reputation. In past centuries, Germany's standing was made largely on the strength of the Rheingau and its large, famous estates like the Kloster Eberbach and Schloss Johannisberg. At the turn of the twentieth century, Rheingau Riesling prices outstripped those of many classified Bordeaux. However, in the twentieth century, many things went astray for Germany, but especially for the Rheingau.

Johannes "Josi" Leitz tells us this as we rumble in his tanklike Mercedes SUV through what he defines as the Lower Rheingau. Here, long terraces of vineyards climb the steep mountain of Rüdesheim, looking precipitously down at the Rhine. In prior generations, Josi informs, these big parcels were many thousands of small, drywall terraced vineyards—a mosaic of tiny plots. During the 1930s, in an effort toward some kind of efficiency, the stone walls were bulldozed in favor of much larger, singular plots. "I think our terroir is amazingly good in Rüdesheim," he says, "but they castrated it. So we maybe only have half of what it used to be."

We can only imagine what it must have been like, then, as what Leitz and his neighbors have now is spectacular. This is the heart of the Rheingau, truly one of the great stretches of vineyards in the world. You feel the power of the landscape as you enter this area, for the Rhine takes a big left turn and starts an east–west run that exposes its towering right bank, unfettered, to the sun. This raises daytime temperatures, while the nights remain windy and cool from the river, resulting in wines with both great ripeness and fruit expression as well as vivacious acidity.

The Lower Rheingau, where the Rheingau's most renowned wines are produced, covers the bend in the river from Rüdesheim to Assmannshausen, which bookend the famous mountain where the steep slopes deliver the Rheingau's most iconic wines. The soils here are primarily red slate with some quartzite and sandstone, which provide these wines—some of the most renowned Rheingau vineyards of Rottberg, Berg Roseneck, and Kaisersteinfels—with their luscious warmth and steely backbone. The Middle and Upper Rheingau continue upstream from here, taking in the villages of Geisenheim (home of the famous oenology university),

Johannisberg, Hattenheim, Erbach, and Eltville. In the Middle and Upper Rheingau, the slope is less shallow and the soils are a little deeper, giving a richer style of wine. As the terrain flattens out into deeper loams and clays, the soil has fewer stones and more moisture, and thus the wines don't appear as mineral (though they can be very racy). This is in stark contrast to the steep-sloped Lower Rheingau and its slate and quartz.

The Rheingau is capable of wines of great power and ripeness, but Leitz, for one, is taking advantage of the new climate and market for dry wines to simply go as dry as possible. "I see the future for Riesling as very light and crisp and dry and precise. There was a decade where I really tried to make bigger, richer wines like you find in Austria. Today we could produce these much easier. But why would we want to, when we can make incredible Rheingau Riesling?"

Nahe

The Nahe river runs north to intersect the Rhine at the town of Bingen, defining the borders of three regions. West of the Nahe is the Nahe region; east of it begins the Rheinhessen. And across the Rhein from both is the Rheingau. The Nahe is a small but important river, as the quality of its terroirs and the skill of its producers have in recent decades brought a previously obscure region into the bright light of fashion.

As with all of these rivers, it seems, we can divide Nahe wines into three regions: Upper, Middle, and Lower, following the direction of the river. We are particularly interested in the Middle and Lower, as they have the greatest concentration of small, artisanal producers who are making incredibly vibrant wines. The character of the wines in these two regions is quite different, making for an interesting comparison. In general, the Nahe is often seen as a place where the style of Riesling transitions between the Mosel and the Rheingau, offering a little of the slate-driven minerality and nervy acidity of the Mosel, but incorporating the generous, ripe fruit and a little body of the Rheingau.

The Lower Nahe includes the areas near the intersection with the Rhine, with vineyards outside of the towns of Dorsheim and Münster. Wines here share some of the power and force of the Rheingau wines, with more muscular bodies and mouth-filling capaciousness. This is apparent in both producers we go to see here, who produce wines emblematic of the region and almost perfect in their own regard.

First, we step into the tasting room of the incredible Caroline Diel (Schlossgut Diel), a winemaker who has since 2006 effortlessly filled the shoes of her famous father Armin, a writer, winemaker, and pioneer for this region. Diel possesses encyclopedic knowledge of her sites, especially the three magical GGs her family owns: Goldloch, Pittermännchen, and Burgberg. The three vineyards are side by side on a massive and steep hillside. "The climate is the same, but the differences in soil are big," says Caroline. "And when you compare the differences, you can see and taste them, but the variable of microclimate has been removed."

All three offer a facet of the Lower Nahe style. Goldlach is stony, with barely any topsoil covering the bedrock. It always produces the most powerful, compact, and fruit-driven Rieslings, full-bodied and straight, with astonishing energy. Pittermänchen has softer textured soils of loam mixed with gravel, quartzite, and weathered gray slate. It's an immensely charming wine, offering delightfully mineral details up front and then gushing with a viscous texture to an ebullient finish. Burgberg is almost the opposite. Intensely mineral and salty in its finish, it offers a drier, more intellectual, and restrained approach, representative of its soil's high concentration of quartzite. Caroline is kind enough to share three vintages with us (2008, 2012, 2015); the wines' most impressive features were their consistency of expression. We give much credit for this to Diel's skillful approach. "It's a major aim of mine not to make them too powerful or overwhelming," she says, "as I want to harness their power to give body to the wines, but refine it enough to always keep the elegance and buoyancy."

Confirming the Lower Nahe's brilliance are the wines of Kruger-Rumpf, now led by the talented young phenom Georg Rumpf. If we were to characterize Rumpf's wines, it's for their ability to maintain balance at high levels of intensity and concentration. Working top sites in his hometown of Münster such as Pittersberg, Dautenpflänzer, and Kapellenberg, Rumpf issues a variety of levels of sweetness in a number of soils. But, as the standout GG Scharlachberg shows, his greatest showcase is in dry wines, where he perfectly captures the potential of the Lower Nahe: exciting wines that deftly offset intensity and grace, using acidity as the balancing rod.

The Middle Nahe boasts an incredible diversity of soils. "What you can say is that the Nahe is a mixture of the Rheingau and the Mosel," says Cornelius Dönnhoff, the young man taking over for his father, Helmut, whose decades of outstanding wines at Weingut Dönnhoff helped establish the Nahe as a force in German Riesling. "So we have similarly cool nights as the Mosel and, during the day, we have warmer temperatures like the Rheingau that the Mosel doesn't have. Therefore, we have the possibility to have high-class dry wines, and, because of this, also high-class off-dry wines." This dynamic gives these wines their elegance and lilting juxtaposition of fine-grained minerality with pure, crystal-clear fruit expression. The cooler climate marks these wines with raciness and grace, but it's the soils that impart the complexity.

On the short ride from the winery in the most iconic of Middle Nahe vineyards, Hermannshöle, Dönnhoff mentions that here "there's an incredible diversity of soils in a very small area—from slate to limestone to volcanic soils, quartzite, and loam. So we can find everything. It's very unusual for Germany." Hermannshöhle, a GG

CAROLINE DIEL
Schlossgut Diel, Nahe

vineyard, is composed of slate with some volcanic soil mixed in; it can pull off both dry and sweet styles with a saline tang. "In Hermannshöhle, the acidity often tastes salty," he says. "I don't know why, and I don't care, to be honest. Even when the free-run juice comes in, you can always tell it's Hermannshöhle because the acidity structure just tastes different from the other vineyards."

The other vineyards each have distinctive personalities, too. Leistenberg is pure slate and produces fruity, graceful wines, perfect for the off-dry Kabinett style of lightweight, zingy, drinkable wines. Felsenberg is pure volcanic stone, keeping the heat from the day and radiating it at night. The warmer microclimate makes for slightly lower acidity—perfect for dry wines. But, as always in the Middle Nahe, look for elegance, even in the powerful GGs.

The Upper Nahe, around the town of Monzingen, is very stony with narrow river valleys and moderately steep slopes, which produce vibrant fruity wines that remind of stone fruits and white flowers. Emrich-Schönleber is the standout producer. And while the wines may seem unusually fruity and quaffable in their youths, they age brilliantly, with the minerality becoming more assertive with age as the wines become savory and complex.

Rheinhessen

After all the steep slate slopes and the towering terraces over tight river valleys, visiting the region producing some of Germany's most exciting Rieslings is a bit of a shock. The Rheinhessen, home to more vineyard land than any other region, is largely flat. Well, flat in comparison to the Mosel, but really it's a giant swath of low, rolling hills. Even more shocking is that the soils in much of the Rheinhessen are deep clay loam with ample water. Consequently, it makes heaps of fruity, rather uninteresting wine. But there are a couple of exceptions.

The first is in the area just twenty minutes northwest of the famous town of Worms. It seems unlikely that this area of featureless, low rolling hills could possibly be home to three of Germany's hottest winemakers—Klaus-Peter Keller, Philipp Wittmann, and Jochen Dreissigacker—but it's true. The secret here? Limestone. In this part of the Rheinhessen, underneath this rich clay loam is a great bed of limestone. "So much of the Rheinhessen's flatland is on loamy soil, giving only fruit-driven wines, but not length or texture," says Wittmann. "Our vineyard sites here are heavily influenced by the limestone, and this gives the personality." It's also warmer here than the Rheingau and Mosel to the north, making ripening fruit less of a problem. Consequently, these three winemakers produce almost exclusively dry wines. That's a function of the microclimate here, Wittmann explains. "I don't produce Kabinett or Spätlese wines anymore for two reasons," he says. "First, we get ripe fruit every year. Second, to make Kabinett we would have to pick too early and the grapes would be too green. And to make Spätlese we'd have to pick too late. Dry is the perfect style."

And indeed, the wines of all three of these guys are electric. The rich, clay soils provide incredible muscle and body to the wines, while the limestone bedrock charges them with thrilling acidity. The flavors can change among vineyards owing to the particular nature of each soil (stony, iron-rich, smooth), but the body and electricity are always there. In a country ever more obsessed with heady dry wines, this is a place that pulls them off most dramatically.

QUESTION OF TASTE

How to distinguish the different regions of German Riesling?

Riesling expresses itself differently in different regions, though it's not always easy to tell. Sweet and dry are no longer enough to make a call, since more and more wines are dry. But, if it's off-dry, you might consider thinking of the cooler regions first: Mosel, Nahe, Saar. First, get a bearing on the wine's weight: is it relatively lighter and more delicate, or does it seem to have more power? A wine with finer minerality and a tendency toward citrus fruits is typical of the Mosel or its tributaries. More structure, body, and girth could take you to the Rheingau. If it's very powerful and dry, it may be from the Rheinhessen.

JOCHEN DREISSIGACKER
Weingut Dreissigacker, Rheinhessen

◇ **JJ PRÜM (MOSEL)** Another legendary producer in a country full of them, Prüm's wines are in some ways the antithesis of Müller's. While concentrated and potent in their own way, these Rieslings are comparatively light and lacy—more about nuance than power. Though lighter in stature, the wines can age for decades, especially the standouts of Wehlener Sonnenuhr and Graacher Himmelreich, which develop capivating notes of quince, pear, and honey over time.

◇ **KNEBEL (MOSEL)** From the vertiginous heights of the Mosel Terrassen, Matthias Knebel is growing incredibly compelling Rieslings that are ripe and mouthwatering, with green apple and limelike acidity. His single vineyards from sites like Uhlen and Röttgen are majestic and well priced at $40 to $50, but you can't beat the quality for the price of his basic Riesling, which can often be found under $20.

◇ **WEISER-KUNSTLER (MOSEL)** Partners Konstantin Weiser and Alexandra Künstler fashion small lots of very beautiful Rieslings in the Middle Mosel. The exquisite quality no doubt comes from the fact that they do everything by hand with incredible meticulousness. The result is a creamy, fluid Riesling of immense precision, that compels the tongue to linger over every sensuous detail.

◇ **EGON MÜLLER (SAAR)** Müller's name is practically synonymous with Scharzhofberg, the massive hill that forms the bedrock of his domaine's Riesling. This cold place produces Riesling of both astounding power and purity. Its potent flavors of lime and lemon and green fruit hit the tongue like a laser beam and push to the back of the mouth. Even after swallowing, the finish can last for minutes.

◇ **MAXIMIN GRÜNHAUS (RUWER)** Focusing on just three vineyards across from the estate—Abtsberg, Herrenberg, and Bruderberg—Carl von Schubert has been able to show the mysterious differences wrought by terroir, especially through the lens of Riesling. Despite their differences, the Rieslings from each place are uniformly a delicious pleasure to drink, as well as always savory, electric, and worthy of extended aging.

◇ **LEITZ (RHEINGAU)** The incredible bundle of energy that is Josef Leitz shows up in his wines, which vibrate and hum with their own internal energy. Besides being a master vigneron, he's great at marketing too, having created wines like Eins Zwei Dry Riesling to appeal to new drinkers at a remarkable $15 price point. But his greatest value is as a steward of the lower Rheingau, where he fashions brilliantly sculpted Riesling from some of Germany's most celebrated vineyards: Berg Roseneck, Rosengarten, and Kaisersteinfels, to name a few.

◇ **EVA FRICKE (RHEINGAU)** A former disciple of Leitz's, Fricke has made a name for herself with a portfolio of sleek, beautifully polished Rieslings that have an effortless lightness atop a mineral core. She makes Riesling on several levels: Rheingau Region; Village (Kiedrich, Lorch, Lorch Wisperwind); and Single Vineyard (Seligmacher, Krone, and Schlossberg). Any one of these is a good place to start.

◇ **ROBERT WEIL (RHEINGAU)** Another of Germany's most celebrated domaines, Weil's wines are noted for their richness and purity, delivering lots of citrus and fruit concentration without ever seeming heavy or ponderous. Kiedrich Gräfenberg is the most famous of the single vineyards.

◇ **DÖNNHOFF (NAHE)** In many ways, Dönnhoff is the name that pushed the Nahe to its current popularity—the domaine produces wines of exquisite balance and precision. Rieslings like Hermannshöhle and Dellchen can offer surprising twists and turns, at first seeming powerful and leaden before lifting off the tongue—or tasting light and ethereal before finishing with great force and length.

◇ **KRUGER-RUMPF (NAHE)** Georg Rumpf is taking his family's domaine to new heights. He's aggressively expanding and replanting in his area, where the Nahe meets the Rheinhessen, but more than that, he's making thrilling Riesling. Wines from the Pittersberg and Burgberg vineyards seem to explode in the mouth with flavor and exuberant acidity.

◇ **SCHLOSSGUT DIEL (NAHE)** This respected house with great history is rising to even higher achievement under the directorship of Caroline Diel. She shows a beautiful touch in sussing out the subtle differences from three vineyards in Dorsheim—Goldloch, Burgberg, and Pittermännchen—that sit side by side on a dauntingly steep slope. While they vary in character, all of the wines are connected by a deep, rich, stony minerality that anchors them at the core.

◇ **WITTMANN (RHEINHESSEN)** A prominent voice in the rise of the Rheinhessen in Germany's Riesling firmament, Philipp Wittmann produces wines of delicate balance. They harness the power of the region, but restrain it just enough so that the wines, while almost austere, are always drinkable and even thirst-quenching. All the wines are dry, and the village Westhofener Riesling is a great place to start.

◇ **DREISSIGACKER (RHEINHESSEN)** Jochen Dreissigacker conveys the drive, certainty, and energy of a zealot, and his wines vibrate with the same urgency. After learning under Klaus Pieter Keller, he made a big bet on Riesling—at a time when it was unfashionable—by replanting his family estate to the grape. Now he's cashing in on that bet in the form of some of Germany's greatest Rieslings—breathtakingly racy, penetrating, and heady wines that never fail to thrill. His single vineyards Morstein and Kirchspiel are worth seeking out, but his village Bechtheimer Riesling is a steal at around $25.

◇ **KELLER (RHEINHESSEN)** The original modern superstar of the Rheinhessen, Keller turned heads starting in 2001 when he took over his family domaine and began releasing full-throttle Rieslings of great density and force. Yet, despite the power, they never lacked for detail or precision, like a racecar capable of cornering tightly at high speeds. His Kirchspiel and Hubacker are particular standouts.

FIVE

SPAIN

If any country can challenge our claim that Italy is Europe's most exciting wine region, without question it's Spain. In fact, Spain may be even more exciting, in a different way. If wine were pop music, the excitement around Italy would be like discovering some old recordings by your favorite band that had been locked away in a vault. The excitement around Spain is like discovering entirely new, riveting genres of music, sung in unfamiliar languages, and played on instruments you didn't know existed.

As with Italy, history plays the largest role in bringing this sense of novelty about. The two countries both had shattering twentieth centuries that afforded little time for oenological exploration. But, if anything, Spain's was worse. In addition to phylloxera and the instability in Europe wrought by the two world wars, Spain was torn apart by a cruel and brutal civil war that raged from 1936 to 1939.

Of course, geography also makes a big impact on the wine. Spain is not only vast, but also is Europe's second most mountainous country. Today, those mountains provide remarkable terroirs in a country that is otherwise scorching and dry, but in the past they served to also keep Spain's cultures somewhat segregated and independent.

The upshot of all this is a wine dynamic similar to Italy's. Ancient terroirs and grape varieties and traditions are just now coming to light (at least for those of us thirsty in the rest of the world). Many of the traditions have been so long buried that the sense of delight in their reinvention is even more powerful today. In many ways, Spain's is a New World wine culture, just one gifted with old vines, dazzling and unfamiliar grapes, and well-worn soils that have a memory of vineyards. It's a heady, thrilling combination, making Spain a captivating playground for young vignerons with ambition, moxie, creativity, and a hard-driving work ethic. Like the innovative chefs who reinvented Spanish food, these vintners have proven up to the challenge at every step: they have displayed, for the most part, great taste and an irresistible sense of style.

All of this makes it difficult to write about Spain as a classic wine region, as even the "classic" regions of Spain, with the exception of Sherry, are either not terribly old or are still moving at a breakneck pace of self-discovery. So we are approaching this section a little bit differently than the others. We are writing what we can about the most stable and traditional wine cultures we've experienced. But more than that, we want to share the mind-boggling and tantalizing wines, terroirs, and vignerons we've encountered, with an eye toward watching them become well-defined terroirs in the future.

RIOJA

To ascend to Rioja Alavesa from the plains below in Rioja Baja is to enter a different world. The path climbs out of a vast, arid expanse of vines into a land of Edenic hills and valleys, where oaks and firs and trickling streams are interwoven with small slivers of vineyards. You leave an area that feels, frankly, like a production zone to find yourself in a bucolic, almost magical, landscape. How can they be part of the same region? That's a story of evolution.

What does the world know of Rioja terroir besides its subdivision into three zones—Alavesa, Alta, and Baja? According to Juan Carlos López de Lacalle, founder of the elite estate of Artadi, two hundred years ago, this sylvan area of Álava *was* Rioja. But as mass transportation came to the area in the nineteenth century, the railroad hub of Haro became the region's distribution center. Soon vines sprouted up all over this zone, which is now considered Rioja Alta, stretching to the Ebro river towns of Haro and Logroño. Rioja Baja and Alta expanded extensively in the mid-nineteenth century when mildew and then phylloxera devastated France's vineyards and oceans of wine were exported to supply Bordeaux's dwindling volumes.

As Rioja's commerce grew, so did the size of its businesses—to the point that it is now so dominated by giant wineries that fifteen of them account for 85 percent of Rioja's wine production. Naturally, these producers have a potent grip on the governing body, hence rules that have limited how specific producers can be on their labels with regards to naming such basic things as vineyard, village, and region. These labeling regulations favor high-production blends over small single-vineyard wines like those produced by Artadi. They drag the more specialized wines down to their level by preventing them from declaring their uniqueness. This is why even most wine lovers know little of Rioja besides its three main regions.

However in 2017 and early 2018, new rules were enacted to begin the process of correcting Rioja's longstanding omission of terroir on its labels. For instance, (under certain conditions) single vineyard wines are now legal, aging requirements are more flexible, and village and zones can be listed. And Rioja Baja, which producers worry is now a pejorative, will be renamed Rioja Oriental (we'll see how well that sticks).

There's still work to do. For instance, while producers can list a village on the label, it must be the village where the winery lies (an often meaningless detail nowadays) and not necessarily where the grapes are grown. But at least the first moves are being taken to acknowledge that Rioja is a collection of terroirs and not just a wine brand. As they say, the first step toward a solution is admitting you have a problem.

PARTICULARS OF PLACE

If you want to explore different terroirs of Rioja, your best bet is to find producers who are making wines from single areas. One such producer is Olivier Rivière, a dashing young Frenchman who trained in Burgundy and Bordeaux and worked for the great Telmo Rodriguez of Remelluri for two years before starting his own label. Olivier's is a modern operation in that he owns or rents small parcels in many parts of Rioja and farms them himself organically and biodynamically. Though he can't list the regions on the labels, he mostly keeps Rioja vineyards and regions separate in the bottle, giving each wine a different proprietary name. "I want the regions to stand out, to have their own identity," he says. "This is what makes wine interesting." For instance, Ganko is a wine made only from Rioja Alta, 50 percent Grenache and 50 percent Carignan. It's got firm tannins and somewhat hard, durable fruit flavors that Olivier says Rioja Alta supplies with ease. It will need time to soften up. Rayos Uva is completely from a vineyard in Rioja Baja and plays the part of a fruity village wine—inexpensive, plump, easy-drinking, and uncomplicated. This is one kind of wine Rioja Baja can excel at, he notes. His Viñas de Eusebio is from the village of Laguardia in Rioja Alavesa. It has plenty of structure, but also a depth of chewy blackberry and cherry fruit, and finely wrought acidity—all hallmarks of Rioja Alavesa.

Rioja Alavesa and Rioja Alta both have clay and limestone soils, tinted orange in many places by ever-present iron oxides. Indeed, the differences between the two subregions are more administrative than geographical. "It's so complex between Alta and Alavesa, because even between one valley and the next it's very different," says Olivier. In general, however, the clay-limestone soils and the cooler elevations make for wines with more acidity, poise, structure, and less alcohol than Rioja Baja (which means "Lower Rioja," referring to altitude, not quality, though the greater heat index here typically makes for less precise wines). This is irrespective of variety, be it the dominant Tempranillo or its usual blending partners Grenache and Carignan (the latter is also called Mazuelo in Spain).

Rioja Baja, says Olivier, "gets a bad reputation, but it also has some very good sites." In general, the bad reputation stems from the fact that Baja's soil is sandy and alluvial, and the climate is much warmer, too warm to raise grapes for fine wines. In the past, though, Rioja Baja played an important role. In years (or eras) when it may have been challenging to ripen fruit in Alta and Alavesa, Baja would be there to provide softer, riper fruit—usually Grenache—to the blend. It still does today, even though its rounder, less structured style is apparent even in wines like Rivière's delicious Rayos Uva.

With single vineyards as a first step, the battle for terroir in Rioja will wage on. As Olivier tells us, "Rioja is huge, you have good spots everywhere. You can't say one spot is better than another one." No, but we at least want to know where they are.

QUESTION OF TASTE

How to differentiate between Rioja Alavesa, Rioja Alta, and Rioja Baja?

Even though most Rioja is blended from the different regions, more and more subzone-specific wines are appearing these days. The heavier, higher-alcohol, lower-acid, often fruitier wines from Rioja Baja are generally easy to spot. Tempranillo especially falls flat here (although plantings are increasing, probably to fill out volumes of simple, industrial Rioja), so keep an eye out for Grenache—with bright red earthy fruit. When it comes to Alavesa versus Alta, it's very difficult even for locals to taste the difference. However, Alavesa comes from heavily limestone-based soils at high altitudes and therefore displays calcareous soil's rare qualities of structure and lift at the same time. Rioja Alta can share these traits, but this region extends down toward some deeper, alluvial regions in the flats, where the wines become a little broader and less electric.

◇ **LÓPEZ DE HEREDIA** One of the great wine estates of the world, López de Heredia is nothing but a force of good in Rioja. They have farmed organically forever, make single-vineyard wines, and age them so well that their white wines often hit the market after their tenth year. These reds, whites, and rosés are simply a marvel, a throwback to when Rioja was taking the world by storm. The reds are classically balanced between leathery earth notes and soft black cherry fruits, and their complexity grows with age. The whites are savory and herb-driven—not racy or high-acid, but refreshing nonetheless. Best, all López de Heredia wines are exceedingly, shockingly affordable, rarely cresting $50, despite the extraordinary quality and aging.

◇ **OLIVIER RIVIÈRE** Rivière's exciting wines are a breath of fresh air in Rioja, as he takes a Burgundian single-vineyard approach to many of his wines, trying to suss out the differences in terroir among vineyards across the valley. His wines are direct and well- made, meaning he doesn't try to pander to the audience with overripe fruit or excessive oak. Rather, he's clearly trying to make balanced wine that shows the site. And in that he's successful—not to mention, the wines are clean, chewy, and delicious.

◇ **ARTADI** One of Rioja's most elite estates, this Rioja Alavesa stalwart was one of the first to push single-vineyard winemaking and other reforms. The style takes advantage of the power afforded by Tempranillo—wines of deep, purple and black fruit, with thick, rich layers of tannin. But there is great purity to all of it—this is pristinely farmed, precisely harvested fruit turned into wine that is meant to age. The vibrant, potent Viña El Pisón is the most famous wine and costs several hundreds of dollars. But the entry-level Tempranillo is also very good (if much less concentrated) and affordable.

◇ **REMELLURI** An icon of high-quality, single-estate winemaking, this beautiful Rioja Alavesa estate is built around the highest altitude vineyards in the region. The estate dates back to the Middle Ages, but its modern history begins in the 1960s, when it was bought by Jaime Rodriguez, who restored the vineyards and instituted organic farming. His son, Telmo, is one of Spain's greatest winemakers and originally worked at Remelluri before leaving for a decade to make his own name. To great fanfare, Telmo returned to the family winery in 2009 and refined the winemaking even more toward quality. The results have been impressive, evident in the Reserva, which is the winery's hallmark—a wine full of black fruit and spice with a rich, luxurious texture supported by a strong tannic spine.

OLIVIER AND KATERINA RIVIÈRE
Rioja

RIBERA DEL DUERO ────────────────◇

In 1990, the young Danish winemaker Peter Sisseck came to Spain from Bordeaux to head up a new project, what today is Haciendo Monasterio. Then, it was just 64 hectares (157 acres) of planted vines. By 1994, Sisseck says, he didn't know where it was going and decided to start something for himself. On his regular drives to and from the north-central Spanish town of Valladolid, Ribera del Duero's winemaking center, he had noticed a vineyard, planted in 1929, that looked promising to the eye. A few years later, he had the opportunity to buy it, and jumped at the chance. In 1995, the resulting inaugural vintage of a wine Sisseck called Pingus almost instantly became one of the world's most hotly desired wines (and still is—at around $1,000 a bottle, if you can find it).

"It really is a great vineyard. I didn't know it was that great, to be honest," the sandy-haired Sisseck tells us one evening over dinner in Valladolid. "The thing with nature and vineyards, it's not that democratic. I got lucky." (We laugh at this line, as Jean-Louis Chave of Hermitage used the exact same words months earlier in the Rhône: "Terroir isn't democratic; you either have it or you don't.") But this small region in the high plain of northern Spain, on the banks of the river Duero, is lucky to have quite a bit of it.

It wasn't all luck, though, as there is a track record here. Pingus wasn't the first Ribera del Duero cult wine. That was Vega Sicilia, an estate that has been around since the mid-nineteenth century and produces Spain's most celebrated wine: Unico. Later, winemaker Alejandro Fernández contributed to the growing reputation of Ribera del Duero with his famous Pesquera red of the early 1980s. And the international and instant success of Pingus in 1995 sealed the deal. By then, international investment was pouring into the region to find the next lightning in the bottle. Many highly regarded wines have been made in the short modern history of Ribera del Duero, but none with the success of those three.

PARTICULARS OF PLACE

Even more than Rioja, Ribera del Duero is Tempranillo country. While Vega Sicilia started from the beginning with Bordeaux varieties in the blend, newer wines focus more and more exclusively on Tempranillo, known as Tinto Fino here. The long east–west valley has a classic continental climate—very cold in the winter and very hot in the summer. Thanks to its situation at an astonishing 2,600 feet of altitude, temperatures can swing more than 40 degrees in a single day, Sisseck tells us, which helps maintain freshness in the wines. "They are always in the ripe spectrum," he says. "It's naturally generous, but we have to be careful of not pushing that generosity into something that becomes too much. [There's] the same problem in California. You must accept some kind of wine made under the sun."

The secret to Ribera del Duero, holding everything in balance, is limestone—though gravel also plays a role. The day after our dinner with Peter Sisseck, we take a limestone adventure through the vineyards of Quinta Sardonia with the brilliant viticulturist Jérôme Bougnaud, who helped find and create the Sardonia property with Sisseck (acting as a consultant) in the late 1990s. Bougnaud shows us limestone in different forms—mixed with sand, crusted into marl, battered into rocks. The key is texture. "The texture of the soil is the same you find in the wine. It's a big correlation," he says. The finer the grain of the soil, the finer the grain of the wine.

Most of the wine coming from Ribera del Duero is big, rich, oaky red, of the kind found all over, from Napa Valley to Mendoza. Ribera del Duero does it well, but it's not that exciting. Easily the most fascinating wine coming from Ribera del Duero these days is not an expensive and lavish red, but rather a simple wine in a style called *clarete* (clah-RE-tay). This combination of red and white grapes was the kind of wine Jorge Monzon's grandfather and the rest of the region would drink at home. A light red or dark rosé, it is bright and fruity, but dry—refreshing and supple, yet with body. "I'm trying to preserve the wine history of this region," he tells us.

Monzon, proprietor of the diminutive Dominio del Águila, has been collecting some of the oldest vines in the region on bony limestone soils and vinifying them in a crazy old winery with a very cramped, dark subterranean cellar. But he's not only making clarete. His other wines are equally interesting and equally historically oriented. Jorge doesn't even have a destemmer to remove the grapes from their stems. Thus, his most serious wine, Canta la Perdiz, can be quite tannic (stems provide extra tannins), but he says that's because the old vines' yields are so low in dry years that there's not enough juice to dilute the tannins.

The presence of Monzon, a true vigneron in the original, Burgundian sense of the word (he himself grows the grapes, works in the vineyard, and makes the wine), is refreshing in a region many have called Spain's Napa Valley, thanks to the millions of dollars of investment in creating sleek New World reds and striking architectural wineries. But in the face of overwhelming novelty and innovation, it's often the lingering past that's the most compelling feature.

How do you distinguish Ribera del Duero from Rioja?

Ribera del Duero wines favor Tempranillo far more than Rioja (though monovarietal Tempranillo is becoming more popular there). This leads to a wine of darker color—purple compared to classic Rioja's dark red—and a much more linear structure, surrounded by a robust layer of flesh. Ribera wines have firm and straight tannins and a more muscular body than Rioja, though at their best they can be soft, plush, and well integrated.

◇ **DOMINIO DEL ÁGUILA (JORGE MONZON)** As described above, Monzon is a vigneron making wines that honor the traditions of his forebears. The Picaro clarete is rosé in color, but don't confuse it with rosé. It's a blend of red Tempranillo and white Albillo grapes, and drinks like a firmer, denser red wine, yet the flavors are all the light, fresh strawberries and raspberries one wants from a rosé, albeit girded with a more serious structure. Second, at around $30 a bottle, its cost is more like a red than a rosé.

◇ **GOYO GARCIA VIADERO** In the same spirit as Jorge Monzon, Goyo Garcia Viadero is looking for something outside the mainstream modern wines of Ribera del Duero. He therefore harvests earlier to preserve natural acidity (at the expense of high ripeness), and mixes red with white grapes to create new textures and concentrations. For his Finca El Peruco, 15 percent Albillo is co-fermented with 85 percent Tempranillo, creating a wine that remains quite dark and has a stiff tannic structure. But atop that frame, the wine seems fluid and gentle like a Burgundy.

◇ **PINGUS** One of the hallmarks of the modern Ribera del Duero, Pingus is an expensive wine for wealthy people. But, like Pétrus in Bordeaux, you can't fault the winemaking or the pedigree. There's a reason demand for the wine is sky-high, and that's because drinking it is an extremely pleasurable experience, as your mouth is lavished by waves of dark fruit, soothingly thick and velvety tannins, and a finish that leaves a tasteful memory of sweet blackberries and vanilla.

PRIORAT

Carles Ortiz was a rock climber from Barcelona when he came to Priorat, looking to be closer to nature. He was in luck. Priorat's very nature is to be rocky with paralyzingly steep rock faces—a climber's dream. While out there, Carles became fascinated with viticulture and started planting vineyards. Later, he met a young winemaker, Ester Nin, and the two partnered in life and in business, creating the wine company Família Nin-Ortiz. Their wines are beguiling. But what's illuminating is to talk to Carles about *costers*.

Costers (pronounced co-STAIRS) are the ancient ways of planting the steep slopes in Priorat. Simply put, costers are just vines planted on the slopes with no effort made to shape the land. Densely planted in rows, they run up the hillsides with little consideration for the treacherous steepness. Over years, they will naturally create their own contours on the hills, almost like little naturally sculpted terraces, but these are slightly mounded bands undulating down the slope. Costers stand in stark contrast to the many terraces built over the last thirty years—steep and attractive steps of vineyard rows shaping the hillsides like staircases with neat, intricately constructed stone walls. The terraces look great (everyone goes crazy for them) and provide a horizontal surface on which the vines grow, but according to Carles, they are far inferior to the ancient costers, which function with a simplicity that belies their effectiveness.

"With the terraces you can only plant 2,500 vines per hectare," he says, "and you get lower quality." This is because the stone walls prevent efficient use of the space and give the vines much more room to grow, allowing them to spread out and concentrate on vegetative production instead of fruit. Costers, on the other hand, can pack in as many as 8,000 vines per hectare, and the increased competition among them allows better ripening, lower per-vine production, and higher quality. "The only downside is you have to use animals to work the vineyards," Carles says, as opposed to the terraces, which can be worked with mechanization. The brutality of working costers is not too much of a problem for him, though, since he's been working with two mules for a decade now and has planted over 25,000 vines this way.

But, after a couple of decades of massive terraces reshaping the slopes of Priorat (and it's still going on), interest in costers has increased. "Ten years ago, when I started, it was only me and Alvaro Palacios [L'Ermita] planting costers," says Carles. "Now there are twenty producers making them."

The collision between ancient and modern is at the heart of the Priorat wines we know today, and the tension between the two is evident in the taste. Ancient are the grape varieties and the spine of minerality that somehow channels the Paleozoic dark slate (four hundred million years old) the locals call *llicorella*. Modern are the winemaking techniques that allow contemporary Priorat wines to be the dark, sleek, clean, and unoxidized beasts they are today. Modernity has resuscitated an ancient place that had dwindled from a peak of 6,000 hectares (14,700 acres) in the nineteenth century to just 2,000 (4,900) today. The culprits of decline are familiar: phylloxera, the abandonment of rural areas for industrial work and war, and economic depression.

When the famous group that would reboot Priorat—Palacios, René Barbier, Carles Pastrana, José Luis Pérez, and Daphne Glorian—gathered in the 1980s, none of them expected such success. But they knew there was something powerful there because it was ever in plain sight—the remnants of those thousands of abandoned costers, subsumed by the tangle of underbrush amassed over the last century and a half. And they knew it from the gravity of those black slate llicorella soils. For its dark, mineral, fruity, expensive wines, Priorat has won much fame. But the rediscovery of its terroirs and what its wine can be has really just begun.

ESTER NIN
Família Nin-Ortiz, Priorat

Priorat may be the most striking wine region of them all (though the Mosel and Ribeira Sacra give it good run). Nestled snugly into a bowl, walled in by soaring mountain peaks, the region is just an hour's drive south and inland from bustling Barcelona, but feels worlds and even centuries away. "It's just a mosaic of microclimates," says Daphne Glorian of Clos Erasmus, from behind the wheel. "It's a big stadium with different hills inside of it."

The stadium is punctuated by nine small villages—Bellmunt del Priorat, Gratallops, El Lloar, La Morera de Montsant, Poboleda, Porrera, Scala Dei, Torroja del Priorat, and La Vilella—perched at various altitudes on platforms of solid, barren rock. In and around them, vineyards speckle the slopes, emerging from crumbling slate soils in small, clenched postures. From a high point, we can see the jagged, teethlike peaks of the Montsant mountains surrounding Priorat like a fence.

To drive, as we are on a cool, sunny December day, out to many of these vineyards involves harrowing rides on chillingly narrow single-lane dirt roads in which one careless turn could lead to a tumble of hundreds of feet. We tell ourselves: Don't look down, and stop thinking what might happen if we encounter a car going in the other direction on one of these "roads." As it is, the paved pathways between towns twist and snake in their own precarious fashion, as no direct path exists between any of Priorat's villages. The valleys that separate them, Glorian explains, go a long way to creating the differences in terroir. And even though they are close in proximity, the differences can be profound.

As Daphne remarks, the village of Gratallops, where she works, is warmer than Porrera. "Gratallops is warmer because it's slightly more open and lower in elevation," she says. "We get the influence of the Ebro while in Porrera they get the breezes from the sea, especially at night. It makes it cooler. It's only 7½ miles by road (only a minute as the bird flies), yet we're three weeks apart in our harvests." We can even feel it on this day, as the warm sunlight bathes our faces in the vineyard.

The exploration of Priorat's microclimates is underway, but it still has a long way to go. Divisions between wines are both stylistic and terroir-driven. Right now, we're seeing new styles emerge—the lighter, lower-alcohol styles of Família Nin-Ortiz and Dominik Huber's Terroir al Limit—alongside the darker, stronger styles of the revolution such as L'Ermita. Also, more and more producers are gravitating back to the traditional grapes of Carignan and Grenache and away from French varieties of Cabernet Sauvignon and Syrah. Priorat's governing body has created a system to accommodate terroir-driven wines called Vins de Vila, but this is more for the future than for today. Village-driven wines are just beginning to appear, as in the Black Slate series created by importer Eric Solomon. But it's early yet to do anything more than generalize about the nature of Priorat terroir.

That said, generalizing is our forte. The coolest villages seem to be Porrera, La Morera, and Poboleda, while the warmest may be Bellmunt or El Lloar. The most defined wines come from Gratallops, Porrera, and Scala Dei. Gratallops, where the modern Priorat winemaking started with René Barbier, is somewhere in the middle between hot and cold. It has the most developed vineyards and style, and its wine possesses the greatest richness and definition, perhaps because it's seen the longest sustained effort. Porrera is one of the coolest spots, and the wines show elevated acidity and more precise definition. Scala Dei is interesting because of the sandiness of the soil, giving it a fine-boned, sandy profile that leads to floral and red fruit notes with softer, more polished tannins.

QUESTION OF TASTE

How do you recognize Priorat wines?

It's still early days with terroir here. But Priorat wines, as they stand now, can be discerned as plush, dark, purple-black wines. The nose will usually give very ripe fruits along the blackberry, licorice, violet, and chocolate spectrum. There may be hints of smoke and sun-warmed rocks on the nose, too. The wines are big and mouth-filling, with high alcohol levels in the 14- to 15-degree range and higher. They sport capacious mid-palates and lots of savory ripe fruits. Tannin is present in high quantities, but it's usually very soft and ripe.

◇ **CLOS ERASMUS** Daphne Glorian's original project, with its first vintage in 1990, is only getting better today. Glorian continues to refine her vineyards, and her winemaking is completely hands-on, crafted in a little cellar under her house. A blend of Grenache and Syrah, the wine is a paragon of Priorat; at once silky smooth and roundly ripe with sweet black fruit, it is centered on a firm underlying core that feels like stones or metals. It embodies the phrase "iron fist in a velvet glove." While the price is high, Glorian's second wine, Laurel, is also deep-fruited, delicious and more affordable.

◇ **ALVARO PALACIOS** Of the clique of wines that skyrocketed Priorat to international fame, Palacios's L'Ermita wine has become the most famous and is often credited alongside Ribera del Duero's Pingus as bringing Spain into the modern wine world. First made in 1993, it's a blend of Grenache, Cabernet Sauvignon, and Carignan. Like Clos Erasmus, it fuses a structured but richly hedonistic fruit expression with the mineral backbone that's the hallmark of Priorat.

◇ **FAMÍLIA NIN-ORTIZ** Not everything in Priorat is ridiculously rare and expensive. The husband-and-wife team of Carles Ortiz and Ester Nin (Nin also serves as viticulturist for Daphne Glorian) is making wines of the people. Both Nin and Ortiz are vineyard-oriented, so the organic and biodynamic-method farming here is meticulous and passionate. This shows up in the wines, which are both full and ripe as well as soft and easy to drink. Planetes is the signature wine, a Grenache and Carignan blend, dark-fruited, crunchy, fresh, and full of vibrant acidity.

◇ **TERROIR AL LIMIT** Another alternative to the famous Priorat cult wines (though with its own growing group of obsessives), Terroir Al Limit is winemaker Dominik Huber's effort at making fresh, direct, transparent wines from different terroirs. He avoids small oak barrels and new oak as much as possible, harvests grapes when they are fresh and bright, and is maniacal about his farming practices. Some of Huber's most compelling wines are white, namely his Pedra de Guix, a blend of native grapes from vines up to eighty years old. This wine proves that Priorat's famed minerality shows up as deftly in white wine as in red.

DAPHNE GLORIAN
Clos Erasmus, Priorat

GARNACHA VINES
at Rumbo al Norte in Sierra de Gredos

SINGULAR WINES OF SPAIN

Even in Spain's well-trodden regions of Rioja, Ribera del Duero, and Priorat, novel styles and terroirs are being discovered. It won't surprise, then, to learn that the rest of Spain is even more wild and wide open. Just as in the regions named above, there is an ancient history of wine production that is just being rediscovered today. The possibilities astonish us.

Consider the Sierra de Gredos. Despite being just a couple of hours outside Madrid, this mountain range is not on most travelers' maps. And rightly so, as there's not much going on in this massive and fairly impoverished-looking area that, like so many rural regions, no doubt lost its rural contingent generations ago to industrial jobs in the cities. The area is now about recreation for city-dwellers, who take advantage of the cool climate of the thick alpine forests, wind-blown mountains of stone, and craggy mountain expanses. Into this remote and rugged land ventured college buddies Daniel Landi and Fernando García, looking for special plots of Grenache to create their brand, Comando G (after a Spanish name for the 1980s Japanese television cartoon *Battle of the Planets*; the winemakers here see G as Grenache, and themselves as explorers of the deep reaches of Spain's Grenache galaxy).

And special plots they found. Inspired by the vision of Grenache embodied in the wines of the famed Château Rayas of Châteauneuf-du-Pape—elegant, red-fruited wine instead of a high-alcohol battering ram—Landi and García farm these extraordinary sites of old vines biodynamically, and extract very lightly in the winemaking to achieve pale, aromatic, ethereal wines, all vinified and bottled by site. There's Tumba del Rey Moro, whose muscular old vines live in a national park with no vineyards for miles around. There's Las Umbrias, a site where similarly old vines stretch out in an old meadow, interspersed with withered old trees. And then there's Rumbo al Norte, one of the most extraordinary and eerie vineyards we've ever seen, in which scraggly, twisted old vines grow haphazardly among massive boulders that appear to have been arranged for some Druidic ceremony by ancient Spanish giants. All told, the Comando G wines are some of the most exciting being made in Spain today, and they are perhaps just scratching the surface (or are at least carving out the high end) for the Sierra del Gredos. Everywhere we went, we saw neglected old vineyards.

When considering the new Spain, you must also think of the continuing ascent of the grape variety Mencia. It reaches its peak in two regions, Bierzo and Ribeira Sacra (in the far northwest of Spain, halfway between Santiago de Compostela in Galicia and Bilbao in the Basque region). The Ribeira Sacra is a river valley as spectacular as the Mosel, where steep terraced cliffs look far down to the river Sil below. Mencia here produces something with the charm of Beaujolais but the seriousness of Hermitage on a lithe, wiry body that often can remind of Burgundy. Its foremost practitioners include the wineries Guímaro and Envínate; both produce wines of great elegance while still channeling the Ribeira Sacra's savory, wild essence. (The white wines here, from the Godello grape, are equally fantastic.) Guímaro's basic Tinto (red) wine costs less than $20 and gives a great sense of the savory, brambly fruit and spicy high tones Mencia can provide in this region. Single-site wines like Finca Pombeiras offer more complexity and richness at about three times the price.

Not far away, Bierzo, another region in a warmed bowl of land surrounded by mountains, finds Mencia taking on a larger, rounder countenance. The great master here is the indomitable Raúl Pérez, who makes fascinating wines in a variety of styles from a number of sites and soils. The entire goal of his company, Bodegas y Viñedos Raúl Pérez, is to help raise the profile of the Mencia grape, which he does expertly with wines like El Pecado. Grown on granite and slate, Mencia takes on a wild, almost feral, quality here, vacillating between lush, wild blackberry notes and earthy, peppery, wild vegetation notes.

There's also the French-trained Grégory Pérez (no relation) making Mencia, under the label Mengoba, from higher up in the mountains, capturing its lean, lithe profile in a lighter style than Raúl Pérez's. These two producers prove Bierzo wines can range from inky dark and heavily structured to a more lacy, graceful style, and also that Mencia, in any style, can be relied upon to supply dense, brambly fruit, good acidity, and sweet tannin.

Finally, we can't forget to mention the emerging wines of the Canary Islands, a part of Spain that lies far off the Atlantic coast, closer to Africa than to the mother country. The impact these wines and the producer Envínate (the same one working in Ribeira Sacra) are having on Raj is monumental. As we closed work on this book, he was experiencing an epiphany about the Canary Islands, and sent the following text about Envínate: "Great guys and AMAZING wines. I compare this to my discovery of Thierry Allemand. Once in a lifetime!"

Envínate's Canary Islands are some of the most surprising wines in the world. Who would think that vines grown on such a bright, tropical latitude could exhibit such grace and beauty? Made from a litany of local varieties on century-old vines grown directly into the rocks above the sea on the island of Tenerife, the wines named Táganan (a red and a white) and single-parcel versions (Parcela Amogoje and Parcela Margalagua) are not just graceful but also dark and earthy, with a complexity that truly boggles the mind and invokes rocks, smoke, the sea, flowers, history, and the interior of the earth. Indeed, they embody everything that is mysterious, compelling, and inspiring about wine.

But Spain's ability to boggle the mind is now a proven fact. We wait thirstily for what must be coming next.

FERNANDO GARCIA AND DANI LANDI
Commando G, Sierra de Gredos

ACKNOWLEDGMENTS

Together, Raj and I would like to thank all the producers we visited on our travels for being so generous with their time, their thought, and their wine. We went on several month-long trips, and we tried to fill every hour with work. Inevitably, this led us to try to see people on weekends and the few holidays that crept up. Amazingly, many producers agreed to see us on these times, cutting into their own family time. Without the magnanimity of these remarkable vignerons, we wouldn't have been able to create this book.

Specifically, we'd love to note a few who were able to go even above and beyond by helping with accommodation, or setting up appointments, meals, translation, and more. These include Jean-Laurent Vacheron, Arnaud and Geraldine Lambert, David Chapel and Michele Smith, Guillaume d'Angerville, Becky Wasserman and Russell Hone, Jeremy and Diana Seysses, Stephane Ogier, Jean and Pierre Gonon, Marc Perrin, Johannes Leitz, Luca Currado, Ricardo Campinoti, Eric Solomon, and the Austrian Wine Board. Even David Feldstein. I also extend a very special note of gratitude to Angelina and Kilian Franzen of Weingut Franzen, who took me to her family doctor when I was so sick I could neither taste nor smell.

We'd also like to thank Ten Speed Press for so enthusiastically publishing this book, especially the sharp editorial team who worked on this book—Emily Timberlake, Anne Goldberg, Carey Jones, and Clara Sankey—as well as designer Annie Marino, and production manager Dan Meyers. And, of course, we were thrilled to work with Joe Woodhouse, who captured the images of this journey brilliantly.

Raj would like to extend special gratitude to dear friend and winemaking partner in Domaine de la Côte, Sandhi, and Evening Land, Sashi Moorman. Also to Pedro Parra, who, through many hours of conversation, has helped him arrive at many of his positions on soil and terroir. And, finally, I'm so grateful to my beautiful wife, Christie, who took care of our house, life, and Fernie for the months and months I was absent, either traveling or chained to my desk. None of this would have been possible without her spirit and support.

—Jordan Mackay

INDEX

Casalte, Le, 272
Cascina Roccalini, 263
Caslot, Emmanuel, 54, 60
Caslot, Stephanie, 54–55, 58, 60
Castello di Verduno, 256
Castiglione Falletto, 247–48, 254, 258
Catell'in Villa, 274
Caveau de Chassagne, 127
Centro Storico, 256
Chablis, 132–37
Chambolle-Musigny, 96–97, 118
Champagne, 159–80
    Aube, 170, 172–73
    classification system of, 79
    Côte des Blancs, 164–67
    Côte de Sézanne, 173
    Montagne de Reims, 168–69
    Vallée de la Marne, 169–70
Chandon de Briailles, 113
Chanrion, Nicole, 146
Chapel, Domaine, 145
Chapoutier, Michel, 209
Chardonnay, 132, 150, 158, 174
Charlemagne, 104–5
Chartogne, Alexandre, 164, 168,
    179, 180
Chartogne-Taillet, 164, 168, 174, 179
Charvin, Domaine, 224
Chassagne-Montrachet, 126–29, 132
Châteauneuf-du-Pape, 219, 221–24
Chauvet, Jules, 139
Chave, 210, 211, 214, 216
Chave, Jean-Louis, 194, 204, 205,
    206, 208, 209, 210–11, 212,
    213, 216, 325
Chénas, 141
Chenin Blanc, 47, 52, 65, 66, 73
Chevalerie, Domaine de la, 54–55,
    56, 62
Chevillon, Robert, 104
Chianti Classico, 266, 271–73, 274
Chidaine, François, 48, 49, 50, 51, 52
Chinon, 53–62
Chiquet, Gaston, 170
Chiroubles, 142
Cighetti, Alessio, 256
Clair, Bruno, 88

Clape, Auguste, 216–17, 218
Clape, Domaine, 207, 209, 216–18
Clape, Olivier, 209, 218
classification systems, 79
Clement, Pascal, 76
Clendenen, Jim, 264
climate, role of, 20
Clos, Les, 135
Clos de la Roche, 92, 93
Clos des Ducs, 112, 119
Clos de Vougeot, 17, 97–98
Clos du Jaugueyron, 196
Clos Erasmus, 330, 332, 333
Closerie, La, 161, 175, 179
Clos Naudin, Domaine du, 48, 52, 53
Clos Rougeard, 63, 66, 67, 68, 69
Clos St-Denis, 92, 93
Clos St-Hune, 225
Clusel-Roch, 202, 209
Coates, Clive, 99, 122
Coche-Dury, Domaine, 106, 122, 155
Coche-Dury effect, 155
Cogno, Elvio, 257
Cogno, Nadia, 257
Colin, Pierre-Yves, 127, 132
Colla, Beppe, 239
Collier, Domaine du, 66, 69
Collin, Olivier, 173
Collin, Ulysse, 173
Comando G, 335, 337
Comté cheese, 150, 156
Conterno, Giacomo, 251, 259
Conterno, Roberto, 251, 259
Corault, Benoit, 74
Cornas, 216–18
Cornelissen, Frank, 275
Corton, 104–6
Cos d'Estournel, 190, 194
Cotat, François, 39, 41, 42, 43, 46
Cotat, Pascal, 46
Côte Blonde, 201, 202
Côte Brune, 201, 202
Côte de Beaune, 80, 104
Côte de Brouilly, 146
Côte de Nuits, 78, 80, 86
Côte des Blancs, 164–67
Côte de Sézanne, 173

Côte d'Or, 16–17, 78, 86, 104
Côte du Py, 143, 146
Côte-Rôtie, 200–203
Cotton, Pierre, 145
Coulée de Serrant, 70, 73
Courtin, Marie, 172
Cramant, 166
Croix, David, 106–8, 109, 110
Croix, Domaine des, 109
Currado, Elena, 241
Currado, Luca, 241–43, 247, 250,
    254, 257–58

D

d'Agata, Ian, 265, 279
Dagueneau, Didier, 46
Dancer, Vincent, 127
d'Angerville, Domaine Marquis,
    115, 119
d'Angerville, Guillaume, 115, 116,
    119, 151
Daumen, Jean-Paul, 221
Dauvissat, René and Vincent, 132,
    134, 136, 137
Defaix, Daniel-Etienne, 135
de Grazia, Marco, 275, 277, 278, 282
de la Morandière, Brice, 126
Delecheneau, Coralie and Damien, 53
de Montille, Alix, 119
de Montille, Domaine, 115, 119
de Montille, Étienne, 100, 105, 109,
    114, 119
de Montille, Hubert, 119
de Villaine, Aubert, 86, 99
di Campalto, Stella, 270–71, 273–74
Diebolt-Vallois, 166
Diel, Armin, 310
Diel, Caroline, 310–11, 312, 317
Dilettante, La, 107
di Marchi, Paolo, 274
d'Issan, 195
Dominio del Águila, 326, 327
Donnecker, Oliver, 301
Dönnhoff, 311, 317
Dönnhoff, Cornelius, 311, 313
Dönnhoff, Helmut, 311

I

Isole e Olena, 274
Italy
    Barbaresco, 259–63
    Barolo, 238–59
    Etna, 275–82
    Tuscany, 264–74
    wine culture of, 237–38

J

Jaboulet, 206, 210
Jaugaret, Domaine du, 196
Jayer, Henri, 94, 100
Jefferson, Thomas, 205
Johnnes, Daniel, 118
Johnson, Hugh, 9
Joly, Nicolas, 70
Jouguet, Charles, 54, 62
Juliénas, 141
Jullien, Guy, 223
Jura, 150–59
Jurtschitsch, 292, 295, 297
Jurtschitsch, Alwin, 293, 295
Jurtschitsch, Stefanie, 293

K

Kamptal, 291–93, 295, 297
Keller, Klaus Pieter, 313, 317
Knebel, Matthias, 304–5, 306, 316
Knoll, Emmerich, 288, 294
kokumi, 29–30
Kracher, Alois, 295
Kracher, Gerard, 295
Kramer, Matt, 9, 12, 21
Kremstal, 291–92, 294
Kroenke, Stan, 105
Krug, 167
Kruger-Rumpf, 161, 311, 317
Künstler, Alexandra, 305, 316

L

Lafarge, Domaine, 115, 119, 139
Lafleur-Pétrus, Château, 191, 192
Lafon, Domaine des Comte, 122
Lafon, Dominique, 122
Lahaye, Benoit, 175

Lambert, Arnaud, 66, 67, 68–69, 71
Lambrays, Domaine des, 94
La Morra, 243, 248–49, 259
Lamy, Hubert, 121
Landi, Dani, 335, 337
Lanza, Piero, 271, 274
Lapierre, 147
Lapierre, Marcel, 92, 139, 147
Lapierre, Matthieu and Camille, 147
Larmandier-Bernier, 166
Lassaigne, Emmanuel, 172
Lassaigne, Jacques, 172, 175
Lassalle, J., 160
Lauer, Florian, 308
Lauer, Peter, 308
Laval, Georges, 170
Laval, Vincent, 170
Ledru, Marie-Noelle, 168
Leflaive, Anne-Claude, 126
Leflaive, Domaine, 126
Leitz, 316
Leitz, Johannes "Josi," 301–2, 303, 309, 310
Leitz, Josef, 316
Lenoir, Jérome, 62
Léoville Barton, 195
Léoville Las Cases, 195
Léoville Poyferré, 195
Leroux, Benjamin, 115
Leroy, Domaine, 98, 99, 100, 101, 113
Leroy, Richard, 70, 74
Le Roy de Boiseaumarié, Pierre (Baron Le Roy), 212
Liger-Belair, Domaine du Comte, 99, 101
Liger-Belair, Thibault, 139
Lignier, Hubert, 94
Lignier, Romain, 94
Lion d'Or, Le, 185
Livingstone-Learmouth, John, 214
Loimer, 292
Loire Valley, 34–74
    Sancerre, 36–46
    Saumur and
        Saumur-Champigny, 63–69
    Savennières and the Anjou, 69–74
    Touraine, 47–62
López de Heredia, 323

López de Lacalle, Juan Carlos, 320
Lorch, Wink, 150, 152
Lukacs, Paul, 10
Lynch, Kermit, 33, 54, 62, 139, 160, 223
Lynch-Bages, 195

M

Macchi, Carlo, 265
Macchione, Il, 272
Machetti family, 269
Maltman, Alex, 19, 20, 302
Manetti, Sergio, 274
Manley, Alan, 247
Mann, Albert, 233
Marchand, Pascal, 115
Mareuil-sur-Aÿ, 170
Margaux, 186, 188, 195
Margaux, Château, 195
Marsannay, 86–88
Martini, Manfredi, 274
Mascarello, Bartolo, 239, 240, 246–47
Mascarello, Giuseppe, 247–48
Mascarello, Maria Teresa, 240, 246–47, 253
massal selection, 82
Matthews, Mark, 10, 13
McGee, Harold, 30
Meadows, Allen, 99
Médoc, 16, 184, 185, 186, 188, 190, 191
Mencia, 336
Menetou-Salon, 37
Méo-Camuzet, Domaine, 99, 101
Merfy, 168
Merlot, 182, 191
Mesnil-sur-Oger, Le, 167
Métras, Jules, 145
Meursault, 119–20, 122, 123
Michel, Guillaume, 133, 136
Michel, Louis, 131, 133, 134, 135, 136, 137
Mignon, Christophe, 179
Milan, Jean, 167
minerality, 2, 19–21, 23, 28–29
Mission Haut-Brion, La, 190
Moines, Domaine aux, 74

Tuscany, 264–74
typicity, 18–19

U

Undhof, Salomon, 294

V

Vacca, Aldo, 263
Vacheron, Domaine, 42, 46
Vacheron, Jean-Dominique, 36–37, 46
Vacheron, Jean-Laurent, 36–37, 39, 40, 46
Vaillons, 136
Vailly, Sylvain, 37
Vallée de la Marne, 169–70, 179
Valmur, 135
Vance, Ted, 65
Vannier, Françoise, 16–17, 76, 77, 88, 118
Vaudésir, 135
Vega Sicilia, 325
Veglio, Paolo, 263
Verduno, 256–57, 259
Vesselle, Jean, 169
Veyder-Malberg, Peter, 288–89, 294
Vieille Julienne, Domaine de la, 221, 224
Vietti, 241, 247, 254, 258
Vieux Château Certan, 191, 192, 196
Vieux Télégraphe, Domaine, 221, 222, 223, 224
Vignieri, I, 282
Villalin, Domaine, 37
Vincent Cuisinier de Campagne, 55
Vin Jaune, 151, 156, 157
Vino Nobile de Montepulciano, 266, 272
Vinoteca Centro Storico, 256
vinous, defining, 174
Volnay, 115–19
von Schubert, Carl, 308, 316
Vosne-Romanée, 99–101
Vouette et Sorbée, 172, 175
Vouvray, 47–48, 51–53

W

Wachau, 287–90, 292, 294
Waltz, Christoph, 285
Weil, Robert, 317
Weiser, Konstantin, 305, 316
Weiser-Künstler, 305, 316
West, Geoffrey, 17–18
Wickhoff, Andreas, 297
Wittmann, Philipp, 313–14, 317

Y

Yvonne, Château, 69

Z

Zind-Humbrecht, 227, 233

Library of Congress Cataloging-in-Publication Data
Names: Parr, Rajat, author. | Mackay, Jordan, author. | Woodhouse, Joe, photographer.
Title: The sommelier's atlas of taste : a field guide to the great wines of Europe / Rajat Parr
and Jordan Mackay ; photography by Joe Woodhouse.
Description: California : Ten Speed Press, [2018] | Includes index.
Identifiers: LCCN 2018011017
Subjects: LCSH: Wine and wine making–Europe.
Classification: LCC TP559.E8 P37 2018 | DDC 641.2/2094--dc23
LC record available at https://lccn.loc.gov/2018011017

Hardcover ISBN: 978-0-399-57823-6
eBook ISBN: 978-0-399-57824-3

Printed in China

Design by Annie Marino

10 9 8 7 6 5 4

First Edition